THE RISE OF AGRARIAN DEMOCRACY:
THE UNITED FARMERS AND
FARM WOMEN OF ALBERTA, 1909–1921

The Rise of Agrarian Democracy is a lucid and persuasive work detailing one of the greatest agrarian and mass democratic movements in North American history. It describes the events leading to the formation of the United Farmers of Alberta in 1909 and explores the UFA's development over the next decade as farmers built a distinct 'movement culture,' organized a large membership, and established the United Farm Women of Alberta. A path is laid from the farmers' inherited ideas and common experience, gender assumptions, class opposition, and agrarian ideals to a collective sense of responsibility, co-operation, and confidence. We follow the growth of a grassroots movement whose astonishing political success culminated in the election of the United Farmers of Alberta in 1921 and in their governing the province for over a decade.

More than an institutional study, this book examines an elemental period in Canadian democracy within the cultural, social, and community context at the core of the movement's inception. It contributes significantly to our understanding of the evolution and politicization of the Alberta farmers' movement and as such is an important investigation in western and agrarian history and economics.

Meticulously researched, this work is of interest to those studying co-operative movements worldwide. With clarity and accuracy, Brad Rennie provides valuable insight into both reform movement and gender history in Canada.

BRADFORD JAMES RENNIE is the winner of several academic awards and has taught at the University of Victoria and the University of Calgary.

The Rise of
Agrarian Democracy

© University of Toronto Press Incorporated 2000
Toronto Buffalo London
Printed in Canada

ISBN 0-8020-4847-1 (cloth)
ISBN 0-8020-8374-9 (paper)

∞

Printed on acid-free paper

Canadian Cataloguing in Publication Data

Rennie, Bradford James, 1960–
The rise of agrarian democracy : the United Farmers and
Farm Women of Alberta, 1909–1921

Includes bibliographical references and index.
ISBN 0-8020-4847-1 (bound)   ISBN 0-8020-8374-9 (pbk.)

1. United Farmers of Alberta – History.   2. United Farm Women of
Alberta – History.   3. Alberta – Politics and government – 1903–1921.
I. Title.

HD1486.C3R46 2000   324.27123′02   C00-931592-6

University of Toronto Press acknowledges the financial assistance to
its publishing program of the Canada Council for the Arts and the
Ontario Arts Council.

This book has been published with the help of a grant from the Humanities
and Social Sciences Federation of Canada, using funds provided by the
Social Sciences and Humanities Research Council of Canada.

University of Toronto Press acknowledges the financial support for its
publishing activities of the Government of Canada through the Book
Publishing Industry Development Program (BPIDP).

To my girls

Contents

Acknowledgments

I would like to thank, first and foremost, Ian MacPherson, who supervised the dissertation on which this study is substantially based. He was particularly helpful in encouraging me to discern broad themes (the proverbial forest), when all I could see was detail (the trees). I am also grateful to Patricia Roy for her painstaking efforts and insightful suggestions. John Herd Thompson, Gerald Hallowell, and two anonymous readers made invaluable comments as well. Jill McConkey was a pleasant and efficient editor; Catherine Frost was an excellent copy-editor; Frances Mundy was a helpful managing editor. I am responsible for the errors and weaknesses that remain.

Several institutions gave generous financial aid. The University of Victoria provided a fellowship for the first three years of my doctoral studies and a President's Research Scholarship. I received a doctoral fellowship for my fourth year from the Social Sciences and Humanities Research Council of Canada. The council also provided the funds for a grant from the Humanities and Social Sciences Federation of Canada to assist with the costs of publishing of this book. The Canadian Association for Studies in Co-operation awarded me the Alexander Laidlaw Fellowship. The University of Victoria Department of History helped to pay for my research trips.

In addition, I would like to thank the staffs at the Glenbow Archives in Calgary, the Provincial Archives of Alberta in Edmonton, the National Archives of Canada in Ottawa, and the Queen's University Archives in Kingston for their capable assistance. Last, but not least, I wish to acknowledge my wife, Faye, and daughter, Sara, who made this project possible and enjoyable.

B.J.R.

THE RISE OF AGRARIAN DEMOCRACY:
THE UNITED FARMERS AND
FARM WOMEN OF ALBERTA, 1909–1921

Introduction

The old country hall stands decrepit, leaning and rotting at the foundation, its windows boarded up, its paint – the little that remains – peeling. The interior, renovated in tacky 1960s fashion, is in shambles from hard use, neglect, and vandalism.

This was once a happy place. Here, with a blue and gold flag hung proudly on the wall proclaiming 'our motto equity,' farmers chatted, smoked, educated themselves, and planned the next co-operative shipment. Here, women overcame loneliness, sewed for the Red Cross, wrote resolutions demanding legal rights, and discussed household efficiency. Here, the junior United Farmers of Alberta (UFA) held debates and shouted, 'Hip hooray, we are members of the UFA.' Here, youth and adults tripped the light fantastic into the 'wee sma'' hours of the night to the tune of 'Yankee Doodle' played on a screechy violin. Here, a sense of community, mutuality, and collective confidence was built. Here, farmers perceived that a truly just society was within their reach and took political action to grasp it.

All that remain are the ghosts of those memories and the sound of the door flapping in the wind.

All eyes were fixed on the doorway of the Mechanics' Hall in Edmonton, Alberta, on 14 January 1909 at the Alberta Farmers' Association (AFA) convention. The weathered delegates shifted in restless anticipation and discussed the imminent event in subdued tones. Suddenly, James Speakman, beaming from ear to ear, appeared at the entrance with the Society of Equity delegates and announced the arrival of 'the other section of the United Farmers of Alberta.' The response was pandemonium. Instantly, a chorus of 'For They Are Jolly Good Fellows' reverberated through the hall as the Equity men marched down the aisles and found seats. Then, after three hearty cheers for both the old organizations and the new one, AFA president Fletcher 'extended the hand of good fellowship to all.'[1] The amalgamation was complete. The United Farmers of Alberta was born.

Its gestation had been lengthy. Since 1905 the two associations had tried to join forces. Most sensed that the new organization had a grand destiny, but none of the 100 delegates who attended the opening of the Legislative Assembly on that afternoon expected that in twelve short years a UFA government would be formed. The UFA and the United Farm Women of Alberta (UFWA) would also see all their candidates elected in the 1921 federal election; would spawn a great co-operative movement culminating in the Wheat Pool; would be responsible for important women's rights, social, and agrarian legislation; and would immutably mould Alberta's political culture.

This is the story of one of the greatest mass democratic movements in Canadian history and one of the most successful state- or provincial-level farm bodies in North American history. Not only did it have a pro-portionately larger membership at its peak than its provincial and many of its American counterparts,[2] but it was a formidable political pressure group in its earliest years, and it held power provincially from 1921 to 1935, while electing a majority of Alberta's members of Parliament in that period. No other agrarian movement in the United States or Canada has enjoyed such political longevity without fusion or an alliance with one of the old political parties. It is also no coincidence that the UFA/UFWA was the first prairie farm organization to establish a wheat pool.

Despite the remarkable record of the UFA/UFWA, this study is the first scholarly book devoted exclusively to its story. Indeed, it is the only book of its kind on *any* of the early post-Confederation provincial agrar-ian organizations, even though in their day they were well known to the literate public, wielded considerable political power, and represented the largest occupational group on the continent. The study begins by tracing the roots of the Alberta movement and covers the period to 1921, when the agrarian revolt broke out. Along the way, like the earlier work of L.A. Wood, it describes the central Canadian background of the Alberta farm movement, and, like the comparative study by Paul Sharp, it shows environmental and American influences. Following W.L. Mor-ton, it tries to illumine the many factors behind the UFA/UFWA; unlike his work, it sees the organization more as a class than as a sectional movement. It elaborates on Ian MacPherson's argument that co-operation shaped the UFA/UFWA, and, like David Laycock's study of prairie populism, it reveals diversity in agrarian thought. Unlike biographies of farm leaders that exaggerate their subjects' influence and importance,[3] this study examines the UFA/UFWA as a grassroots movement. It does not ignore the role of leadership, but concentrates on the rank and file by analysing convention voting, letters to the editor, and local secretaries' reports. It rejects some scholars' contention that farmers were simply entrepreneurs whose main aim was to improve their status within capitalism through scientific techniques, pressure tactics, and 'managerial capitalism.'[4] It favours the view that farmers sought popular political control and wanted to protect their families, communities, and way of life from corporate hegemony. At the same time, it recognizes that farmers often used business methods to preserve their traditional values and lifestyle.[5]

Most published studies on the UFA/UFWA focus on its politics, not on the organization itself. In particular, they say little about the UFWA and concepts of gender in the movement.[6] They also abstract farmers from their local and social context; they fail to explore links between the UFA/UFWA and the rural economy and do not examine, in any depth, relations between different groups of farmers and between farmers and other 'classes.' Moreover, they barely consider the dynamic role of education in the movement. This book seeks to fill these gaps.

The main theme of the study is that the UFA/UFWA had a 'movement culture' that helped it to grow and develop. As a mass movement, the UFA/UFWA was a 'group venture extending beyond a local community or a single event and involving a systemic effort to inaugurate changes in thought, behavior, and social relationships.'[7] It arose because farmers' demands for reform were frustrated by what they felt was an unresponsive political system. In mobilizing to meet this challenge, they created a unique culture, a movement culture.

Lawrence Goodwyn argues that American farmers' co-operative experience spawned such a culture, one that led them to support the Populist movement. Critics have revealed weaknesses in Goodwyn's argument about the strength of the co-op movement in Populist states, but other scholars confirm the existence of a Populist movement culture, arguing that it stemmed from different sources,[8] not necessarily co-operative enterprise. This study similarly affirms that the UFA/UFWA movement culture emerged from farmers' class, hinterland, agricultural, community, co-operative, and movement experiences and from various intellectual and cultural influences. It was grounded in a material, social, and local context, yet was affected by a range of factors.

The UFA/UFWA movement culture helped the movement to develop in three phases.[9] In the first phase, the 'forming of the movement,' which spanned the three decades from 1879 to 1909, farmers started to question the economic and political status quo and acquired a nascent movement culture that prodded them to create several farm associations. Organizational rivalry brought on the final act of movement formation – the birth of the UFA. In the second phase, the 'building of the movement,' which lasted from 1909 to 1918, the organization gained a solid membership base, established a women's section, built its culture, and came to the brink of independent political action. In the 'politicizing of the movement' phase, which began in 1919, farmers committed themselves to such action, were confirmed in this decision by their interpretation of events, gained women's political support, created political structures, and entered the 1921 elections.

Understanding the movement culture that helped to push farmers through these phases is challenging because, as Robert Darnton points out, people of other cultures 'do not think the way we do.'[10] Non-elite, early modern Europeans enjoyed torturing cats; we find the idea repulsive. The eighteenth-century popular French mindset clearly differed from our own, but we rarely think that major groups in recent history in our own country might have had a different world view from ours. Yet the UFA/UFWA culture was distinct from our early twenty-first-century, urban outlook.

We can perceive that cultural gap by applying Darnton's maxim: 'When you realize that you are not getting something – a joke, a proverb, a ceremony – that is particularly meaningful to the natives, you can see where to grasp a foreign system of meaning.' It is worth considering whether we really 'get' the following statements and if they have such a 'foreign' meaning:

> Ours is a great world movement which will make a nobler civilization ... We are in the midst of a great civic, a great national, awakening; a silent revolution is in progress throughout the whole civilized world.

> It is fitting that we ... should dedicate ourselves with a firm determination to do our share in lifting humanity from the dismal swamp of political

debauchery where rule supreme the powers of darkness; dedicate ourselves to a higher ... conception – a conception of universal brotherhood
and sisterhood.[11]

These statements, written by Alberta farmers, may sound to us like self-
justifying rhetoric or quaintly naïve mumbo jumbo. This assessment contains a grain of truth, but our negative or vague impressions of the writings of intelligent and earnest farmers should alert us that we are not
quite 'getting' their 'foreign system of meaning.' In fact, by deciphering
their language, we see that they were not foolishly utopian. Nor was their
discourse empty or merely self-serving. It was 'meaningful' – to them.

The point is that we are dealing with another culture. How many of us
would talk about our organizations as these farmers spoke of theirs?
People do not respond mechanically to their circumstances; a culture
mediates their responses to their environment. Some labour historians
recognize this fact; few scholars of rural life have done so.[12]

The UFA/UFWA movement culture, which comprised assumptions,
beliefs, and metaphors, expressed farmers' class interests and was a
weapon in their pursuit of political power, drained off their tension by
providing scapegoats, such as 'big business,' and sustained them in their
struggles by conjoining them and assuring them of ultimate victory. It
also helped them to communicate their agenda to the public. It was a
response to sociopsychological 'strains' arising from frontier experience, environmental disaster, price squeezes, the Great War, corporate
economic and political control, and the general culture's inability to
explain these pressures.[13]

At the heart of this movement culture were feelings of community; a
sense of class opposition; assumptions about gender roles and traits;
commitment to organization, co-operation, democracy, citizenship, and
education; a social ethic; religious convictions; agrarian ideology; and
collective self-confidence. The emergence and evolution of these sensibilities helped to 'form,' 'build,' and 'politicize' the movement – helped
it to move through the forming, building, and politicizing phases – as
follows.

From pride in their districts, collective and local projects, mutual aid,
social ties and activities, and economic bonds rooted in occupational
pluralism and non-staple exchange, farmers developed a sense of community and mutuality. This sense provided cohesion that enabled them
to work together to form and build the movement and ultimately to
take direct political action.

Farmers' feelings of community and experience with state and business power helped to foster a sense of solidarity and class opposition to corporate economic and political control. This class consciousness formed, built, and politicized the movement by drawing farmers to it for protection and action, eventually political action. The UFA/UFWA maintained its fighting strength by accommodating among producers differences resulting from ideology, ethnicity, economic status, and agricultural specialization.

Assumptions about gender reinforced farmers' sense of class opposition and otherwise shaped the movement. Aspiring to be 'manly,' farm men formed and built the movement and supported UFA politics to defend their families, class, and country. Women used the movement to protect the home, to gain gender rights, and to promote agrarian interests. Though the UFA never granted them equality, it endorsed their agenda, including their equal rights demands, because of their maternal ideology, political support, and their community, reform, domestic, and farm work. By their unpaid work in the home and field, women made the rural economy, and hence the movement, viable; by joining the UFWA and voting UFA, they built and politicized the movement.

Both sexes believed that agrarian organization would give them great collective power. Consequently, beginning in the 1890s, farmers created several associations, but organizational rivalry led them to form the *United* Farmers of Alberta. They then built the movement, convinced that if they recruited most farmers, they would become a powerful political pressure group. When their influence proved limited, they were politicized, certain that every farmer brought into the movement would vote UFA.

Through organization, farmers hoped to create a co-operative society. Radical and co-operative ideology, the social gospel, and collaboration among farmers and between farmers and other groups forged a co-operative ethos, an ill-defined notion that co-operation should replace competition in economic, political, and social affairs. This idea built the movement by attracting producers to it. Farmers were later politicized when they perceived that only direct politics could usher in the co-operative commonwealth. Co-operative enterprise strengthened farmers' co-operative ethic and formed the movement by hastening the creation of the UFA, built the UFA/UFWA by providing an economic incentive to join, and politicized farmers by elevating their sense of possibility.

They sought a democratic as well as a co-operative society. Part of their agrarian heritage, farmers' commitment to democracy was developed by their class experience and the democratic example of the UFA/ UFWA, which they felt Canadian politics should emulate. They were drawn to the movement and built it to bring about this truly democratic political system, and when the old parties appeared beyond redemption, farmers were politicized and took independent political action. The post-war UFA/UFWA philosophy told them that a 'class'-based political strategy would usher in the co-operative, democratic order they sought.

Farmers' belief in citizenship was a conviction that it was their duty to work for a more democratic society. Initially, this meant electing good candidates in the two main parties and building the movement into an effective political pressure group. When this action did not produce the desired results, farmers' citizenship sensibilities prodded them to take direct political action through UFA/UFWA constituency associations, so that farmers themselves, rather than plutocrats or professional politicians, controlled who represented them and what they did.

Farmers' belief, based on popular tradition, that education would empower them to solve their problems further encouraged them to form and build the movement. Education, including that supported by corporations and the state, trained them for this work and helped them to come to a consensus about key issues, which, in turn, prompted them to act. After the war, farmers' learning about independent politics and their need for it politicized the UFA/UFWA.

While educating themselves, farmers developed a social ethic: a belief that state action could reform society. Wartime idealism and anxiety, state intervention, maternal and other ideology, economic hardship, charity work, and veterans' needs inclined them to seek greater freedom, public morality, and equality of opportunity and condition through social reform, libertarian and welfare legislation, and progressive taxation. Farmers built the movement to lobby for these measures and were politicized when they felt compelled to enter politics as a movement to implement most of them.

Religious beliefs strengthened farmers' social ethic and built the movement by giving it a moral impulse while convincing members that their demands and critique of society were just. Starting in the war years, many farmers were inspired by a social gospel message of social regeneration through legislation or class action. Some saw the UFA/UFWA as a quasi-religious institution. Later, farmers caught a millennial vision of a redeemed society rising out of wartime sacrifices and were politicized to take independent action to realize their Christian ideas about society.

Agrarian ideology – the agrarian myth and the ideas of the country life movement – also inspired farmers. The agrarian myth told them they were the source of national prosperity and virtue, which attracted new members and energized farmers to build the movement. Moreover, the myth helped them to justify their program; since agriculture was the nation's main industry, what benefited farmers surely would benefit everyone. During the war, the movement was built as farmers were drawn to its country life ideas and sought to implement them. After the war, farmers were politicized once they concluded that country life solutions required UFA/UFWA political action.

Farmers' agrarian ideology, their legislative, co-operative, and community successes, and their movement education imparted self-respect and collective confidence – the cornerstones of any successful movement. Such feelings emboldened farmers to build the movement and then to enter politics.

The UFA/UFWA movement culture also had a radical and a liberal ideology. The pre-UFA associations articulated one or the other of these doctrines, both of which were brought into the UFA/UFWA. The ideologies were poles on a cultural continuum; many farmers were not purely radical or purely liberal in their thinking, although most favoured the assumptions of one or the other ideology.

Alberta radicals, drawing on British and North American radical traditions, castigated monopolies and opposed 'special privileges' for corporations. Following the labour theory of value – that labour creates and should retain all value – they saw themselves and workers as fellow producers. This belief led them to call for a farmer-labour political alliance to implement their program of radical monetary reform and state ownership to redistribute wealth. Radicals were stronger civil and women's rights activists than liberal Alberta farmers and were very suspicious of big business. Some sought the end of capitalism.

Prominent UFA/UFWA radicals included the intrepid ex-American mechanic, W.R. Ball; the English single taxer and second UFA president, W.J. Tregillus; Strathcona pioneer Rice Sheppard, an enduring warhorse; the Danish-born, ex-Chicago socialist, John Glambeck; Emma Root, a brilliant UFA/UFWA membership recruiter; the distinguished-looking ex-Populist Kansas governor, John Leedy; and the sharp-featured, quick-witted former Shetland Islander, William Irvine. These and other men and women sustained a vibrant radical ideology that influenced the whole movement.

Ideological liberals had more faith than radicals in the benefits of a truly competitive capitalism. At the same time, owing to a 'Tory touch' or the 'new liberalism,'[14] they supported state interventionism and ownership, where necessary, to ensure equality of opportunity and greater equality of condition. Their favoured solutions for farmers' economic ills included self-help through improved farm production and, especially, co-operative buying and selling. Before 1919 they preferred pressure politics to independent political action.

Notable liberals included Daniel Warner, an Alberta Farmers' Association president and UFA officer, who, judging by appearances, should have been a sheriff in his native Nebraska; the first UFA president, James Bower, a workmanlike farmer-co-operator with a substantial moustache; James Speakman, the articulate, grandfatherly third UFA president; Irene Parlby, a UFWA president from an upper-middle-class English background, who commanded great respect; Margaret Gunn, a country life advocate; S.S. Dunham, a lawyer and irrigation farmer; and the lanky, Lincolnesque Henry Wise Wood, the greatest UFA leader of all, whose sincerity and homely charisma attracted mass loyalty.

The numerically dominant liberal wing usually convinced the UFA/UFWA to adopt its agenda, although towards the end of the war the radicals persuaded the liberals to endorse independent political action. Until that point, there was tension between the two wings over politics and sometimes other matters, but there was never a rupture; the organizational rivalry of the pre-UFA era convinced farmers that they needed to maintain unity.

Women were not formally part of the Alberta farm movement until 1915. Once in the organization, they espoused the same movement culture as the men, including the radical or liberal ideology, while concerning themselves with women's rights and domestic and social issues associated with their 'sphere.' Their sense of class was generally stronger than their gender loyalty, although neither predominated in all situations. Both women and men simultaneously had class, movement, gender, religious, community, ethnic, racial, and other identities; and any could come to the fore in a particular circumstance.[15]

Chapters 1, 2, 5, and 8 are chronological chapters that analyse the Alberta farm movement as it evolved through the forming, building, and politicizing phases. Chapters 3, 4, 6, and 7 are thematic and discuss subjects that were important throughout the period of study and helped to develop the movement. Chapter 1 covers the forming of the movement, which occurred from 1879 to 1909. Chapter 2 covers the first part of the building of the movement, which occurred from 1909 to 1913. Its main theme is the growth of collective self-respect. Chapter 3 shows how a non-staple rural economy moulded a sense of reciprocity on which the movement relied. Chapter 4 reveals how local activities and relations among farmers and between the UFA/UFWA and other local and regional groups promoted feelings of community and co-operation, which also strengthened the movement. As well, the chapter reveals the limits of farmers' sense of community, while arguing that the UFA/ UFWA generally maintained its solidarity and effectiveness by accommodating differences between producers. Chapter 5 explores the second part of the building of the movement, which took place from 1914 to 1918. It examines the origins and early development of the UFWA and how the movement culture, shaped by the war, edged the UFA/UFWA towards independent political action. Chapter 6 considers how co-operative enterprise and ideology affected the movement; chapter 7 considers the role of education. Chapter 8 deals with the politicization of the movement after the war, and chapter 9 describes the post-war UFA/ UFWA philosophy and its politicizing effect. The epilogue briefly looks past 1921 and summarizes the study's main arguments.

Chapter One

The Forming of the Movement,
1879–1909

The trouble may be expressed in one word, monopoly.[1]

1880. The future Alberta was on the fringe of the North American frontier. The tiny settler population clustered around fur-trade posts, mission stations, and Mounted Police forts. Calgary and Edmonton combined had only a few hundred souls. The railway had not yet arrived; the era of big cattle barons had not begun. Politically, the territory was a colony of Ottawa.

In this context, the fiery Frank Oliver, a former journalist for George Brown's *Globe*, that gritty organ of Ontario Liberalism, established the *Edmonton Bulletin*, which became a major force in the 'forming of the movement.' It initiated and popularized local and regional farm organizations, expressed agrarian and western discontent, and provided space for farmers to debate issues.

The movement-forming era in Alberta, which spanned the three decades to 1909, involved the emergence of newspapers like the *Bulletin* and of farm associations that questioned the economic and political status quo. Two approaches and ideologies developed that would form the two wings of the United Farmers and Farm Women of Alberta (UFA/UFWA). Radical organizations – the Patrons of Industry, the Farmers' Association of Alberta (FAA), and the Society of Equity (S of E) – advocated state action, co-operative enterprise, direct politics, and farmer-labour collaboration, while enunciating producerism, anti-monopolism, and equal rights.[2] In contrast, liberal groups – the Territorial Grain Growers' Association (TGGA), the Alberta Farmers' Association (AFA), and to some extent the *Bulletin* – promoted pressure politics and improved marketing and production, while opposing socialism and a farmer-labour alliance.

Farmers developed a nascent movement culture that led them to form these organizations. In particular, they acquired a sense that corporations and middlemen exploited them, a feeling of class opposition heightened by their conviction that the land would otherwise make them prosperous. A larger western farm movement formed the Alberta movement institutionally and culturally by entering Alberta and creating myths that imparted collective self-confidence. Farmers came to believe that organization would make them powerful – if their competing farm associations could be united. This realization prompted the final act of movement formation: the creation of the UFA.

The early Alberta farm movement was part of a larger North American agrarian movement that arose from the 'efforts of farmers either to protect themselves against the impact of the evolving commercial-capitalist economy or to catch step with it.' From the mid-nineteenth century, North American farmers were increasingly subject, as producers and consumers, to the credit system and markets of industrial capitalism. Shaped by this context, the emerging Alberta movement was also formed by the culture of the Grange, an American farm organization that first arrived north of the border in Ontario in the 1870s. The taproot from which subsequent Canadian farm associations emerged,[3] the Ontario Grange demonstrated the possibilities of farmer co-operative trading, made education an agrarian tradition, and, by prohibiting politics and partisan discussion, fashioned an anti-political current in farm circles that rendered many Alberta producers wary of direct politics.

In 1879, the year the Canadian Grange peaked, the first step in the formation of the Alberta farm movement was taken when the Edmonton Agricultural Society (EAS) was organized. This was the seed from which the Alberta movement would develop: EAS members would later be prominent in the Alberta Patrons of Industry, the Strathcona TGGA, the AFA, the S of E, and the UFA. The EAS eulogized northern Alberta's agricultural potential in its exhibition advertisements, an image of the land that farmers embraced; they yearned, as frontier men and women, to be proud of and feel attached to their districts. Agricultural surpluses in the Edmonton area in the 1880s reinforced their faith in their farms, but they had to restrict production because there was no railway to take their produce to outside markets.[4]

Frustrated, they formed the EAS into an incipient protest body. In

1884 it demanded a link to the Canadian Pacific Railway and complained that farmers could not bid on government contracts. The *Bulletin* strongly supported the EAS in this and other endeavours and helped farmers to see themselves as part of a larger western movement by keeping them abreast of producers' struggles in Manitoba. As they read about the grain trade and the CPR 'monopoly' in the *Bulletin*,[5] farmers developed their sense of opposition to corporate power.

The railway finally reached South Edmonton (later renamed Strathcona) in 1891, but high freight charges dashed local farmers' hopes that it would open up lucrative markets. Their disillusionment was heightened by their belief, confirmed through their success at the Winnipeg agricultural exhibition, that without this impediment their land would make them prosperous. They responded by attending a meeting called by Daniel Maloney, a former EAS president, at which they demanded lower freight rates. The CPR did reduce rates – but only slightly.[6]

Farmers near Sturgeon River, just north of Edmonton, sought a more effective and flexible organization than the EAS to deal with such problems. They met in December 1891 under George Long, an EAS leader and future UFA officer, and considered establishing a farmers' union to improve farm production, obtain cheaper imports, and secure better prices by finding new markets. In the next year, after studying the constitutions of several farm associations, they organized a branch of the Patrons of Industry. The Patrons, like the Grange, began as an American organization. It spread into Ontario in 1889 and rooted itself in Manitoba two years later. The Ontario Patrons established a binder twine company, which, until its collapse in 1912, provided an impressive co-operative example to farmers across the country. The Manitoba and Ontario Patrons also took direct political action, the former winning a provincial by-election in 1894 and two seats in the 1896 provincial election, the latter winning seventeen seats in the 1894 provincial election.[7]

Patron ideology was grounded in late-eighteenth-century English and American radicalism, which blamed political oppression for economic problems. In concert with many American labour and agrarian movements from the 1860s on, Patrons enunciated producerism, depicting farmers and workers as fellow producers with a common cause against the non-producing rich, who exploited them. Articulating the labour theory of value, Patrons argued that labour was the source of all value and that producers consequently were entitled to the wealth they created. Echoing other radicals of the age, they also articulated anti-monopolism, denouncing corporate power – what they called 'monopolies' – while demanding 'equal rights,' that is, no 'special privileges' for big business.[8]

Although it never gained a foothold in Canada, American Populism, the largest nineteenth-century American farm movement, was a further influence on the Alberta movement. Its national electoral defeat in 1896 revealed, as did the Ontario and Manitoba Patron defeats in the later 1890s, the apparent folly of third-party action. The lesson was not lost on the Alberta TGGA, the AFA, and the early UFA. Moreover, like the Grange and the Patrons, Populism advocated farmer co-operation and established agrarian ideals in North American farm culture. Following the paths of the Anti-Monopoly parties and the Greenback party of the 1870s, it also made equal rights, producerism, and anti-monopolism key radical agrarian notions, which the FAA, the Alberta S of E, and UFA/UFWA radicals would adopt. Furthermore, Populism, the Patrons, and their predecessors reinforced farmers' suspicions about banks, middlemen, lawyers, and speculators; strengthened their opposition to inequitable taxation, public debt, and corruption in government; expressed their desire for economy in government and for civil service and tariff reform; deepened their antagonism towards the corporate 'East'; raised their class consciousness; and confirmed their conviction that through organization they could ameliorate their lot. By promoting these sentiments and ideas in Alberta – where they mingled with British co-operative, labour, and socialist thought, Ontario free trade liberalism, and European populist antipathies towards elites[9] – the Patrons of Industry helped to form the early Alberta farm movement.

Following the Sturgeon River farmers, Patron lodges sprang up like wild oats around Edmonton starting in 1892, and by 1894 organization was under way along the Calgary and Edmonton Railway line. Like other western farmers, the Patrons attacked high tariffs and freight rates. An Alberta lodge petition read in the House of Commons in 1893 declared that the dominion government should not promote western settlement unless freight charges and duties on farm machinery and binder twine were lowered. Alberta Patrons were also involved in meetings to form co-operative creameries, and in 1894 they requested a bridge to provide northern access to the railhead at Strathcona, while threatening to elect candidates to the Territorial Assembly in support of a demand for an Edmonton normal school. A Patron county association called for a division of the District of Alberta into two electoral jurisdictions to give northern Alberta farmers fair representation in Parliament against the southern ranching community.[10] Already, north-south tensions, which would be exacerbated by controversies such as the choice of provincial capital, were evident in Alberta.

Inspired by Ontario Patron political victories in 1894, Alberta Patrons helped to elect Daniel Maloney to the Territorial Assembly. Two years later, they supported Frank Oliver as a federal candidate. Like many Alberta Patrons, Oliver was less radical and more liberal than most Manitoba and Ontario Patron leaders; he called himself an 'independent liberal' and endorsed the Liberal party's provincial rights stance, its Manitoba school policy, and its tariff-for-revenue plank. Invoking the agrarian myth, he argued that lower tariffs were needed because agriculture was Canada's wealth-producing industry. He also called for an end to the CPR monopoly.[11]

Oliver's victory was the high-water mark of Patron success in Alberta and the culmination of an important period of movement formation. The Patrons had mobilized farmers and captured their imaginations, fashioning them into a collective force. But the Patrons and their political movement would be cut short. After 1896 no Patrons ran for political office in Alberta, and the Patron movement outside Alberta was practically wiped out. Improved economic conditions dampened farmers' sense of grievance, and the Liberals co-opted the Patrons with the Crow's Nest Pass Agreement and the Fielding tariff of 1897, which reduced duties on farm articles.[12]

In short order, however, a war erupted with the CPR and the grain trade that opened a new chapter in the formation of a prairie farm movement. In identifying with the struggle, Alberta farmers developed a culture of class awareness and opposition and gained pride from the legislation that resulted. Stories emerging from the events amplified these feelings, attracted new recruits, and sustained producers in subsequent skirmishes. The CPR fired the first volley in 1897, when it decided it would no longer take grain from flat warehouses at centres with grain elevators.[13] In response, James Douglas, a member of Parliament from Assiniboia elected with Patron support, moved first reading of a bill in February 1898 that sought to force railways to receive grain from flat warehouses and farmers' vehicles. The CPR conceded farmers' right to load grain from wagons,[14] and the bill was dropped. Unsatisfied, Douglas introduced another bill in the following year; besides demanding flat-warehouse privileges, it called for a chief inspector to supervise the grain industry. The House agreed to have the issue considered by a committee, which approved the proposal for an inspector but rejected the flat-warehouse clause.[15]

Douglas and Frank Oliver were livid. Oliver lampooned the committee members who had voted to protect 'the western farmer from the mistaken idea that he ought to have a free market for his produce.' In response to such criticism, the government appointed the Royal Commission on the Shipment and Transportation of Grain. At the hearing in Edmonton, farmers complained about prices and weighing of grain and about the railway's announcement that it would impose extra charges if cars were not loaded or unloaded in twenty-four hours. Although attendance was low at the hearing, partly because of farmers' lack of an effective organization, their representation had some effect: the CPR did extend the loading time for Edmonton.[16]

The commission's report formed the basis of the Manitoba Grain Act of 1900. The act provided for improved supervision of the grain industry and the erection, under specified circumstances, of flat warehouses and loading platforms. While the act was a partial victory for farmers, it did not end their discontent. Difficulties in enforcing it gave rise to new grievances, which led them to conclude that producer-owned grain companies, and ultimately direct political action, were needed to solve their grain shipping and handling problems.[17]

The act also could not help farmers in a dispute about the oats market in 1901–2. This controversy did more to develop Alberta farmers' opposition to the grain trade than conditions leading to the Manitoba Grain Act had done. The incident began in December 1901 when, after a sharp rise in prices, the bottom fell out of the oats market. Frank Oliver accused the Manitoba 'grain combine' of paying high prices to dissuade farmers from selling to the government under its contract to supply oats for the South African War. Having ensured that the contract could not be filled, the combine allegedly controlled the market and dropped its prices. In addition, the Grain Standards Board, a tool of the combine according to Oliver, announced that all damaged oats would be classified as No. 1 or No. 2 Alberta – which implied that most damaged oats were from Alberta. The Board also graded virtually all Alberta oats as injured. Oliver saw all this as an attempt to depress Alberta oat prices.[18]

Alberta farmers and businessmen protested the grading of Alberta oats, especially after they learned that an Edmonton oat exhibit had won first prize at a Paris exhibition. Once again, farmers' faith in the land fuelled their anger; they believed that the Board had stolen the wealth created by their productive farms. The government responded by finding new markets and lowering its standards for purchases for

South Africa, and it removed oats from the Board's control. Despite this action, the oats episode left lingering animosity among farmers that made them receptive to new farm associations[19] – thus helping to form the movement.

As the oats controversy came to a head in late 1901, the Grain Growers' movement was born at Indian Head, just east of Regina. This movement would help to form the Alberta movement as it spread into Alberta and imparted its mythology. Movements create myths and write their own history to foster commitment among members. Tales about the Grain Growers would develop western and Alberta farmers' sense of class solidarity and pride. The stimulus for the creation of the Grain Growers was the CPR's difficulty in handling the record 1901 crop. Because grain could be loaded most quickly from elevators, the company refused to allot cars to farmers shipping from warehouses and platforms. Oliver attacked the CPR in Parliament for this policy, and farmers took action at Indian Head by forming the Territorial Grain Growers' Association (TGGA). Ottawa responded to TGGA demands by passing amendments in 1902 and 1903 that provided for more loading platforms and warehouses while requiring railways to issue cars in the order they were applied for, so that railways could no longer favour elevator companies over farmers in distributing cars.[20]

The 1902 crop was even heavier than that of 1901, and the 'freight car famine' was more acute. The TGGA proved in the Sintaluta court case that the CPR had violated the 1902 act, which forced the company to obey the law. David had slain Goliath! For years, the western farm movement considered this victory among its 'most treasured possessions'; it gave farmers collective self-respect. With the prestige gained from the Sintaluta case, the TGGA spread like wildfire across the Territories and into Manitoba. Its progression into Alberta, however, was comparatively slow. The first Alberta TGGA branch was not formed until 1905, partly owing to the competition of the Farmers' Association of Lacombe, 'the forgotten forerunner of the U.F.A.'[21]

The leading force behind this organization was the colourful J.J. Gregory, another Ontario influence on the Alberta movement, like the Grange and the Patrons. Gregory – 'the Colonel' – moved to the Lacombe district of central Alberta in 1893 and was one of several who tried in 1898 to establish the Lacombe Co-operative Society, a multi-faceted co-op based on Rochdale principles. The Society collapsed the following year because of poor finances, lack of farmer support, credit problems with wholesalers, and the opposition of banks and merchants.

But this failure did not deter Gregory from trying to create a farm association. Increasing agrarian unrest in 1902–3 convinced him to act. He did not establish a TGGA branch, however, believing that the TGGA was primarily intended for wheat producers and that Alberta farmers wanted a local organization.[22] As a radical, he was also averse to the TGGA's liberalism and avoidance of direct politics.

A letter by William R. Ball that appeared in the *Bulletin* in December 1902 triggered Gregory's organizing efforts. Ball, a Strathcona area farmer and ex-American mechanic, would be largely responsible for establishing key ideas of the movement's radical wing, notions that remained intact well into the UFA era. Virtually absent from the historical record and a self-styled 'crank,' Ball was as important in developing radical Alberta agrarianism as William Irvine would be in later years. Ball's letter articulated the themes he would preach for over a decade. In the language of producerism and the labour theory of value, he called on 'the toilers and producers' who 'create all the wealth' to form a protective union. Further, he expressed a belief in organization, based on agrarian and labour tradition, that would become a central movement culture axiom. He noted that other classes had combined and promised farmers that organization would secure measures such as government railways and loans. He also revealed the Christian foundation of his critique, arguing that God intended 'the profit from the large crops for those who tilled the soil' rather than for 'a few immensely rich men.'[23]

In early 1903 Ball raised farmers' class awareness at several rallies in support of government ownership of railways. He compared CPR rates with those of the Intercolonial Railway to suggest how much the West would save if its railways were state owned. He urged farmers to hold meetings to discuss railway problems and tried to organize a political society to address farmers' difficulties. Likely in response to this agitation and to Ball's letter in the *Bulletin* calling for a protective union, Gregory and his son-in-law, F.B. Watson, organized the Farmers' Association of Lacombe in April 1903, which soon expanded to become the Farmers' Association of Alberta (FAA).[24]

The FAA was a re-creation of the Ontario Patrons, with which Gregory and Watson were familiar. Like the Patrons, the FAA sympathized with labour, supported co-operative enterprise, and entered politics. After a successful recruiting campaign, the FAA nominated Gregory as its candidate for the Strathcona riding in the 1904 federal election. Henceforth, the Liberal *Bulletin* referred to the FAA as the 'Farmers' Alliance,' the farm movement behind American Populism, to cast Gregory's candidacy in a negative light by associating him with a politically defeated organization. Undaunted, Gregory carried on. His platform called for state railways and loans, aid for farmer co-ops, more government creameries and experimental farms, and the opening of B.C. markets for Alberta produce. Of Loyalist stock, Gregory promised to maintain the British tie and resist undesirable American influences.[25]

It was a mistake to play the anti-American card in a constituency where a third of the population was American. This fact plus weak organization, a lack of funds and newspaper support, and the popularity of the old parties led to Gregory's crushing defeat, which killed the FAA.[26] Its demise and that of the Ontario Patrons and American Populism created a strong aversion to independent politics among liberal Alberta farmers.

Gregory's defeat did not mean that farmers were content with their lot. The large harvest of 1904 confirmed their faith in the productivity of their land, but they were disillusioned when they were denied their 'just portion' by unfair weighing, grading, and dockage. As prices also were low for livestock, farmers could not meet their obligations. Consequently, they 'got a little excited and wanted some action taken.'[27] The result was a new era of movement formation.

It began in the Poplar Lake area north of Edmonton in the fall of 1904, when several school trustees discussed 'the low prices and ... meagre returns for labor on the farm.' Believing that a combine existed in the Edmonton grain market, a subsequent meeting of electors appointed a committee to gather information about farm associations. Soon after – in late 1904 or January 1905 – some farmers of the district established a branch of the American Society of Equity (S of E). Founded in 1902 in Indiana by J.A. Everitt, the Society spread into several American states and gained a smattering of followers in Saskatchewan. The Poplar Lake farmers had been influenced by W.J. Keen, secretary of a local school district and a subscriber to the official Equity organ; some had also been exposed to Equity ideas in Nebraska, where they had emigrated from. The Society's central doctrine, 'controlled marketing to compel profitable prices for all farm products,'[28] involved setting prices for farm products and holding them off the market until those prices were obtained.

Reacting to the same conditions prompting the Poplar Lake farmers to take action, Strathcona pioneer Rice Sheppard, in a letter to the *Bulletin*, called on farmers to organize. W.J. Keen, the Alberta Society secretary, responded with a letter promoting the S of E. Sharing with Ball and Sheppard a belief in the power of agrarian organization in the language of anti-monopolism and equal rights, Keen declared that the Society platform sought 'justice and equity to all' and would, when backed 'by a million or more strongly organized farmers,' carry such weight that 'no political party, no railway monopoly, no implement trust' would 'dare oppose' it.[29] Such rhetoric was characteristic of the Society and would be taken up by UFA/UFWA radicals.

Sheppard replied that the S of E was suitable only for conditions in the United States. He exhorted farmers to establish a branch of the TGGA, which he, Ball, and several other farmers subsequently did at Strathcona in March 1905.[30] The activities, rivalry, and efforts to unite the TGGA and S of E would form the Alberta movement into the UFA.

Sheppard would be an important leader in the TGGA, AFA, and UFA. He emigrated from England to the Edmonton area in 1898, where he became a successful farmer. A radical, he was one of the first UFA officers to support independent politics. He was an effective speaker, 'his highly emotional disposition' helping him to 'dramatize the need for rural organization in a way few others could have done.'[31] As was the case with Ball, Sheppard's intensity and radicalism flowed from religious convictions. He became secretary of the new TGGA branch, and Daniel Warner was elected president. Warner, a future UFA officer and UFA member of Parliament, moved from Nebraska in 1898 and became a prosperous farmer near Edmonton. W.F. Stevens, a giant of a man, was an early director of the Strathcona TGGA. Possessing an acute intellect, he would display impressive ability as secretary of the Alberta successor to the TGGA. Another early TGGA director was the volatile Joshua Fletcher. Young and impetuous, he gained a reputation as a skilful orator and was elected president in 1907.

The importance of these men lay mainly in the future. Meanwhile, they had to contend with the aggressive organizing of the S of E. By the spring of 1905 the Society had grown enough to hold a convention, and its executive, aiming to implement controlled marketing, decided to draw up a list of minimum prices farmers would accept for the next crop. The price of oats was so low that an Equitist exhorted farmers to join the Society by arguing that their being at the mercy of a few grain dealers did 'violence' to their 'manhood.'[32] It was unmanly to be ripped off by middlemen; real farm men should join the S of E.

The Society's strength was evident in its prominence in the parade held in Edmonton to celebrate the birth of Alberta as a province. For

Equitists, it was a moment of pride, but they obtained 'the place of honor' in the procession only when they agreed to show their name as 'Farmers" rather than 'American' Society of Equity. This was merely one instance of the Society's difficulty in promoting itself in Alberta. The majority of farmers in the province were Canadian or British born,[33] and many were wary of anything American. The Society later changed its name to Canadian Society of Equity, yet a taint of Americanism remained to hinder recruitment.

Notwithstanding, the Society had much to offer farmers. It bought binder twine co-operatively and its locals shipped members' grain. Moreover, in 1905 it convinced the Strathcona TGGA not to sell farm products below certain prices. This joint effort, though not very successful, revealed the Society's influence: it had convinced the TGGA to concede 'the very principle on which the rival organization was founded,' namely, controlled marketing. The two organizations also collaborated to try to improve the unprofitable hog market. In April 1905 the Strathcona TGGA appointed a committee to determine how many hogs Alberta exported and the volume of pork products Edmonton merchants imported. The Society supported the TGGA committee and asked it to publish its findings, which it did. The two associations later worked together on a submission for the Tariff Commission hearings.[34]

These efforts suggested to farmers that they would have greater success if they had a united movement. Accordingly, the major theme of the last four movement-forming years was the struggle to merge. The Strathcona TGGA initiated the first attempt in late 1905, which failed because the Society felt that the provincially oriented Alberta Farmers' Association (AFA) broached by the TGGA could not effectively control markets. Equitists believed that controlled marketing, to be truly successful, must be managed by a worldwide body. They were also suspicious of the close government links the AFA would have under the proposed constitution. For its part, the TGGA refused to join the S of E, maintaining that world prices could never be controlled and that Canadian governments would more likely listen to a Canadian association than an American one.[35] Society secretary W.J. Keen also played a role in the merger failure. At a meeting of TGGA and S of E representatives, he opposed a motion supporting the amalgamation and asked for the withdrawal of the AFA draft constitution. In correspondence to the locals, he argued that the constitution downplayed controlled marketing and that adopting it would be 'cutting loose from our Society.' He also suggested that the AFA would be a political organization and would be less democratic than the Society.[36]

The failure to merge was not complete. In December the Clover Bar branch of the S of E joined with the Alberta TGGA to form the AFA. Soon after, the new organization and the Society made separate presentations to the Tariff Commission. The AFA employed liberal jargon to argue that 'freedom of trade is a natural right.' Invoking the agrarian myth that farming was the 'fundamental industry,' it asserted that farmers' interests should have first priority in Ottawa, which would mean lower duties on lumber, farm implements, and other goods. Consistent with its generally pro-British perspective, the Association called for more trade with the empire. Overall, it wanted a 'tariff for revenue,' while asking, somewhat inconsistently, that the duty on hogs and pork be maintained. In contrast to the AFA's liberalism, the Society used radical rhetoric: It declared that capitalists 'unjustly' extorted labour and money through high tariffs, and it demanded that duties be made more 'equitable.' This moral economy notion about fairness contrasted with the AFA's market discourse. Finally, the Society requested a lower tariff on farm machinery and protested a proposed hike in the duty on lumber and fruit.[37]

After the commission hearings, the AFA launched a vigorous recruiting campaign. As the rival organizations vied for farmers' allegiance, much name calling and infighting ensued. Both bodies grew steadily, expanding even into southern Alberta. The Society claimed over 1,000 members in March 1906; the AFA listed 1,200 by May.[38]

In 1906 the AFA began work on one of its major preoccupations: the western shipment of produce, for sale in British Columbia and abroad. The AFA and its successor, the UFA, were imbued with 'the myth of the Japan market.' They believed that Japan's 40 million people would soon demand huge quantities of Alberta's agricultural products. Accordingly, the AFA called for a coastal terminal and changes to the Inspection and Grain acts to promote shipment to the coast. In testifying before the Agricultural Committee in Ottawa, Joshua Fletcher asked that farmers' car distribution rights for shipping east apply to western shipments. The government granted this demand and Fletcher's request for a classification for Alberta winter wheat.[39]

While emphasizing western markets, the AFA was concerned with a variety of issues. Its 1907 convention called for forest conservation, a commission to manage the trunk telephones, an investigation into interest rates, changes to the irrigation laws, and a coyote bounty.[40] This wide-ranging program contrasted with the S of E's rather narrow fixation on controlled marketing and state ownership and control: it demanded government elevators, terminals, meat-packing houses, telephones, railways, and loans, as well as compulsory hail insurance and graduated land taxes.

Several Equitists convinced the Society to accept this comparatively radical agenda, including the ex-American Populist R.C. Owens, the ex-Patron supporter George Long, and that old FAA warrior, J.J. Gregory – the 'Colonel,' no less. But the most influential person in this regard was W.R. Ball, who had defected from the AFA to the S of E by early 1906. Ball had never been comfortable with the liberal TGGA/AFA market philosophy. The idea of controlling the market was more palatable to his radical taste; he saw the strategy as an anti-monopolistic tool. 'Monopolies,' he declared, 'are our one common enemy and it is not necessary to emphasize to thinking men the importance of being in touch with farmers of all countries, thereby aiding one another to secure profitable prices.'[41]

Committed to controlled marketing and state interventionism, the S of E was less interested in finding new markets than the AFA was; it felt it would one day control the markets at hand, while governments would eliminate other forms of exploitation by owning and operating key industries. Because of this radical emphasis, the Society was less concerned than the AFA about local issues. Unlike AFA conventions, S of E conventions did not consider matters like herd laws, stray ordinances, fire control, and pests. The AFA's willingness to deal with such community issues and its stress on improving markets and correcting abuses in the grain trade contributed to its growing success.

Meanwhile, in May 1906 the AFA proposed a renewed attempt at amalgamation. The two associations agreed to hold simultaneous conventions for this purpose in the fall at Lacombe. It was not to be. The rock on which the merger talks in Lacombe foundered was an 'ultimatum' the AFA sent to the S of E. It conceded the name proposed by W.J. Keen – the Farmers' Union of Alberta – but stipulated that the new organization must not interfere with farm organizations outside the province. When a motion was moved at the Equity convention to accept these terms, Keen objected on the grounds that they compromised the Society's 'essential principle.' He argued strenuously that 'for the Society to accomplish its purpose – the central control of the market prices of farm produce – it was absolutely essential that the field of operations be not limited to Alberta or any other province, as their scope must be worldwide.' An Alberta-only organization, he asserted, 'would be fatal.'[42] A majority of Equitists agreed.

The AFA was equally unwilling to compromise. It wished to work with the Grain Growers' Associations in Saskatchewan and Manitoba; it did not want to link up with the American Society, which Equitists insisted a united Alberta movement must do. The AFA feared that a multinational farm organization might conflict with the Canadian movement. The AFA focus on western markets, especially its belief in the myth of the Japan market, also worked against a merger on S of E terms. AFA president Warner explained that

> We want an Alberta organization to look after the interests of the farmers of Alberta. Until recently we have been looking to the East for our markets, but now we are beginning to look to the Orient, and this matter of markets alone is of sufficient importance to warrant the continuance of an all-Alberta association. Our interests in this matter are vital, and to look after them we must have a distinct society, not one interested in Eastern Canada or in the United States, but in Alberta and in Alberta alone.[43]

Analysis in the press clarified the deeper philosophical reasons for the failed merger. One writer contrasted the S of E's unsuccessful attempts to dictate prices with the liberal and implicitly more successful AFA approach: co-operating with other farm organizations to secure 'every cent' for farmers' grain 'that market conditions warrant.' A pro-Society article dismissed the AFA's contention that farmers could never 'exert any controlling influence upon the price of their produce.' Noting that the Association's goal was 'unrestricted competition,' it argued that prices were governed, not by the law of supply and demand, but by the 'law of offer and demand.' It concluded that the 'proper way for the farmers to deal manfully with the trusts' was to adopt their method of collectively refusing to sell until buyers paid minimum prices.[44] This idea of controlling the market by organizing all farmers would be central to the pooling movement of the 1920s, but the AFA liberal market strategy was more popular in the pre-UFA era.

The AFA tried to make the market work for farmers by informing them about prices and buyers so that they could get top dollar for their products. In this way, middlemen could not 'make a haul' out of farmers' ignorance.[45] The Association also stressed that farmers had to produce the best product to get top prices, and it taught them through meetings, seed fairs, and stock judging schools how to increase the quantity and quality of their goods. Believing that increased production would only lower prices and benefit a few, the S of E was less interested in farm improvement. One local president, in response to a letter about Department of Agriculture seed fairs, argued that 'the government should try to get us better prices for what we raise now instead of trying to get us to raise larger crops.'[46]

The AFA emphasis on better farm methods was a product of the country life movement and progressivism, which suggested that farmers would succeed if they became good businessmen. Consistent with this notion, the AFA acted as a lobby group, approaching governments 'in a business way, the same as manufacturers or merchants do.' The S of E, in contrast, did not lobby consistently; its faith was in controlled marketing and government ownership of key industries. It is revealing that the Society failed to appear before the 1906 Grain Commission.[47] Partly by default, then, the AFA effectively became the Alberta farmer's voice before the state.

The AFA also effectively promoted a liberal version of controlled marketing. Starting in 1906, it proposed, not to dictate prices according to S of E doctrine, but to help farmers to keep their products off the market until prices went up. By 1907 even the Society had apparently moved towards this approach. W.J. Keen explained that through the Society farmers could 'get good prices for their products, by selling at opportune times and avoiding overstocking the markets.'[48] The S of E's failure to fix prices and the growing popularity of AFA policies appear to have moved the Society away from its determination always to 'control' prices.

The AFA never really worked out its controlled marketing strategy. In 1906 AFA leader E.N. Barker encouraged farmers to insist that their implement and other notes be carried forward to the spring, so that their debts would not come due when grain prices were low. He also described how some farmers obtained bank loans against their grain in storage, giving them the wherewithal to wait until prices improved before selling.[49] This idea of orderly marketing became a key doctrine of UFA/UFWA co-operative ideology. Selling when prices were high, rather than in the fall, when markets were glutted and prices supposedly depressed, was a maxim that culminated in the pool movement of the 1920s.

The AFA's brand of controlled marketing, its concern about local issues, its efforts to improve markets and production, as well as its liberalism, business image, and lobbying ultimately made it the dominant

Alberta farm body. This ensured that the AFA's ideas and strategies would predominate in the Alberta movement, making the UFA's liberal wing its main wing.

At the 1907 AFA convention, secretary Stevens outlined the Association's major successes. It had gained legislation to benefit Alberta grain producers, had arranged the appointment of D.W. Warner as a government agent to expand B.C. markets for Alberta produce, had helped to secure investigations of the grain and beef trades, and had given advice that led to the establishment of several government creameries. In the following year, it obtained lower freight rates.[50]

Such accomplishments attracted farmers to the organization and motivated them to work for it by instilling self-respect. The AFA's official organ, the *Saturday News*, captured this pride, boasting that the Association had become 'a source of no ordinary strength.' Having enlisted 'some of the ablest, most intelligent, and most energetic representatives of the world's premier industry,' it stood 'in such a position as to be able to reap for the benefit of the farmers of the province the results of the months of early effort.' And by co-operating with other farm organizations beginning in 1907, the AFA disproved the Equity accusation that it was narrow and provincial.[51]

The AFA also had culture on its side. A product of the Grain Growers' movement, it had a rich heritage that gave it credibility. Had not the Grain Growers defeated the CPR in the Sintaluta case, and had they not reformed the grain trade? The S of E could not point to such a history of struggle and victory. Nor could it compete with the AFA's legislative record. All it could do was offer a radical stew of state ownership planks and promise that it would one day control the world's markets. The Society also suffered from an unsympathetic press; consequently, in 1907 it started publishing its own newspaper, the *Great West*, to counter AFA propaganda and erase the image of American control that reliance on the Indiana paper, *Up-to-Date Farming*, fostered.[52] But it was not enough to compete with the AFA.

With this knowledge, the Alberta Equity leadership decided to launch a series of ambitious co-operative projects through a company called the Canadian Society of Equity Limited, which they incorporated at the end of 1906 or in early 1907. Possibly inspired by M. Wes Tubbs, the American Society secretary and a strong advocate of co-operative marketing, they planned to 'build and operate elevators, warehouses, mills, stock yards, etc., to buy and sell all manner of farmers' supplies, to operate cheese factories and creameries, and generally to carry on all kinds of business.' W.J. Keen enthused that the company would 'change our position from one of helplessness to one of great power.' Its main purpose was to 'take the place of the middleman' and secure for its shareholders the profits that had previously been 'wrongfully' carried off by the 'speculators.' Building on this radical rhetoric, the prospectus appealed to a budding sense of class consciousness, expressed in antimonopolistic terms. 'If the farmers of Canada,' it proclaimed boldly, 'stand together and fight the trusts with their own weapons, they cannot fail to receive a just and equitable proportion of the general prosperity hitherto denied them.' At the same time, it warned producers that 'if they offer nothing but a disjointed and individual opposition to their enemies, they will fail and deservedly fail.'[53]

The founders of Equity Limited, including its president, John Moran, vice-president, W.R. Ball, and secretary, W.J. Keen, believed that the company would fulfil an aim described in the Society's constitution: to build and operate granaries, elevators, warehouses, and cold storage houses 'so that farm produce may be held and controlled for an advantageous price.' Keen promised that the company would soon determine prices in 'all the farmers' markets in Alberta.' In actuality, it would prove to be the most ill-advised endeavour in the history of the Alberta farm movement. Agriculture in Alberta was not sufficiently developed to support the grandiose schemes proposed, and the Society lacked the members and money to implement them in the first place.[54]

At the outset, however, all seemed to go well and company shares sold briskly. But in May and June the campaign began to unravel when letters condemning the company from the American S of E district manager as well as the American S of E president, J.A. Everitt – who was fighting a similar move to start co-ops in the American Society – were sent to Alberta Society members and leaked to the press. The letters pointed to the inadequacy of the capital stock for the projects described and accused the Canadian affiliate of seeking secession and departing from Equity principles.[55] 'By daring to endorse co-operative action and the elimination of the middleman, the Alberta executive collided sharply with the Everitt conception of "controlled marketing."' Everitt blasted:

[Even] IF IT IS CONCEDED THAT THEY WILL BE ABLE TO CARRY OUT THE UNDERTAKING ALONG THE LINES PLANNED, IT MEANS THAT THEY MUST DESTROY ALL THE INSTITUTIONS NOW ENGAGED IN THESE LINES BEFORE THEY CAN SUBSTITUTE THE NEW PLANTS OR INSTITUTIONS. IN DOING THIS, THEY NATURALLY WILL ARRAY AGAINST THEM ALL OF THESE POWERFUL

INSTITUTIONS, CORPORATIONS, AND INDIVIDUALS. THIS IS CONTRARY TO
THE DECLARED PURPOSE OF THE AMERICAN SOCIETY OF EQUITY, WHICH IS TO
NOT INTERFERE WITH ESTABLISHED BUSINESS BUT RATHER TO REGULATE
ESTABLISHED ... INSTITUTIONS AND USE THEM ... FOR THE PEOPLE.[56]

Once the letters became public property, financial support for the co-op
dried up, putting it on a tailspin to bankruptcy. Yet its failure helped to
form the movement by discrediting the cause of Equity, which eventually led the Society to seek amalgamation with the AFA.

Arrangements to wind up the Equity company were made in November 1907 at the Society's convention, where labour leaders, likely at the
behest of R.C. Owens and W.R. Ball, encouraged the S of E to affiliate
with the labour movement. The Equity leaders believed that an alliance
would politically benefit both groups and deflect attention from the failure of the co-op. As it turned out, disillusionment resulting from that
debacle made many Equity delegates more open to socialism and a coalition than they otherwise would have been. The delegates also heard
from T.A. Crerar, president of the recently formed Winnipeg-based
Grain Growers' Grain Company. He told his company's story, one that
became, like the tales of the Manitoba Grain Act struggles and the early
Grain Growers' movement, part of a western agrarian culture of solidarity and self-respect that the UFA/UFWA would share. He described the
company's expulsion from the Grain Exchange, the dark hour that followed when buyers boycotted the company, its heroic determination to
hang on, and the final victory.[57]

The delegates listened attentively to Crerar, but the labour men had
already stolen the spotlight. They advocated socialism and proposed a
'mass meeting of the farmers and trades.' W.R. Ball endorsed this plan,
and the delegates agreed to have the rally on the next evening. The
meeting supported a farmer-labour coalition, although a tall, spare
Equity delegate, who would one day become the most influential UFA
leader of all, opposed the idea. Henry Wise Wood argued that 'farmers
did not come off nearly so well as the labor men.' Noting the lack of
rural schools and the need of farm youth to work early in life, Wood
declared that he was 'going back to his union to preach Equity,' and he
hoped that the others would do likewise.[58]

The showdown came on the next and final day of the convention, when
'brother Wood strongly recommended that the Society refrain from joining forces with the labor men on account of the principles involved, arguing that the farmer was an employer and capitalist.' Several other

'The Grain Trade "Zoo,"' by Arch Dale. *Grain Growers' Guide*, Dec. 1908, 4. In this era, a western agrarian sense of opposition to the grain industry began to emerge from farmers' personal experiences with the elevator and railway companies, and from episodes such as the debates over the Douglas bills, the oats dispute in Alberta, and the expulsion of the Grain Growers' Grain Company from the Grain Exchange. Stories about these events and cartoons like this one further developed this oppositional culture.

delegates agreed, and in response a proposed affiliation resolution was shorn of its most radical clauses. In its original form the resolution used producerism to assert that farm and industrial 'workers' must join together to agitate for collectivism and popular political control:

> Whereas, we the delegates of the Canadian Society of Equity ... recognize the identity of interests between the workers of the world; and ...
>
> Whereas, the Trades and Labor Congress of Canada has unequivocally declared their absolute independent political action on the part of the working class, separate and distinct from the present two old parties ... both of which stand for the present form of property ownership; and
>
> Whereas, we believe that only in the collective ownership of the things used collectively (with production for use instead of profit) lies the solution of the problem confronting the workers. Therefore be it
>
> Resolved that we reaffirm the position and attitude of the Canadian Trades and Labor Congress of Canada and pledge ourselves to affiliate if possible and do everything in our power to wrest the reigns of government from the domination of the ruling class.

The resolution also urged Society members to buy goods with a union label.[59]

The clauses removed from the resolution because of Wood's protest proclaimed an identity of interest between farmers and workers, noted that the Trades and Labour Congress (TLC) would take independent political action, and favoured collective ownership. Most delegates endorsed the remaining clauses, but Wood argued that the TLC 'had everything to gain, the farmers were getting nothing,' and that 'co-operation would be no good to the farmer.' To dissociate themselves from the proposed alliance, Wood and his supporters presented a report in which they regretted that the convention had committed the S of E to socialism and a boycott of non-union farm journals. They protested that these decisions had been made without consulting the locals, contending that the TLC had unduly influenced the delegates. The convention committee responded with an even milder resolution, which simply stated that the Society should cultivate cordial relations with the TLC and carefully study their common interests with a view to co-operating in those areas. This motion carried, although it was still unacceptable to the Wood camp. A letter was also sent to a labour representative, promising that Equitists would demand a union label and refrain from patronizing non-union farm newspapers.[60]

In the end, the TLC accepted the Society as an affiliate, though little came of the alliance. The convention debate on the matter, however, was a notable movement-forming episode. The controversy reinforced an ideological division that carried over into the UFA. Radicals established themselves as proponents of a farmer-labour alliance and socialism; liberals took a stand against such objectives. More important still, the split weakened a Society already hurt by the co-operative debacle. Equity was now mortally wounded; the outcome of the third attempt to form the movement by merging the S of E and the AFA was 'practically a foregone conclusion.'[61]

While the Society's fate was sealed, the AFA grew in prestige and stature, partly owing to its efforts to establish a government meat plant. Pragmatism and a liberal belief in state aid to ensure market competition moved the AFA to take up this cause; a 'Tory touch' led it to justify its demand by citing past government involvement in other industries. Similar notions were behind the AFA's request that the province operate farmer-built grain elevators, although by 1908 it wanted the government to build, own, and run a line of elevators, which was the policy of the Inter-provincial Council of Grain Growers' and Farmers' Associations to which the AFA's belonged. The AFA's position on the meat plant showed a similar pattern of initially offering farmer assistance and then demanding a straight government plant. The Association felt that since the province had taken full responsibility for building a telephone system, it should help farmers by constructing a meat plant.[62]

The AFA meat plant campaign effectively started in 1906, when the directors asked the locals if they wanted a government pork-packing and beef-canning plant. About twenty locals responded, all in favour, but the minister of agriculture rejected the idea. Prompted by a locally initiated meeting, the AFA secretary then called on locals to meet the minister in March 1907 at a seed fair, where forty farmers appeared to demand a plant. AFA evidence at the Beef Commission sittings in June and July similarly favoured one or more government canning and packing houses. The commission, which had been appointed by the Alberta and Manitoba governments to investigate an alleged combine among livestock dealers, recommended that the Alberta government consider building at least one pork plant. The AFA claimed a victory, even though the commission did not suggest that the province undertake beef canning. The government's response was to appoint another commission to examine the swine industry. The commissioners, one of whom was prominent AFA man James Bower, heard evidence starting in

July 1908, and they reported in early 1909, shortly before the merger of the S of E and the AFA. They found the hog industry in a sorry state and proposed that the province construct a pork plant when producers agreed to supply 50,000 hogs per year.[63] The AFA now passed the baton to the UFA. It would be up to the new organization to ensure that the government followed the commission's recommendation.

The S of E also called for a government plant, as early as 1905, but it did not progress beyond passing resolutions. By forfeiting the chance to take a significant role in the campaign, the Society lost ground to its rival. It also suffered from mediocre leaders. W.J. Keen, John Moran, J.J. Gregory, and even W.R. Ball simply did not have the leadership skills of AFA men such as W.F. Stevens, E.J. Fream, D.W. Warner, James Bower, and James Speakman. The only strong leaders the Society produced were W.J. Tregillus and Henry Wise Wood.

The AFA, however, had problems with its president, Joshua Fletcher; in 1908 he attacked W.F. Stevens for resigning as AFA secretary to become livestock commissioner. Fletcher publicly accused Stevens of having been bribed to keep quiet about the government meat plant campaign with the promise of the position. Mud flew between the two men in the press, causing dissension in the AFA, which 'damaged its strong position in the province' and hastened its merger with the 'tottering Society of Equity.'[64] The incident made necessary the final act of movement formation.

Appropriately, the two men who initiated the amalgamation negotiations were the Society's W.R. Ball and the AFA's Rice Sheppard. Ball first proposed another merger attempt with Sheppard at a fair in Edmonton in the summer of 1908. By August Sheppard was actively promoting the idea, and in September AFA and Equity officials adopted a draft constitution for consideration during the upcoming AFA convention, when Equity delegates would be present to try to effect an amalgamation.[65]

At the convention, which opened on 13 January 1909 at the Mechanics' Hall in Edmonton, AFA president Fletcher and E.A. Partridge, founder of the Grain Growers' Grain Company, urged the delegates to approve the merger. After prolonged debate, the draft constitution was endorsed, and a committee of representatives from both associations was appointed to name the proposed organization. During the committee deliberations, Society delegate R.C. Owens insisted that the word 'equity' be in the name. Rice Sheppard, another committee member, found a name acceptable to all. He later related that he believed 'the name was God given,' since he had 'asked God to give us a name, and the name that came to me was the United Farmers of Alberta, Our Motto Equity.'[66]

On the morning of 14 January, after both organizations had approved the report of another committee appointed to facilitate the amalgamation, James Speakman was sent to invite the Equity convention to the hall. He appeared with the Equity delegates a few minutes later and announced the arrival of 'the other section of the United Farmers of Alberta.' The Equity men found seats and the AFA president 'extended the hand of good fellowship to all.'[67] It was the final act of movement formation. A decade of movement building was about to begin.

During the three decades leading up to 1909 an agrarian movement formed in Alberta as several farm organizations and periodicals began fighting for farmers' interests. Two approaches emerged: the Patrons, the FAA, and the S of E promoted a radical program and ideology; the TGGA, the AFA, and the *Bulletin* promoted liberal views and solutions. These two factions continued their activites into the UFA era, helping to form the UFA/UFWA's two wings, but the liberal wing would dominate, because the AFA was stronger than the S of E.

Besides the liberal and radical ideologies, farmers' nascent movement culture included a sense of opposition to corporations that denied them their land's wealth, which prompted them to establish the early farm associations for protection. The larger prairie agrarian movement helped to form the Alberta movement by establishing the TGGA in Alberta and by imparting myths that spawned feelings of solidarity and self-respect. Through these myths and their experience, Alberta farmers concluded that organization could make them a powerful force, a point driven home by the associational rivalry of the pre-1909 years. The result was the creation of the UFA – the last act in the forming of the movement.

Chapter Two

The Building of the Movement,
1909–1913

Truly it can be said that the farmers are making themselves heard.

'A CONVENTION WHICH WILL GO DOWN IN HISTORY — THE UNITED FARM-
ERS OF ALBERTA A REALITY.'[1] So rang the headlines about the creation of
the United Farmers of Alberta (UFA) in January 1909. At last the movement was fully formed. It had united and developed two ideologies and
a larger nascent movement culture. In the next five years, the UFA constructed this culture, which penetrated much of rural Alberta and, in so
doing, built the movement. The most vital cultural development was the
fostering of collective self-respect, which produced mass commitment.
This development and the continued growth of a sense of class opposition, strengthened by gender assumptions, spawned grassroots recruiting and an independent political campaign. The latter was cut short by
farmers' fear of direct politics and their belief that direct legislation
would make the political system as democratic as the UFA. Farmers also
took steps to establish a women's section.

In amalgamating, the Alberta Farmers' Association (AFA) and the Society of Equity (S of E) agreed to a new constitution based mainly on the
Society constitution but with key clauses from its AFA counterpart. Like
its predecessors, the early UFA would consist of locals, a central office,
an executive, and a board of directors. The board's composition
changed over the years yet always included the president, one or more
vice-presidents or executive committeemen, and directors, who generally represented federal constituencies. The executive included the
president and other officers, such as the secretary, directors, or the vice-

presidents or executive committeemen. The women's section would later be represented on both the UFA executive and board. Local officers, of both the UFA and the United Farm Women of Alberta, included at least a president, vice-president, and secretary-treasurer.

Every January delegates selected by the locals attended the annual convention, the ruling body of the organization. The first UFA convention continued the S of E tradition of designating the locals 'unions' and kept the membership fee at $1.00 to attract new members.[2] Most important, it chose the *Grain Growers' Guide* as an official organ, ensuring that the UFA would be part of the larger prairie farm movement. The AFA's strength over the S of E was revealed in the convention's election of two ex-AFA men, Rice Sheppard and James Bower, as vice-president and president, respectively. Bower, who hailed from Ontario, settled in central Alberta, where he helped to organize the Red Deer Co-operative Association in 1909. Elected as a vice-president of the Canadian Council of Agriculture in the following year, he was an effective debater and a conscientious and generally well-respected UFA president – despite his strong Liberal partisanship – until his retirement in 1912.

The officers were soon embroiled in a public debate about the location of the agricultural college, an incident that strengthened farmers' self-respect and opposition to 'partyism.' At the centre of the controversy was the outspoken William J. Tregillus. Born in England, Tregillus settled on the outskirts of Calgary in 1902, where he built up a model dairy farm and the city's first pasteurized-milk business. He also served as chairman of a Calgary school board, was a city alderman in 1913, and opened a brick plant before the war. An agrarian radical, Tregillus joined the S of E in 1906, was UFA vice-president from 1910 to 1911, and was president from 1912 until his untimely death in 1914.

At the 1910 UFA convention, Tregillus proposed, in so many words, that the college be built in southern Alberta. He felt that an independent college would be better than one joined to the university in Strathcona. Above all, like many southern Alberta farmers, he wanted a college in the south for reasons of convenience, pride, and benefit. The dispute was one more episode in Alberta's north-south rivalry, which had developed earlier from struggles over the location of the capital and the university. To sidestep this controversy, the convention endorsed Edward Michener's resolution asking the UFA board to confer with the government on the matter. Tregillus accused the premier and university president of inspiring Michener's motion because they wanted the college at the university and thus did not want the Tregillus motion approved. He suggested that the premier had friends with land in Strathcona who would benefit from a college located there and that he had lied about how the site was chosen. These accusations, coming as they did shortly before the Great Waterways Railway scandal of 1910,[3] cast doubt on the government's integrity and planted a seed of movement opposition to 'partyism' that would culminate in the agrarian revolt of 1921.

Equally important, the resolution of the issue enhanced the UFA's credibility. The UFA board eventually agreed to the university location for the college if agricultural schools were built in different parts of the province and if farmers were represented on the college board. The Liberals agreed to these terms, suggesting to farmers that 'the U.F.A. is respected in government circles and their wishes will be considered.'[4]

The greatest moment of movement self-respect came on 16 December 1910, when 800 or more farmer delegates from the prairies and to a lesser extent from Ontario, Quebec, and the Maritimes 'marched four abreast up Parliament Hill' in the 'siege of Ottawa' to meet Prime Minister Wilfrid Laurier. The farmers were following up Laurier's tour of the western provinces during the preceding summer when he had been besieged by producers demanding tariff reform. In Ottawa, before their encounter with the prime minister, the delegates had unanimously endorsed a great symbol of the movement, the Farmers' Platform – a product of debate in locals and conventions across the country, in the *Guide*, and in the recently created Canadian Council of Agriculture[5] – which they presented to the ageing statesman when they arrived in the House of Commons. It demanded reciprocal trade with the United States; lower duties – ultimately free trade – with Britain; dominion construction, ownership, and operation of terminal grain elevators and the Hudson Bay Railway; a flexible Bank Act; co-operative legislation; an end to freight rate discrimination; and a government chilled-meat export system.

Laurier's response was vague and non-committal; he promised only to construct the Hudson Bay Railway, and, while favouring lower tariffs, he would do nothing about the tariff for the time being. Plainly, the farmers had obtained little, despite having mustered their full strength, but they were not discouraged. By creating a national movement, agreeing on a platform, organizing a mass demonstration, and getting a hearing in Ottawa, they had provided, according to one UFA man, a 'concrete example to those who always say, "oh, the farmers can't unite to do anything.'" From this success grew tremendous self-respect, as a *Guide* article suggested: 'Canada sat up on Friday morning and rubbed its eyes to see that the farmers were at last coming to the front and were capable of doing business at Ottawa ... Although their clothing was not of the latest cut, nor their whiskers trimmed in the most approved style, they realized the part they were playing in the upbuilding of the nation, and their feeling of dignity did not desert them.'[6]

As farmers thought retrospectively about the 'siege,' they mythologized it, augmenting their sense of possibility. One local UFA secretary proclaimed that the farmer 'who has carefully studied the attitude taken by the powers at Ottawa recently will not have much difficulty in noting how the wind blows.' Exhorting farmers to 'unite, unite, unite,' he speculated: 'If this much can be accomplished while we are yet in the green blade, what shall we say of the time in the near future when the green blade will become full ear?' Some farmers believed that the 'siege' had national and international significance. Tregillus argued that it had 'awakened the people of this great Dominion' to 'their possibilities and their duty' and that it would benefit the British Empire and be 'worldwide' in its influence.[7]

The power of the 'siege' as a symbol of self-respect did not fade with time. In 1913 local UFA leader C. Blunden asked the *Guide* for the booklet, 'Siege of Ottawa,' so that he could 'look at it in the years to come and say, "that was the time when the farmers were beginning to think for themselves."' The siege, thus, became part of a shared noble past that inspired farmers. They were so proud of it that they held a second 'siege' on the third anniversary of the first one.[8] The 1913 'siege' rekindled the feelings inspired by its predecessor, feelings of dignity that drew farmers to the farm movement and energized them to build it.

The agrarian myth, of which Tregillus was the chief UFA propagandist, also imparted self-respect. At picnics, on speaking tours, and in articles, he told farmers that they alone produced wealth and that farming – the most ancient, honourable, and healthful profession – instilled integrity, character, and highmindedness. Tregillus concluded that given the importance and potential of agriculture, 'we estimate ourselves too low and others take us at our valuation.' Farmers were further exposed to the myth through cartoons and poems in the *Guide*. Bert Huffman, a prominent UFA man, penned the following lines:

> The city's stifled throngs go by
> With empty heart and aching eye;

The burning street, the maddening roar,
The killing routine, o'er and o'er ...
But, O, so near that surging tide
There lies the restful countryside ...
A freer life, a higher view,
A wider outlook calling you –
And health and life and gladness wait
Inside the country's open gate![9]

The agrarian myth made farmers feel good about themselves, inspiring them to build the organization, while attracting new members. Additionally, the myth helped farmers to justify their movement-building efforts; it told them that their program would benefit the nation. Invoking the myth, the Farmers' Platform argued that agriculture should not 'be hampered by tariff restrictions,' since other industries were 'so dependent' on its success.[10]

In January 1911, shortly after the 'siege' of Ottawa, the federal government struck a trade agreement with the United States, which bolstered farmers' self-confidence, while its subsequent defeat elevated their sense of class opposition. The deal promised to establish reciprocity, mainly in natural goods, thus opening the American market to Canadian farmers. Though unhappy that it would not lower duties on much of what they bought, most farmers saw the agreement as a step in the right direction. Pleased with its economic benefits, they were ideologically favourable to lower tariffs, having absorbed free trade doctrines in Britain, Ontario, or the United States.

The agreement strengthened the confidence of farmers across the country; many believed that their lobbying had pushed Ottawa to sign it. Opposition to reciprocity grew, however, as railways, fearing loss of east-west traffic, and protected industries, fearing that the deal might lead to free trade in manufactured goods, invoked pro-British rhetoric to argue – often shrieking hysterically – that reciprocity would mean American control and probably annexation. UFA officers, on the other hand, told members that it was their duty to support the measure in the 1911 election. President Bower suggested that they would be 'less than men' if they went back on their position and failed to vote for it. Manliness, for Bower, involved consistency, resolve, and adherence to principle. He and James Speakman also contended that reciprocity would increase railway competition, thus reducing freight rates.[11]

Alberta farmers' critiques of protectionism reflected their ideologies.

'Canada's Prosperity – and Its Foundation,' by Dick Hartley. *Grain Growers'*
Guide, 3 Aug. 1910, 9. The agrarian myth, depicted here, was part of the culture
of the Alberta and larger North American farm movements. It contributed to
the development of agrarian self-respect.

Farmers of the liberal wing used market discourse to argue that tariffs 'put an artificial value' on goods and that unviable companies should not be protected, since 'capital should be invested in such enterprises as are naturally advantageous.' They also maintained that the tariff was an inefficient source of government revenue and that its removal would create more competition.[12] Expressing anti-monopolism, radicals emphasized that duties 'produced trusts, combines, and mergers.' They employed Jacksonian equal rights rhetoric to condemn protection as a 'special privilege' and to demand 'equity' through freer trade.[13] They also drew on a Jeffersonian image of manufacturers stealing from producers in order to assert that lower tariffs would 'drive out the vultures who fatten on our toil.' Employing an old radical metaphor and strong class analysis, one radical described protectionists as rich members of an upper caste living a pampered existence at the expense of the masses. He was glad that farmers were 'outspoken in denunciation of the plug-hatted aristocracy,' who were 'always ready to spend freely to prevent anything from injuring the protected interests of the privileged classes.' Other radicals saw tariffs as a tax on the poor. Still others, and liberals, felt that protectionism bred corruption and dishonesty.[14]

Prairie farmers had little sympathy for B.C. fruit growers' support for tariffs on their produce.[15] Not wanting to pay high prices for fruit, UFA members did not show solidarity with protectionist fellow producers. Nor was there much enthusiasm in the organization for the idea of bonuses for prairie farm products. Most farmers did not want such 'special privileges' and knew that asking for them would contradict their freer trade stance.

Though a majority of Albertans voted for reciprocity, it went down with the defeat of the Laurier Liberals, confirming the tariff as a symbol of oppression for farmers, raising their sense of class awareness and opposition, and weakening their faith in the old parties. Even the Liberal party lost agrarian support, because protectionist Liberals had opposed the agreement. By inciting the hostility of farmers to corporate economic and political control – especially farmers in Ontario, Saskatchewan, and Alberta – the defeat of reciprocity marked 'the first act' in the post-war agrarian revolt.[16]

Farmers called for a single tax on land values to replace tariffs and all other taxes, a partially successful campaign that fostered movement-building pride. Henry George, the self-educated popularizer of the single-tax doctrine, was born in Philadelphia in 1839. His publications, most notably his 1879 book, *Progress and Poverty*, sold millions of copies

'Putting on the Screws: How the Farmer Benefits by a Protective Tariff,' probably by Arch Dale. *Grain Growers' Guide*, 20 Apr. 1910, 4. The tariff was more than
an economic impediment for farmers; it was a symbol of metropolitan corporate
and political oppression. In this cartoon, the manufacturers and the government work together to put the squeeze on farmers.

and were highly influential in the United States, Canada, Australia, and Europe, and they were available to Canadian farmers through the *Grain Growers' Guide* book department. George argued that a single tax – a heavy tax on land values alone – would return to society the 'unearned increment' of rising land values that enriched big landowners and would also force them to put their land to productive use. The result would be a great reduction in the gap between rich and poor and prosperity for all. Caught up in this utopian vision, W.J. Tregillus enthused that a single tax would promote industry and 'throw open to labor the illimitable field of employment which the earth offers' and do 'away with involuntary poverty, raise wages to the full earnings of labor, make overproduction impossible until all human wants are satisfied, render labor savings inventions a blessing to all, and cause such an enormous production and such an equitable distribution of wealth as would give to all comfort, leisure, and participation in the advantage of an advancing civilization.'[17]

Farmers also felt that a single tax would drive out speculators, who, by holding land off the market, impeded development and forced settlers to locate far from existing services, while profiting from rising land values created by producers' work and risk taking. In addition, farmers believed that a land value tax would shift the tax burden from farm to urban land because the latter rose most in value and would therefore be taxed at the highest rate. Moreover, by eliminating tariffs, the single tax would destroy monopolies. It would also simplify tax gathering, reduce fraud and government costs, and make the wealthy pay more taxes. Furthermore, farmers could improve their farms without penalty under a single tax, since land values, not improvements, would be taxable.[18]

A convention resolution and the unions' responses to a survey show that most UFA members, like organized farmers throughout the West, wanted all government revenues raised by a single tax – a land value tax – and a surtax on unoccupied land.[19] The Henry George bug had bitten Alberta farmers. The articles in the *Guide*, the addresses and discussions in the locals and at conventions, and the reading of George's works on long winter evenings had done their work.

The Alberta government responded to the UFA's single-tax demands. It allowed cities to implement land value taxation,[20] established the single-tax system for villages and towns in 1911–12,[21] enacted an unearned increment tax in 1913 and a wild-land tax the following year to curb speculation,[22] and provided that all districts organized under the 1912 Rural Municipalities Act would tax land values alone.[23] Following Alberta's lead, Saskatchewan passed similar laws.[24] Such legislation,

'The Finance Minister Should Fish in the Main Stream,' by Arch Dale. *Grain Growers' Guide*, 30 Sept. 1914, 6. Alberta and western farmers believed that the tariff was not only unjust but also, as suggested here, an inefficient means of raising government revenue. In contrast, land value taxation – the single tax – would drive out land speculators and increase government income so that the tariff could be reduced or eliminated.

Paul Sharp notes, was envied by American farmers and 'was one of the most important, though infrequently mentioned, victories of the agrarian reformers.'[25] It was a source of prestige for the western farm movement.

Farmers' self-assurance was further strengthened as the UFA convinced the provincial Liberals to act against corporations. It influenced the government to pass legislation in 1912 to implement municipal hail insurance rather than completely privatize the business as planned,[26] to continue its efforts from 1909 to 1911 to recover taxes from the CPR,[27] to agree in 1910 to take the Grand Trunk Railway to court over a fire allegedly started by a train, and to disallow, in that same year, mortgage clauses in implement agreements.[28] Particularly impressive was the UFA's record for 1913: it succeeded in its long fight – one also being waged by the Saskatchewan Grain Growers – for legal protection from industry contracts that allowed farm machinery companies to avoid responsibility for their products,[29] and it induced the province to pass co-operative trading and direct legislation acts. And though the government refused the UFA's request for a public elevator system, it helped to finance the Alberta Farmers' Co-operative Elevator system.[30] These and other political successes built the movement by giving farmers a 'sense of power' and by giving the UFA credibility that attracted new members.

The UFA had some success with the federal government as part of the national farm movement, which was further cause for satisfaction. In response to demands by the prairie farm associations and the Dominion Grange and Farmers' Association in Ontario, the government provided for a parcel post system in 1913.[31] Earlier in the year, Ottawa announced a $10 million grant to assist with the costs of agricultural education throughout the country.[32] But western farmers' biggest victory with the Borden government had been won the previous year.

The struggle began in early 1912, when representatives of the Manitoba and Saskatchewan Grain Growers and the UFA informed the government that they wanted state-owned terminal grain elevators and a commission to supervise grain handling. They were disappointed when the government's proposed act allowed grain mixing, which they believed lowered the prices paid to them. They were particularly alarmed that the act permitted suspension of the railway-car order rules to speed up grain movement when necessary. The farmer spokesmen, including UFA secretary E.J. Fream, lobbied successfully against the contentious clauses. The amendment to the car order section was dropped, and the grain-mixing provision was rendered temporarily inoperative. The resulting Canada Grain Act of 1912 created, as the farmers had requested, a Board of Grain Commissioners to control the grain industry under strict new guidelines. Under the act, the government also constructed, from 1913 to 1916, a terminal elevator at Port Arthur, interior elevators in Saskatchewan and Alberta, and a transfer elevator in Vancouver.[33] All told, the western farm associations had done much to shape the new act and to encourage terminal construction. This activity built self-respect; farmers had influenced even the party that had defeated reciprocity.

Farmers wanted the Board of Grain Commissioners because they believed that expert bodies could be neutral parts of the state, a belief formed by their confidence-building successes with the Board of Railway Commissioners. In 1909 the UFA asked the Board to force the completion of an Alberta Railway and Irrigation Company branch line. The

Board responded by ordering the company to provide better service and lower rates. This was seen as a 'splendid victory.' The UFA also expressed concerns to the Board about fencing, cattle guards, and other matters. Here, too, 'the rulings were in favor of the complaints supported by the association.' Another boost for self-assurance! Later the Board began to deal with UFA demands about railway fireguards.[34]

Farmers were especially impressed with the Board's chairman, Judge Mabee. At a 1910 hearing in Edmonton, D. Mackenzie, a local farmer, complained that the Grand Trunk would not give him a proper crossing at his homestead. Mabee found this assertion to be true and discovered that the railway had blocked Mackenzie's road. 'You engineers,' he rebuked the railway representatives, 'get out in the country and act like a lot of vandals. You'll have to build a crossing there within thirty days and construct a road allowance according to regulations.' Because of such experiences, western farmers sought greater jurisdiction for the Board over freight rates and cases involving killed stock, and they called for independent commissions to operate government terminals and the Hudson Bay Railway.[35]

It became apparent, however, that commissions did not always favour farmers. In 1912 the Railway Board increased demurrage charges – the fines farmers had to pay for taking more than twenty-four hours to load a railway car; the year before it had refused a UFA request for lower minimum railway car weights; and in 1914, despite many petitions from prairie producers, it upheld the CPR's right to levy discriminatory freight rates.[36] These decisions made farmers wonder if the Board was as free of corporate influence as they had thought. Their suspicions grew, eventually fuelling a post-war belief that only a new political system could ensure that the state acted for farmers.

But before the war, the actions of politicians, not those of commissions, stimulated farmers' animus to the state and the 'interests' behind it. Fundamental to this sense of opposition was the UFA's frustration over the issue of livestock hit by trains. The organization, in concert with the Canadian Council of Agriculture, lobbied hard for laws to force the railways to install effective fences and guards by making them liable for animals killed on the track. Amendments meeting these demands were introduced in Parliament in 1911, but they were withheld and postponed from session to session.[37] Canadian farmers were still working – with increased exasperation – for effective legislation in this area after the war.

Western farmers were also frustrated by their inability to gain federal

'How the Country Is Governed: The Real Rulers Send Their Messengers to the People,' by Dick Hartley. *Grain Growers' Guide*, 10 Aug. 1910, 12. This cartoon reflects organized farmers' suspicion that corporate interests controlled both political parties. Here, a railroad magnate, backed by other big businessmen, informs Borden and Laurier of what they are to tell the electorate. Such concepts of political reality combined with farmers' political frustrations to forge their sense of class opposition.

co-operative legislation. As was the case in their campaign for livestock laws, bills were introduced but not passed. They were also angry that Ottawa allowed grain mixing before investigating the matter[38] and would not, despite their pleas before the Banking Committee in 1913, permit producers to borrow on the security of their livestock and grain – it seemed that the bankers had the cabinet 'tied hand and foot.' Moreover, Alberta farmers discovered the limits of their influence with the provincial Liberals, who turned down their requests for government loans and a law to make machinery notes due in the spring.[39]

Farmers' direct experience with corporate power further informed their sense of class opposition. In 1910 certain terminal companies were convicted for illegally mixing grain. Here, it seemed, was proof that prairie farmers had been swindled out of their hard-earned dollars. On a speaking tour of UFA locals, T.L. Swift of the Grain Growers' Grain Company told stories about the incident that became part of western farmers' oppositional culture. At Stettler, he described

> the machinations of the grain elevator combines, which resulted in great loss and fraud to the farmer. By means of illustrations ... he proved that the recent developments and reports by the warehouse commissioner ... had been an overwhelming indictment of the methods of the grain elevator companies ... The speaker ... riveted the attention of the audience, and his remarks were convincing when he urged upon all the need for co-operation to throttle the octopus.

Swift also developed farmers' culture of opposition by relating the history of his company and its fight against the nefarious grain trade. To the Wellsdale UFA local, he outlined 'the beginning and development of the Grain Growers' Grain Company from a small corporation of farmers to secure the highest prices for their products on the world markets. The company, Mr. Swift said, had not attained its present condition without opposition, but in spite of the opposition had steadily developed ... How had all this been accomplished? By co-operation.'[40]

Western farmers faced other opposition in 1912 when the Credit Men's Association circulated a petition asking for amendments to the car distribution clause of the Grain Act, which it blamed for a recent railway car shortage. The UFA saw this as 'a deliberate attempt to take from the farmers one of their hardest fought for privileges.' Parties supporting the Credit Men's request argued that farmers tied up cars by taking too long to load them. E.J. Fream refuted this claim by showing that fewer than 5 per cent of the cars handled by the CPR had demurrage charges.[41]

The UFA sense of opposition that developed from such incidents was reinforced by the growth of monopolies. Truly this was 'the day of mergers.' The *Guide* revealed that there had been 135 mergers in Canada in 1910. Farmers were convinced that these 'trusts' paid producers low prices and charged consumers inflated prices. One such monopoly, the 'Mountain Mill Lumber Combine,' allegedly forced retailers to refrain from stocking American lumber so that it could dictate prices. By demonstrating that no U.S. lumber had been brought into Alberta, Fream exploded the company's contention that the country had been swamped with cheap American wood.[42]

Assumptions about gender also shaped farmers' oppositional culture.

'Sleight of Hand at the Lake Front,' by Dick Hartley. *Grain Growers' Guide,* 11 May 1910, 12. The discovery that terminal elevators were illegally mixing grain confirmed farmers' beliefs about the duplicity of the grain industry. Here, the terminal elevator 'manipulator' (in the centre) expresses the hope that the farmer (on the left) 'won't expose the trick' now that he has seen 'how it's done.'

UFA men were admonished to exert their manhood against class oppression and other adversity. Any man who did not 'kick' was 'either a fool or a coward,' because real men did not take difficulties 'lying down': 'Farmers! Acquit yourselves like men.' UFA men – 'true men' – were to take vigorous action to defend their interests.[43] They were not, however, to be the rugged individualists of the self-made man or frontier myths. The movement's co-operative ethos had transformed traits celebrated in these myths – assertiveness, resourcefulness, and self-reliance – into ideal collective characteristics. UFA men were to embody these as an organization and class, not as independent yeomen.

Other ideals about manliness highlighted progressiveness. True UFA men practised scientific agriculture, educated themselves on subjects such as political science, and supported the farm movement. With 'hearts of manhood,' they had 'broad minds and high aspirations' and acted justly and with integrity. They could even view arguments against female suffrage as unmanly – 'hardly ... up to the standard of men.'[44]

Farmers' oppositional culture, reinforced by their sense of male toughness and responsibility, combined with their self-respect to ignite a grassroots 'mania for organization.'[45] The directors oversaw recruitment in their constituencies and there were official UFA organizers, but local farmers spontaneously did most of the organization work.

Drawing on agrarian and labour culture, farmers believed that if they built the Canadian farm movement by organizing most of their class, they would become an unstoppable force for agrarian and national reform. The formation of the *United* Farmers of Alberta from a divided movement and the growth and success of the national farm movement reinforced this belief. 'I will bet anyone five dollars to a doughnut,' one local UFA secretary mused, 'that as soon as we are organized thoroughly and systematically from Winnipeg to Hudson Bay, from Lethbridge to Athabaska landing, there will be no trouble getting Sir Wilfrid to ... declare he is in favor of everything we demand.'[46]

Imbued with this conviction, UFA locals organized their neighbours. In other cases, several farmers got together and formed themselves into a union. One farmer appointed himself an organizer. 'I have been watching ... some of the farmers' organizations,' he informed the central office, 'and as I do not wish to be classed among the drones, I have concluded to make an effort towards organizing a branch of the U.F.A.' Many locals held contests among members or with other unions to increase membership. In one district, the unions held a convention that appointed area organizers.[47]

Disappointments like the defeat of reciprocity spurred farmers to greater organizing efforts. Victories could have the same effect. Fream noted that during his successful fight in Ottawa over the Grain Act the farmer spokesmen 'were told time and again that they represented the views of only a few.' 'What is the thought that suggests itself?' he asked rhetorically. 'Is it not that we should organize, organize, organize?'[48]

Organize they did. Official membership rose from about 2,100 to 9,400 from 1909 to 1913.[49] The UFA's real membership, however, was and would always be higher than the official figures, which were based on paid membership. Letters that Fream received in 1911 indicated that many more farmers were active in locals than had been able to pay dues. Following settlement patterns, the UFA grew fastest in southern Alberta in 1910 and during the next year crept into the northwest part of the province, while gaining strongly in the southeast. Lack of funds and local help for outside organizers kept the movement from growing even faster, although unions organized by locals proved more resilient than those 'brought to life on the spur of the moment by a fluent organizer.'[50]

Farmers of the liberal wing believed that organization could make the UFA a powerful political pressure body. The early constitutions described the association as a lobby group and, in the tradition of the Grange and the AFA, rejected independent politics. Unhappy with this approach, radicals took direct political action. One study suggests that the UFA executive under Tregillus initiated this campaign, but it began in 1910, when most UFA officers opposed it. Except for Rice Sheppard, none directly involved in the political movement was an officer. At a 1912 board meeting, George Bevington proposed that the UFA organize mass meetings to draft a platform and select political candidates. No one – not even Tregillus – seconded the motion.[51]

Though a supporter of independent politics, Tregillus did not overtly propose a third party in his UFA speeches until 1914. While he broached the idea in a Calgary newspaper in 1910, organization and co-operation were the main themes of his addresses as a UFA leader. Keenly aware of partisan loyalties among members, he was not about to wreck the UFA by creating a new political movement. Even if he had actively promoted direct politics, his influence would have been limited. The UFA convention ignored his call in 1914 for a third party.[52] Moreover, it seems he was not as interested in a new party as he was in defeating certain Liberals, which is why he worked for Premier Arthur Sifton's Conservative opponent in a 1910 by-election rather than organize an independent campaign.[53]

The early agrarian political movement, though encouraged by the moral support of Tregillus and other radical leaders, was primarily a grassroots affair. Local radicals, such as W.R. Ball, John Glambeck, and W.J. Glass, convinced their unions and sometimes their districts to endorse direct action. Many of their supporters were ex-Americans who were familiar with populist politics, and because they had settled mostly in southern Alberta, the independent movement was strongest there.

Political activists' usually began by calling for aggressive agrarian action through the existing parties, sometimes in conjunction with a political association. A few promoted independent politics from the outset; all, or nearly all, soon wanted a new party. The main catalysts behind this increasingly radical stance were the Great Waterways Railway scandal of 1910, which tarnished the image of the provincial Liberals, and the defeat of reciprocity in 1911. T.K. Rogne was one who initially thought it did not matter what party a candidate belonged to if he were a farmer. Like other radicals, however, he soon called for a farmer-labour party, and he articulated a fundamental tenet of UFA radicalism:

reform required direct political action. 'Direct legislation is O.K. if we can get it,' he wrote. 'Cheaper money on farm security also. Nearer and larger markets, less protection to the trust is all desirable, but to obtain any and all of these ... we must have real farmers to legislate.'[54]

Though a few independent farmer candidates were nominated before the war, and one, Robert Patterson, an independent Conservative and 'farmers' association' candidate, gained a seat in the legislature in 1910, the agrarian political movement was stillborn. Partisan loyalties remained strong, and few farmers were interested in direct politics; fewer still wanted the UFA involved. Radicals' attempts to convince conventions to allow the organization to support or place candidates were defeated,[55] partly because members already had the right to take any political action if they did not associate it with the UFA. At the same time, liberal leaders discouraged third-party politics. Vice-president W.S. Henry argued that a new party would perpetuate the evils of partyism, and P.P. Woodbridge, the central secretary, told a local secretary that his union's call for a farmer party was unconstitutional and if persisted in might destroy both the UFA and farmers' ability to get anything from the party in power.[56]

The anti-political heritage of the Grange and historical example also discouraged UFA political action. The downfall of the American Farmers' Alliance, the Patrons of Industry, and the Farmers' Association of Alberta appeared to prove that independent politics killed farm groups. Furthermore, farmers' belief in organization suggested that pressure politics and showing 'our controlling power by standing together ... would perhaps be better than a third party at present.'[57]

Above all, the political movement's failure stemmed from farmers' conviction that direct legislation – the initiative, referendum, and recall – would ensure the passage of good laws under the two-party system. The UFA's direct-legislation campaign began when the 1910 convention called for the measure. Soon after, a multiclass direct-legislation league was formed, with W.J. Tregillus as president. In the following January the convention forced all candidates for UFA office to declare themselves on direct legislation. All, of course, were in favour, and the newly elected officers committed themselves to getting a direct-legislation act on the statute books. Later, farmers signed a UFA petition requesting an act, prompting the Alberta legislature to endorse the principle of direct legislation in 1912. After further demands by the 1913 convention, the province finally passed a direct-legislation act in that year.[58]

Organized farmers in the West and Ontario overwhelmingly favoured direct legislation. They had learned about it from articles in the *Guide*, from the propaganda of the Manitoba-based Direct Legislation League, and from its use in several American states, including South Dakota, Montana, Oklahoma, Missouri, Colorado, and especially Oregon, where 'its first effect was to paralyze the political machine.'[59] Increasingly critical of 'partyism,' Alberta farmers were attracted to direct legislation because it promised to 'enforce their will in government.' Believing that even independents or reform parties would become corrupt if not under direct democratic control, radicals felt that the measure was compatible with direct political action. They were also convinced that direct legislation would ensure the establishment of government-owned industries. Farmers of the liberal wing considered direct legislation to be the 'key that would open the door to all our reforms.' They thought it would make independent politics unnecessary by forcing existing parties to respond to producers' demands.[60]

Despite these different ideological perspectives, direct legislation united the Alberta farm movement. Farmers saw it as a 'non-partisan' reform that all could agree on. Indeed, radicals, despite their emphasis on independent politics, concurred with liberals that, for the time being at least, direct legislation was 'the first plank in our platform.'[61] In this way, direct legislation diverted farmers from direct politics, taking the wind out of the independent political campaign.

Farmers' faith in direct legislation, partly a response to corporate political influence, owed much to their experience with direct democracy in the UFA. They believed that direct legislation would give them the same power over politicians as they had over their organization and leaders. Robert Irwin argues that a technocratic leadership dominated the Saskatchewan Co-operative Elevator Company and that centralized managerial control may have been more prevalent in the farm movement than has been thought. This argument may be true, but it does not apply to the UFA, which was truly democratic; the members, not the leaders, gained ultimate control, despite one author's conclusion that the UFA executive determined the organization's policies. At the 1909 convention, prominent UFA leaders moved, seconded, or amended over half the resolutions – more than they would in subsequent conventions – but on the important question of which paper would be the official UFA organ, the delegates rejected two suggestions by officers, including one to let the board decide, and they chose instead the *Grain Growers' Guide*. Similarly, the 1910 convention defeated a proposal that an appointed UFA committee and the government devise a better hail insurance plan and insisted that the locals have input.[62]

Even the adoption of a resolution stating that the next convention would consider only resolutions written by locals or by the resolution committee under the president's instruction did not weaken delegate democracy. While prohibiting spontaneous motions from the floor, the resolution forced unions to consider issues more carefully before the convention – a good move from a democratic point of view. And through the resolution seemed to give the president and resolution committee great power to set the agenda, that power was more apparent than real. Fewer than 10 per cent of the 1910–1913 convention resolutions were presented by the resolution committee, and they were not necessarily the most significant ones. A third of them were simply consolidations of several local resolutions with a similar meaning.[63] Given this limited role, it would have been hard for the committee to control the convention agenda.

Furthermore, in only two cases, both of which occurred at the 1911 convention, can it be argued that the president might have strongly affected convention decisions through his alleged control of the resolution committee. In the first case, president Bower may have influenced the committee to water down a resolution favouring a farmer-labour alliance referred to it by the delegates. The committee's redrafted resolution, which the convention carried, asked simply that discussions be held with labour to 'ascertain if there be any neutral ground on which to work out our common interest.' In the second case, a resolution was moved calling on the executive to take steps towards securing UFA stockyards. The committee's revised resolution, which was also approved and may have reflected Bower's input, merely asked the executive to try to convince the municipal authorities to establish the needed facilities.[64]

These cases aside, the influence of the executive and president over the resolution committee was quite limited. Though appointed by the president or other officers, the committee generally was composed of independently minded local leaders. Their autonomy was evident at the 1913 convention when they endorsed a resolution that implied that unless the Grain Growers' Grain Company became a 'purely cooperative association,' farmers should not approve the UFA executive's plan to have the company establish government-supported elevators in Alberta. Moreover, conventions did not rubber-stamp resolution committee motions; three times they refused to adopt committee proposals before 1914.[65] Aware of this delegate independence, resolution committees and UFA officers rarely moved resolutions unless they knew that there was strong support for them.

The rank and file – not the resolution committee or the central officers – set the UFA agenda. Throughout the year, locals submitted resolutions that were published in the *Guide* and mailed to all unions for discussion, and many were forwarded to the conventions for consideration. The great majority of convention resolutions came from locals, not from the leadership or resolution committee. At the same time, members occasionally complained that leaders unduly influenced conventions to approve or defeat certain resolutions. Rice Sheppard argued that opponents of the pledge form to supply hogs for the proposed government pork plant were not given sufficient time at the 1910 convention to air their objections, and Henry Sorenson maintained that president Bower 'suddenly' called for a vote on compulsory hail insurance at the 1911 convention before the merits of the compulsory plan could be presented.[66] There is likely some truth to these complaints, but the bottom line is that the 1910 convention endorsed the pork plant contract because a majority of delegates believed it should be submitted to farmers for their consideration, and the 1911 convention opposed compulsory hail insurance because a majority of delegates did not feel that producers – especially those who specialized in livestock – should have to pay hail tax on land they used for grazing. In short, it is unlikely that the officers determined the outcome of the vote on these issues. And only once did a union accuse the executive of failing to follow convention instructions to forward resolutions to the unions for discussion. The accusation was without foundation; the resolutions appeared in circulars that were printed in the *Guide* and sent to the locals.[67]

The bedrock of UFA democracy was the delegate system. Each local was entitled to send one delegate to the convention for every ten paid-up members.[68] Most locals, having discussed the resolutions to come before the convention, told their delegates how to vote, while assuming they would exercise some discretion based on convention debate. Other unions simply asked delegates to use their judgment, knowing they would represent their locals' views. Most unions elected delegates and raised money for their expenses, usually through dances or socials, so that the best persons, regardless of economic status, could be delegates. Some locals, however, endorsed individuals as delegates simply because they were willing to pay their own way. This practice weakened delegate democracy; it meant that some unions were represented by members who might not have been chosen if ability had been the only consideration.

The most serious limitation to delegate democracy was lack of representation in the convention. Before the war, fewer than half the locals sent delegates in a given year, and while the percentage increased slightly, many locals had no delegates in some years, and many more failed to send their full quota every year. Sometimes expense was a factor, although women's locals formed during the war sent delegates in higher proportions than UFA locals did,[69] suggesting that apathy was a reason for the failure of many men's unions to send representatives. The 1911 convention considered but wisely rejected proxy voting as a way of providing more local input in conventions.[70] Proxy voting would have allowed locals to vote on complex issues without hearing the convention discussion, thus producing less informed decisions. Moreover, it would have reduced convention attendance, lowering the quality of debate and its educative effect. Most seriously, fewer farmers would have learned about democratic citizenship by electing and instructing delegates and raising money for their expenses. This experience trained farmers, without their awareness, for the political campaigns of 1921.

While rejecting proxy voting, UFA conventions took steps to make future conventions more democratic. To improve the accessibility of conventions for all unions, the 1911 convention equalized travel expenses by pooling railway rates. In addition, it decided that the board, not the president, would appoint the resolution committee, making it more likely that the committee would reflect a range of views. The 1912 convention adopted a revised constitution that stipulated that the delegates, rather than the president or an appointee, would elect a chairman. The constitution also indicated that, for the first time, the convention would elect the entire executive except the secretary.[71]

The democratization of the UFA effected by these measures, by the delegate system, and by rank-and-file control over resolutions and policy making, built the movement by inspiring farmers to try to make the political system as democratic as the UFA. They aimed to control governments as they did their delegates, conventions, and leaders, and they felt that they could do so through direct legislation. When experience with direct legislation later proved that it was less than a democratic elixir, they concluded, after the war, that a new political system was needed to allow constituents to 'dictate' to politicians.

Farmers' Christian beliefs helped them to justify their early support for direct legislation and other causes. Bert Huffman felt that direct legislation expressed the 'God given powers of the people.' Daniel Boiss-vain argued that 'in the Bible we are told that for the great ones to exercise authority is wrong.' 'The old Book also states,' he reasoned, 'that a house ... divided cannot stand. Could not these words be taken to mean the great value of direct legislation?'[72]

Religious beliefs encouraged farmers to build the movement by strengthening their convictions about their agenda. Austin Droney could not understand 'how any people calling themselves Christian ... can vote for protection and keep the other Christian's product out because he did not happen to be born in his backyard.' W.R. Ball hoped that the political associations he envisaged would create a 'good and pure government' based on 'the principles ... of Jesus Christ.'[73]

Ball's appeal to the church to 'condemn sin in high places' reflected the evangelical outlook shared by most UFA members. Before the war, very few farmers used social-gospel rhetoric about building a kingdom of God on earth. Instead, they stressed that persons and institutions must follow biblical principles. This was the standard by which they judged right and wrong in social, economic, and political affairs.

The campaign for equal homestead rights for women revealed how farmers' prejudice contravened that standard and how Christian ideals could work against nativism. During the campaign, which began in 1911, some farmers were angry that non-Anglo-Celtic men could home-stead while British and Canadian women could not. 'Mother Scot' com-plained to the *Guide* about how unfair it was 'to give to these outlanders the privilege of homestead and deny that privilege to their own race and blood when it happens to be of the other sex.' She asked sharply, 'Is not the mother of sons and daughters of British blood at least as worthy of a ... gift as the hordes of men of alien race who are given free home-steads without condition?' Isobel Graham, a *Guide* editor, shared this view and made sure that a 'homesteads for women' petition being circu-lated in the West demanded homestead rights for women of British birth only. H. Ahern, on the other hand, a UFA man, argued that attempts to get a homestead law benefiting only British women indi-cated a 'lack of Christianity.' Others agreed that the British-birth clause was prejudicial.[74]

The homesteads for women campaign was an early step in the build-ing of a women's section of the UFA. It exposed men to an important demand of women, mobilized and trained women to work for a cause, and encouraged women to consider joining the agrarian movement – especially since many UFA men signed the homesteads for women peti-

tion. M.E. Graham, a local women's leader, found only two men at a picnic unwilling to sign it. Moreover, she claimed that 'several prominent
men of the district' had done most of the work obtaining 114 signatures
of men and 48 of women. The first-prize winner of a *Guide* competition
for the best letter on women's homestead rights was also a UFA man.[75]

There were limits, however, to male support for equal homestead
rights. Many men opposed the campaign, including delegates to the
1912 Saskatchewan Grain Growers convention, and those in favour in
Alberta were not sufficiently concerned to see a resolution on the subject brought before a UFA convention, although the UFA later endorsed
UFWA homestead resolutions. Women asserted that equal homestead
rights were a matter of 'common justice.' One woman argued that those
rights would provide the assurance of a home to women married to a
'ne'er-do-well.' Men, especially, were aware that if married women could
homestead, families could cheaply expand their farms.[76] Here was an
economic incentive for men to back the campaign.

Some men supported women's rights, including the right to join the
farm movement, because they recognized the value of women's work.
The 1912 UFA convention resolved:

> Whereas the women in the rural homes of Alberta are sharing with the
> men the burden of the struggle for better conditions and equal rights;
>   And whereas we believe that under the law our women should enjoy
> equal privileges with the men;
>   Therefore be it resolved that we believe that the wives and daughters of
> our farmers should organize locally and provincially along the lines of the
> U.F.A. for the improvement of rural conditions, morally, intellectually, and
> socially, and we urge all our members to assist in every way the develop-
> ment of such an organization.[77]

By arguing that organized farm women would improve conditions
'morally' and 'intellectually,' W.J. Tregillus and Rice Sheppard, the
mover and seconder of this resolution, expressed farmers' conviction
that women in the movement would elevate society's ethics and reform
rural schools because of their innate purity and maternal instinct. Farmers also expected that women's charitable and aesthetic sensibilities
would promote mutual aid and culture in the countryside, and they felt
that women would benefit the UFA 'socially.' Already in some locals
wives prepared refreshments for meetings, picnics, and functions. Their
efforts were usually appreciated and often acknowledged: 'Three cheers

for the ladies!'[78] Women also sang and played instruments and participated in plays, recitations, and readings in UFA locals. Farm men believed that women, if organized, would make further contributions in these and other areas.

Ideology and culture prodded some UFA men to invite women into the movement. Radicals, including Tregillus and Sheppard, were usually strong believers in women's right to be in the organization. Agrarian tradition reinforced their position. There had been prominent female American Populist platform speakers – such as Mary Ellen Lease, who urged farmers to raise 'less corn and more hell' – and four women officers in every Grange local. In Alberta, women had participated in S of E social activities.[79]

Even before the UFA called on women to organize, some farm women were involved in clubs. A Women's Institute was formed in Alberta in 1909, and by 1913 there were twenty-two provincial Institutes, which aimed to 'promote the interests of home and country' and improve 'the standard of housekeeping.'[80] Some Institutes assisted UFA unions or acted as UFA auxiliaries. A number of women attended local UFA meetings and occasionally gave talks on subjects such as dairying. Moreover, at least two women's auxiliaries were formed in association with UFA locals before the 1912 convention invited women to organize.

That invitation bore little fruit, partly because farm men had not yet grasped the possibilities of having women in the movement. The UFA board at this point envisaged women creating homemakers' clubs rather than a class-conscious female section of the UFA, but that vision began to change. The 1913 convention renewed the UFA's commitment to organize women and instructed the board to encourage this work, so that many women would attend the next convention and possibly hold their own meeting. Later in the year, the executive indicated that the women's convention should decide whether to form new Women's Institutes under a government department or club auxiliaries under UFA auspices.[81] Women's choice of the latter alternative would inaugurate an important development in the building of the movement during the war.

The 1909 to 1913 years were foundational for the building of the movement in Alberta. The unity and growth of the organization, its legislative successes and agrarian ideals, and the 'siege' of Ottawa attracted farmers to the movement and built collective self-respect, which mobilized members. Farmers' sense of opposition, shaped by notions about manliness, developed through their failures with governments and encounters with corporate power. They responded with a grassroots recruiting campaign. Radicals also promoted independent political action, but most farmers, because of agrarian political defeats and the potential of direct legislation, preferred lobbying. They believed that direct legislation could make the political system truly democratic, like the UFA. This belief built the movement by inspiring farmers who hoped to create a more democratic political system. Their Christian convictions provided further motivation by giving them a sense of moral rightness about their efforts. Aware of women's potential contributions to rural society and the farm movement, the UFA also took steps to organize a women's section.

Chapter Three

The Rural Economy and the Movement

As we all know, wheat is not our mainstay, nor can it be for generations to come.[1]
James Bower to the 1910 UFA convention

Many historians use the staple thesis to argue that a wheat economy was the basis of early prairie development and agrarian protest.[2] Such arguments must be modified for Alberta. Its agriculture was more diversified than the wheat staple interpretation implies, and this diversity shaped its farm movement. Even after wheat became the main Alberta farm commodity during the war, non-wheat production remained crucial to the rural economy, an economy that included subsistence activity, wage labour, non-farm business endeavour, and formal and informal exchange – all supported by women's work. This multifaceted economy helped to form, build, and politicize the movement, partly by developing its sense of community and commitment to co-operation. Emphasis on the wheat staple, in short, cannot illuminate the Alberta farm movement to 1921; in fact, it blinds historians to complex economic factors behind the movement and makes them see farmers as they would be later – strongly affected by a wheat economy – rather than as they actually were.

If any province had a wheat economy before the 1920s it was Saskatchewan, although new research may qualify the validity of this argument even there. Alberta was generally the least wheat-oriented prairie province. Examination of the agricultural census data of these two provinces reveals the inapplicability of the wheat staple thesis to Alberta's early development.

Most of the great cattle barons of central and southern Alberta disappeared after 1900, but the farmers and small ranchers who replaced them, and who strongly supported the farm movement, raised proportionately more livestock and animal products than producers in Saskatchewan did. This was especially true in the movement-forming years before 1909, when the livestock industry was the foundation of Alberta's rural economy. In 1900 livestock and animal products sold or slaughtered in Alberta were valued at $3.2 million, $500,000 more than Alberta's land products (vegetables and field crops). In Saskatchewan, animals and their products were worth only $2.9 million, $1.7 million less than that district's land products. By 1901 the average value of livestock per acre of improved land in Alberta was three times that in Saskatchewan, and the average number of livestock per farm was much higher.[3]

Crop data further reveal that Alberta did not have a wheat economy. In 1900 only 23 per cent of the field crop acreage was in wheat; it was 74 per cent in Saskatchewan. Moreover, Alberta produced over four times more oats than wheat, while Saskatchewan produced nearly twice as much wheat as oats. By 1910 wheat had become a more important part of Alberta's economy, and more farmers were specializing in its production, but it was still not a dominant staple. Though about 40 per cent of the value and acreage of field crops was in wheat, the percentage was roughly 50 per cent higher in Saskatchewan. And while the total value of wheat in Alberta slightly exceeded that of oats, the volume of oats was almost twice that of wheat. In Saskatchewan, the volume of wheat exceeded that of oats, and its value was nearly three times as great.[4]

Also in 1910 the value of animal products and animals sold or slaughtered in Alberta – almost $30 million – continued to be much higher than the value of land products: about $18 million. In contrast, Saskatchewan's land products were worth about $81 million – $63 million more than those of Alberta – while its livestock products and livestock sold or killed were valued at $5 million less.[5] The Alberta economy, then, was not wheat based into the early UFA era. The main farm outputs in those years were livestock, their products, and oats.

During the war, however, wheat production came to the fore. After declining from 1911 to 1914, wheat acreage began to increase sharply.[6] The average number of acres in wheat per Alberta farm more than doubled from fifteen in 1910 to thirty-eight in 1916. Wheat production per farm, which had been 147 bushels in 1910, soared to 979 bushels in the bumper crop year of 1915, and the proportion of the value of crops in wheat, which had been 39 per cent in 1910, was 61 per cent five years later. Still, even though wheat was the main farm product in much of southern Alberta, it did not yet dominate the provincial economy as it did in Saskatchewan. The average value and amount of wheat per Alberta farm in 1915 remained less than half that per Saskatchewan farm. And while the total value of Alberta wheat was nearly one and a half times the value of the province's livestock and livestock products, the corresponding ratio for Saskatchewan was four times. Furthermore, the total value of Alberta livestock and livestock products plus the value of oats in 1915 exceeded greatly the value of wheat.[7] Clearly, the Alberta agricultural economy relied on a variety of products rather than on a single staple.

This situation held even after the war, although wheat played an ever-increasing role in the economy. Alberta farmers seeded 57 per cent of their crop acreage to wheat in 1921, but collectively they were not wheat specialists like Saskatchewan producers, who sowed 66 per cent. In 1920 Saskatchewan farmers grew fifty-five more bushels of wheat per capita of rural population than Alberta farmers, who still produced large quantities of non-wheat products. Per rural dweller, Alberta farmers produced more barley and fifty-four more bushels of oats than Saskatchewan farmers. In addition, the average number of livestock per farm remained higher in Alberta,[8] as did the average value of livestock products and livestock sold or slaughtered per farm. It is significant that the average value of animal products and animals sold or killed per Alberta farm, plus the average value of other non-wheat products per farm, equalled the average value of wheat.[9] Thus, although wheat had become the most important agricultural commodity and the major source of farm income, it was not the only important farm product. Alberta's agricultural economy continued to depend on many goods.

The growth of wheat production stemmed partly from positive price trends. Canadian wheat prices, generally following world prices, climbed from 65 cents per bushel in 1896 to 75–85 cents in 1907, to $1.20 in 1912. In the financial crisis of 1913 the price dipped below $1.00 per bushel but recovered thereafter, reaching $1.28 in 1915 and over $2.00 for several years after 1916.[10] High wartime prices and patriotic appeals for food production were major catalysts for wheat growing across the West.

On the southern Alberta plains, the environment favoured wheat. Lack of water and natural protection from severe winters limited the number of livestock a farmer could care for, and the arid climate, which was hostile to many midwestern crops, produced high grades of wheat. Additionally, the treeless terrain facilitated the use of machinery for wheat production. The introduction of Marquis wheat in 1911, which resisted drought better and ripened earlier than other strains, was a boon to wheat growing throughout the prairies.[11]

Wheat was also cheaper and easier to transport to distant markets than most non-grain farm products. Moreover, compared with livestock raising, wheat growing had lower production costs, turned a quicker profit, and needed less labour – important considerations in a debt-ridden frontier society where land was cheap and labour expensive. Furthermore, unlike mixed agriculture, which necessitated year-round work, wheat farming was seasonal, making it easier for farmers to work at other occupations or to seek warmer climes in the winter.[12]

While environment, frontier conditions, transportation, and markets account for the rise of wheat growing, similar realities explain the continued importance of non-wheat production. In central, northern, and southwestern Alberta, an abundance of shelter and water facilitated mixed farming and livestock raising; and Chinook winds, especially in the south, periodically melted the snow, exposing grass for grazing. Where there was no railway, as was the case around Edmonton before 1891 and in the far north until the First World War, farmers had little choice but to produce a variety of products for home use and the local market. During the war, high prices encouraged most farmers to produce at least some livestock as well as feed crops.

Alberta's urban centres also encouraged mixed farming. By 1906 over 30,000 Albertans lived in its five cities and another 28,000 in its eighteen towns and thirty-three villages. Saskatchewan, despite having 72,000 more inhabitants than Alberta, had nearly 10,000 fewer urban dwellers and only four cities with 12,000 fewer persons than Alberta's cities.[13] Manitoba's urban population as a percentage of its total population was somewhat higher than that of Alberta, but most of its urban dwellers lived in Winnipeg. Farmers who could not ship cheaply to the city did not have as many good local markets as most Alberta producers did. Nor did they have a substantial market outside the province, as Alberta farmers and ranchers had in British Columbia. In 1912 British Columbia received 37,000 head of cattle from Alberta, while another 65,000 were sold in Alberta for local consumption. In the preceding year, British Columbia and the prairie provinces had need of 'everything which Alberta could raise,' and Alberta producers had shipped 289,000 cattle, horses, sheep, and hogs, most of which went to the 'home market of the

Canadian West.'[14] This market – in Alberta and the other western provinces – stimulated non-wheat production because it absorbed a wide range of agricultural goods.

Metropolitan propaganda and culture reinforced the economic incentives to produce non-wheat products. Newspapers, the farm press, railways and banks, schools and departments of agriculture, and other state bodies preached mixed farming through articles, fairs, courses, experimental and demonstration farms, and trains with displays on farm improvement. Western farmers were often receptive to this message, particularly before the war; many had come from mixed-farming regions in Ontario, the American Midwest, or Europe, where they had learned that diversified agriculture was the ideal and that one-crop farming harmed the land.[15]

Wheat specialization had other disadvantages. Greater distance from the ports on Lake Superior meant that Alberta farmers had to pay more to ship their wheat to foreign markets than their prairie counterparts did, especially before the completion of the Panama Canal in 1914. The vagaries of nature also discouraged wholesale wheat growing: frosts, pests, disease, and unpredictable levels of rainfall caused greater variation in the quantity and quality of wheat in Alberta than in the other western provinces. In 1910 Alberta had the lowest average wheat yield per acre in the West: ten bushels. In 1915 it had the highest yield, at thirty-one bushels, only to experience unprecedented crop failure in 1918 and 1919: seven and eight bushels – again the lowest averages on the prairies. Yields rebounded in 1920 to twenty bushels per acre, but plummeted once more to another prairie-wide low of just over ten bushels in 1921.[16] Such variation, which was even greater in certain districts, made reliance on wheat precarious. Production of other goods, at least as an adjunct to wheat, promised greater income stability.

This volatility in the yield of wheat and other grains shaped the Alberta agrarian movement. Frequent crop failure and high debt loads resulting from recent settlement and wartime expansion made some United Farmers and Farm Women of Alberta (UFA/UFWA) desperate and therefore receptive to radical monetary and political solutions. This desperation partly explains their keen interest in soft money and group-government doctrines after the war. Crop and income variability also ensured that the UFA/UFWA worked for all its members, not only its elite leaders. Because of environment, farmers in a given area might need off-farm income or government aid in one year and labourers to harvest their large crops in the next. This happened in much of southern Alberta in 1914–15. Such experience fostered an egalitarian and co-operative culture. Knowing they could be the next to have a bad crop, most UFA/UFWA members and leaders had personal reasons for supporting other members who were experiencing difficulty.

Alberta's diversified farm economy was at the heart of the formation of the movement before 1909. In 1901–2 a dispute about the price and grading of Alberta oats raised farmers' sense of opposition to the grain trade. Partly in response, J.J. Gregory created the Farmers' Association of Lacombe in 1903, believing that the Territorial Grain Growers' Association (TGGA) could not meet mixed producers' needs. In the next year, northern Alberta farmers who were convinced that a combine existed in the grain market, especially for oats, established a branch of the Society of Equity (S of E) to control the Edmonton market for several farm products. Also in 1904 Strathcona farmers reacted to depressed prices for wheat, oats, pork, beef, and eggs by forming a TGGA local. A year later, feeling that the TGGA focused too much on wheat-related matters and desiring to have 'an Association that will embrace every farmer whether a grain grower or a stock grower,'[17] the Strathcona TGGA transformed itself into the Alberta Farmers' Association (AFA).

The S of E, the TGGA/AFA, and their predecessors were heavily involved in mixed-farming causes, such as trying to increase the price of various farm products and lobbying the government to establish creameries and to promote the sale of different agricultural goods. In 1906 the province responded to AFA requests for help in selling surplus oats by sending Association president D.W. Warner on a successful marketing mission to British Columbia.[18] Also in that year, the AFA launched a campaign for a government meat plant, a cause the UFA took up. Farmers' desire for a united farm movement to deal with such diverse agricultural matters led to the merger of the S of E and AFA in 1909.

The first UFA constitution made it clear that the new organization would continue to 'forward the interests of the producers of grain and livestock.'[19] It would not neglect wheat specialists, but its efforts to address the concerns of all farmers built and politicized the UFA/ UFWA by attracting new members and fostering commitment. Frustration over wheat and non-wheat issues and low prices for a variety of agricultural products ultimately drew the movement into politics.

In its earliest years, the UFA concentrated on non-wheat causes, since few members specialized in wheat. The directors, in fact, had difficulty in finding pure wheat producers to speak for the organization at a Calgary conference in 1909 on western grain shipping. 'You know we are not so well organized in the large wheat growing districts of the south as we are in the mixed farming districts,' president Bower explained to the 1910 convention. 'Consequently, we were somewhat in the dark as to who would best represent the wheat growers.' It was not long before more wheat specialists joined the UFA/UFWA, but as late as 1915 mixed-farm constituencies still contained nearly half the UFA membership.[20] And although the organization soon had its strongest support in southern Alberta, it always had substantial representation in central and even northern Alberta,[21] where livestock, oat, and other agricultural production remained crucial. As a result, the UFA/UFWA never lost sight of non-wheat concerns.

The early UFA's non-wheat focus was evident in its efforts to find new markets in British Columbia for several farm goods. To that end, Bower went to British Columbia in 1909 at the government's expense and discovered large quantities of hogs, meat, and hay entering the province from the United States. To break monopoly control over Alberta products so that they could be more competitive in British Columbia, Bower and the UFA advocated lower freight rates, a government pork plant, municipal abattoirs, standardized inspection of hay, as well as licensing and bonding of commission merchants.[22]

Farmers' support for these and other non-wheat issues shows that the early UFA was not driven by a wheat economy, as does Bower's remarkable statement to the 1910 convention:

In making this province a prosperous mixed-farming province, we are more vitally interested in dealing with British Columbia than we are in terminal elevators at Fort William or Hudson Bay, or even line elevators through the prairie provinces. If we build up an interprovincial trade with British Columbia, we build up a western export grain route at the same time, but as we all know, wheat is not our mainstay, nor can it be for generations to come. Our chief line of production is in our live animals, in our hay, and in our coarser grains, and in the west, and through the west, lies our market.

Reflecting this non-wheat focus, the early UFA campaigned for a government chilled-meat system and railway compensation for killed horses and cattle, while passing resolutions about matters such as coyote bounties, strays, and herd laws. Moreover, UFA leaders argued that farmers should support reciprocity in 1911, partly because it would greatly benefit the livestock industry.[23]

'A Slim Chance: "Monopoly" Is Liable to Get a Pointed Hint,' probably by Arch Dale. *Grain Growers' Guide*, 12 Jan. 1910, 4. This cartoon shows the importance of both the livestock industry and the B.C. market to the early UFA. Here, the UFA, with the support of organized farmers in Manitoba and Saskatchewan, hopes to break monopoly control of eastern and western livestock markets.

Non-wheat UFA activity did not wane, even as wheat production increased. Thanks to wartime demand and the opening of the American market to Canadian cattle in 1914, UFA members sold tens of thousands of head of livestock through their locals, co-ops, and elevator companies. When the U.S. market effectively closed in 1921, the UFA sought a government-assisted co-operative chilled-meat scheme and urged the province to make trial beef shipments to Britain. During the war, the UFA affiliated with the Western Live Stock Union and lobbied Ottawa to pay more for warhorses and to change the Bank Act so that farmers could borrow on the security of their livestock.[24]

The UFA/UFWA also worked to facilitate members' selling, mainly of non-wheat products, in local centres. In 1910 Broken Hill union wanted a crossing to give farmers a direct route to Vermilion, where they hoped to find 'a better market' than at Manville. Two years later, Olds union agitated for a railway to connect local farmers with a 'ready market' for milk. In the southwest, unions enjoyed lucrative markets for hogs and other goods in Crow's Nest Pass towns. Across the province, farmers sold to contractors, especially in the heady pre-war boom years. Onoway union decided in 1910 to ask members to 'hold the produce they are selling to railway contractors at ... hay $12 to $15 per load, potatoes, carrots, turnips, beets, at fifty cents per bushel, and onions at 2 1/2 per pound.'[25]

The UFA association helped farmers to market their non-wheat goods in larger urban centres. In 1913 it blocked a by-law that would have prohibited individual farmers from selling meat in Calgary, and it arranged for the Grain Growers' Grain Company to sell UFA members' products at the Calgary public market. It also organized outlets for produce in other centres, including Red Deer and Edmonton,[26] and called for a parcel post system to ship perishable goods to urban markets. During the war, UFA/UFWA locals sold eggs to urban centres through a government marketing service. Towards the end of the war, the UFA formed a milk and cream committee that negotiated prices with Calgary dairy companies. Later, the UFA helped to create the Calgary Milk Producers' Association and affiliated with it and similar bodies in Medicine Hat and Lethbridge.[27]

These efforts to assist members in marketing their non-wheat products brought new challenges and required much organization, locally and between unions and central office. This activity formed bonds of mutuality and an ethos of co-operation that built the movement as farmers learned to work with each other and the organization. In so doing, they developed relationships, a sense of commitment, and skills they used for other movement purposes.

Buying and selling among UFA/UFWA members also built feelings of collectivity. 'Has any member anything he wishes to sell?' – the UFA constitution suggested that this question be asked at every local meeting. Farmers sold to and bought from each other equipment, farm produce, and other items. Settlers purchased many supplies from neighbours during their first year, and even in subsequent years few farm families produced all the local goods they needed. UFA/UFWA unions provided forums and developed social links that promoted this trade. Furthermore, locals did business with each other. In 1910 Cowley union purchased a car of potatoes from the Red Deer UFA Co-op; Kasimir local ordered a car of hay from the Farmers' Exchange Company of Barons; and Claresholm Five Mile UFA union bought potatoes and vegetables worth almost $500 from Leduc, Alberta.[28] Such exchanges between members and locals developed feelings of solidarity and co-operation as farmers economically supported fellow members.

The UFA central office helped farmers to buy and sell. In drought years, it acted as an information bureau, bringing together buyers and sellers of seed and feed. In 1910 it tried to get freight rates reduced on hay and grain shipped within the province for local use. Occasionally, it advertised products such as cordwood, posts, pickets, and lumber, which farmers produced for sale from clearing the land.[29] By assisting members with this non-wheat buying and selling, the UFA association fostered loyalty to the movement, since farmers felt that it was working for them.

Wage labour also strengthened the movement. Scholars have shown that farmers relied on wage work in central and eastern Canada in the late nineteenth century and in Alberta from the 1920s. Such work was critical for Alberta producers in the period under study. The UFA constitution recommended that members be asked at every meeting: 'Does any member wish to employ a hand to work? Does any member wish a job to work or know of a person who does?' In the earliest settlement years, many farmers were 'farm labourers and farm owners concurrently.' They needed to earn money to make improvements and support their families until they could market their livestock or harvest their first good crop. That is why Rice Sheppard criticized regulations that required a homesteader to spend six months of the year on his land when he could be away 'earning good wages' on another farm.[30]

Few farmers totally escaped their reliance on wages. When crops failed, they left their districts to look for work, making it difficult for UFA locals to hold meetings. Some farmers needed wages because their farms were not large enough to sustain a family. Therefore, they worked routinely for more established or well-to-do farmers, even in better years. Occasionally, the UFA office helped farmers to find employment. In 1916 it published a notice in the *Guide* from a local secretary indicating that some members of his union wanted work at haying time. The response was overwhelming, and a number found jobs as a result.[31]

The importance of wage labour prompted a few UFA members who were dependent on farm employment to request a minimum wage for farm work and legal priority for farm wages over other creditors' claims. Such demands, however, received little support in the UFA/UFWA as a whole. Most UFA men were farm owners whose main income was from farming, not wage work, and their identity, at least for the liberal majority, was that of entrepreneur, not worker. Accordingly, the UFA, along with other western farm organizations, sought to establish a maximum wage rate in 1921.[32]

Farmers also sought non-farm wage employment, such as working on irrigation canals and doing road and other work for Local Improvement Districts (LIDs). In 1910 the LID Association, whose officers included UFA secretary E.J. Fream and future UFA premier, Herbert Greenfield, passed a resolution favouring an eight- rather than a ten-hour day, since districts were having difficulty in competing with railways for men. One UFA local on the edge of the northern frontier raised money to hire some of its members to build needed roads and bridges. Around Lethbridge farming and mining were 'closely intertwined,' and near Drumheller some coal miners homesteaded and gradually became full-time farmers.[33]

Farmers earned income in all sorts of ways. A few were pound keepers, some earned commissions getting *Guide* subscriptions, some plowed railway fireguards, and some farm wives and daughters did housework and chores for their neighbours or women in the towns. For homesteaders in the dry belt after the war, off-farm earnings were a matter of survival. There, locals clamoured for road, railway, and irrigation work 'to tide them over ... and make it unnecessary for them to leave their farms.' Some UFA farmers wanted to be relief officers.[34]

The diary and accounts of Wilfred Sutton are particularly revealing of the multiple sources of rural wage work. Sutton, a prominent member and sometime officer of the Winona UFA local, emigrated from England and settled near Edgerton on the eastern edge of central Alberta in 1910 or 1911. In June 1911 he broke sod for an unnamed 'boss,' and from September to January 1913 he worked for R.B. Gunn, a farmer-merchant, at a wage ranging from $10 to $25 per month. During his final two months of working for Gunn and in February 1913 he also laboured for another party for $20 per month.[35] In September of that year, he received $19 in wages, apparently for harvest work, and paid $10 for room and board. The following 10 January he did some sawing and was paid $1. Sutton did much, if not all, of this wage work while homesteading.[36]

Sutton's diary also shows the pervasiveness of the local exchange economy. In March and April 1913 he bought one bushel of potatoes, thirty bushels of oats, two dozen eggs, thirty and a half bushels of oat chop, eleven bushels of flax, and twenty pounds of beef from four farm families. He also borrowed his neighbours' equipment, a practice that was not without obligations: he helped Dan Mackenzie to stack hay on 16 August 1911 'in return for the use of his mower and rake.' This example is suggestive of Nancy Osterud's argument that farm men kept close tabs on their labour exchanges as if they were market transactions.[37] Thus, Sutton dug a well for 'Henton' on 12 November 1913; two days later he wrote that 'Henton is hauling a load for me in payment for work done at the well.' On 22 November Sutton recorded another kind of informal economic arrangement: 'Went over to Henton's and made a deal for him to haul 4 loads of wheat for school tax.'

N. Rich from the Manville area east of Edmonton was another UFA supporter who exchanged labour with his neighbours, and, like most farmers, he bartered goods. Unable to sell his oats, he traded 'some for a cow, some for a sheepskin coat, some for threshing, some for a pig, and some ... for a wedding present.' In payment for wintering cattle, he got an ox, which he traded for a pony.[38]

Money was short on the frontier. Most settlers arrived with little of it and had heavy initial expenditures. As a result, many got into debt. All experienced erratic cash flows amid price and climatic fluctuations. Trading labour or goods with other farmers, bartering produce for store merchandise, or working off rather than paying local taxes were ways of coping.[39]

Such informal exchanges of equipment, labour, and goods moulded farmers' sense of rural community; the interaction and interdependence fostered by these activities forged bonds of mutuality on which the forming, building, and politicizing of the movement rested. Even wage-labour relationships could create ties of reciprocity rather than conflict, especially when farmers both hired and worked for their neighbours. Moreover, while hidden in the census and largely missed by the wheat staple thesis, informal exchange kept the rural economy going, making the farm movement possible and enabling farmers to produce the wheat and other goods the census reveals.

UFA/UFWA locals were based on local exchange relationships. Virtually every person with whom Sutton had formal or informal economic dealings was a UFA member.[40] In some cases, farmers, having developed economic and community ties among themselves, joined the UFA/UFWA as a group or formed a new union. UFA/UFWA locals, in turn, reinforced members' connectedness by strengthening economic relations between them, enhancing their sense of community, solidarity, and co-operation.

The local exchange economy could have a very direct impact on unions and ultimately on the movement. In 1919 Dora Burkholder, president of the Excel UFWA local, described an experience of recruiting new members:

My husband asked me to go over to Mr. So-and-So's for some seed potatoes, so I started out to get the potatoes from a farmer about four miles away. On the way, I called on one of our neighbours and led the conversation to the subject of U.F.W.A. She became so interested in the work of our association that she paid her membership fee that very afternoon.

I then went on with my errand, but was fortunate enough to secure two new members, a mother and her daughter, at the farm where the potatoes were for sale. It was quite late by this time, but as I was driving home I could not resist the temptation of making the attempt to get another member. Before I could bring the subject up myself, my hostess, who is our U.F.A. secretary, said, 'Oh! Mrs. Burkholder, my daughter wants to join the U.F.W.A., but she has gone home now. Perhaps you can see her later ...'

Of course I ... made a special visit to my new prospect, thus securing another member. On this trip, I also visited three others who promised to attend the next meeting and join the club.[41]

All this because of a trip to buy potatoes from a local farmer!

In addition to local exchange, non-wheat staple production, and wage labour, small-business activity was an important part of Alberta's rural economy. Such activity revealed some farmers' progressive 'business' outlook, but for most it was simply a pragmatic form of occupational pluralism; like wage work, it helped them to survive or prosper while they were farming. Farmers ran sawmills, freighted, located homesteads, speculated in land, or sold machinery. Many farmers cut telephone poles or railway ties on a subcontract basis. In 1919 Junkins local asked the railways to deal directly with farmers rather than through a contractor. Some farmers, such as R.B. Gunn, for whom Sutton worked, were merchants. A few, including UFA vice-president Samuel S. Dunham, were lawyers, and others, such as another vice-president, Percival Baker, were 'farmer-preachers.' Farming was a sideline for some of these professionals and businessmen, but it was the main source of income for most. Certain kinds of work made it hard to tell where petty capitalism ended and wage labour began. Was F.B. Sulman, a UFA man, working as an independent contractor when he ploughed a neighbour's field for a money payment, or was he a casual labourer?[42]

One of the more important businesses for farmers was custom threshing. As grain growing spread, there was great demand for this service, since few farmers could afford their own threshers. The Lien Act of 1916, which gave threshermen preference as creditors, made the business even more attractive. To take advantage of these opportunities, some UFA locals collectively bought and operated threshing units.[43]

Business activity was especially significant in northern Alberta, where many farmers, including some women, trapped during the winter. By the war years, farmers caught most of the fur taken in Canada. In 1915 alone, over 306,000 muskrat pelts were sold in Alberta, and the province paid wolf bounties. The fur trade was sufficiently important to farmers that the 1921 UFA convention protested a pelt tax.[44] The mover of that resolution was W.F. Bredin, a UFA director engaged in farming and fur trading. Farmers near Lesser Slave Lake caught fish in the winter for sale. One girl claimed that her father and brother had landed '2,700 big ones.' In 1919 it was estimated that there were over 10,000 part-time commercial fishermen in the prairies, most of whom were 'farmer-fishermen' dependent on fishing for their livelihood. The Water Glen district northwest of Calgary was reminiscent of the pre-capitalist age, when farming and cottage industries were inseparable. It was 'rich in experienced spinners and weavers' and had a home woollen industry based on local sheep raising.[45]

Farmers did not always stick with one job or business, including farming, for extended periods of time. George Bevington, who became a UFA credit expert, exemplified many farmers' multi-occupational experience. Born in the United States, Bevington arrived in Edmonton at the age of fifteen in 1893. Sometimes he lived on his parents' homestead, but he 'worked out most of the time, farming in the summer, at bush work, coal mining, etc., in the winter.' Suggestive of the importance of adolescent labour for farm families, Bevington gave most of his earnings to his parents. At age twenty, he struck out on his own, hauling freight for Klondikers to Athabaska, after which he rented and operated a farm for two years. Then, after working at railway construction for a season, he ran a sawmill business and 'engaged in a variety of enterprises – hotel and livery, coal mining, and so forth.'[46] Later, Bevington farmed for many years in the Edmonton area.

Such multi-occupational experience affected the farm movement. Because farmers could be agriculturalists, businessmen, or wage earners – at different times or simultaneously – barriers between classes in rural areas were slow to emerge. This facilitated the development of farmers' sense of community and reciprocity on which the forming, building, and politicizing of the movement depended. Moreover, occupational pluralism fostered ideological diversity. Many UFA/UFWA radicals were, or had been, involved in the labour movement, and many liberals were, or had been, businessmen. This experience helped farmers to collaborate with other groups on projects of mutual interest, contributing to the notion, fully expressed in the post-war UFA/UFWA social philosophy, that co-operation could be the animating principle of all human relations – social, economic, and even political.

Like occupational pluralism, subsistence work was fundamental to Alberta's rural economy. Ian MacPherson and John Herd Thompson argue that some prairie farm families were largely self-sufficient; others were mainly commercial; and still others were something in between: 'commercially oriented but strategically flexible.' They contend that even families on mainly commercial operations 'satisfied many of their consumption needs from their own farms.'[47] Analysis of the UFA/UFWA confirms these arguments and shows that subsistence activity was not limited to food production. With considerable variation, depending on region, environment, economic status, and culture, farmers were self-sufficient in many ways – even if they were 'commercially oriented.'

Self-sufficiency was practised most completely, mainly for cultural and economic reasons, by central and eastern European peasants who settled in east-central Alberta. Other settlers on the fringes of the frontier were fairly self-sufficient out of necessity. Until railways arrived, they had to hold back commercial production and concentrate on subsistence work. Yet even where railways existed, most farmers desired some self-sufficiency. In a paper read to the Macleod district UFA convention it was proposed that farmers establish co-operative mills to produce flour for home consumption. 'We can then eat our bread,' the author concluded, 'whether we can get money or not, and we can afford to take our chances of the market.'[48]

Some farmers extracted coal from river banks and surface mines for their own use and sometimes for sale. One local arranged to have its members dig from a nearby mine. In addition, farmers cut hay and gathered wood from unoccupied land, which is why Great Bend union favoured 'reserving the vacant government lands in the vicinity for wood, etc.' Great Bend also discussed wild game, a topic central office encouraged all locals to consider. Game was an important part of many farmers' diet, including that of UFWA president Irene Parlby's family. Like many farm women, Parlby also gathered wild berries.[49]

As well, the Parlby family and other farmers fished for their own consumption. In 1910 F.C. Clare moved a resolution before the UFA convention asking the province to take action against parties who were polluting rivers. Clare's union later told the Fisheries Commission that pollution and illegal fishing had depleted fish stocks in the North Saskatchewan River. The union requested that steps be taken to restore the population, since fish provided 'a welcome change of food.'[50]

Besides fishing, hunting, and gathering, farm families produced much of what they needed on the farm, including grain, meat, fruit, dairy products, and garden produce. UFA member F.B. Sulman made furniture from willows and soap boxes. Self-sufficiency was most important before the war as farmers established themselves commercially. During the war, families consumed more garden produce, coarse grains, fish, and game in order to conserve meat and wheat for the war effort. For farmers facing crop failure or low product prices, especially after the war, subsistence activity was a matter of survival. The census hints at the magnitude of the post-war subsistence economy, revealing that an average of 2,250 pounds of whole milk were consumed on each Alberta farm in 1920.[51]

Tradition also prompted farmers, including those bent on commercial production, to practise some self-sufficiency. Fishing, hunting, gathering, and livestock raising were part of rural life in Ontario and the American Midwest.[52] Additionally, subsistence work was a way of getting ahead; it freed up money for other uses. Why buy food when you could produce it yourself and invest the money you saved in farm equipment or household appliances?

Subsistence activity, occupational pluralism, and local exchange facilitated the forming and building of the movement by helping members and prospective members who could not have survived as pure commercial wheat growers to stay on the land. Moreover, these activities helped to sustain the national economy. Because of them, farmers could receive less for their products and still buy tariff-protected metropolitan goods. Lower prices for farm products – which subsistence work, occupational pluralism, and local exchange made possible – also kept food prices low. This raised the disposable income of non-farmers and put downward pressure on wages, which increased investment and profits and stimulated the economy. Non-wheat economic activity also enabled wheat specialists to keep going in hard months and years, so that they could contribute to the western wheat boom that boosted the Canadian economy before the war.

Understanding the diverse nature of Alberta's economy reveals the significance of women's and children's work. The wheat staple thesis, emphasizing wheat production for foreign markets, highlights men's work in the fields and largely ignores childrens' and wives' domestic and subsistence activity and their small-commodity production.[53] Women cooked, canned, cleaned, and laundered; looked after the children; made clothes and soap; acted as doctors, nurses, and teachers; picked berries; and hauled water. They milked cows and were largely responsible for keeping busy the government and, later, the co-operative and private creameries. They raised most of the garden produce and poultry that farmers sold in markets, such as the Calgary public market, in which the UFA was involved. They gathered eggs and sold them by various means, including through the government egg-marketing service supported by the UFA/UFWA.

Women and children also did field work, particularly in earlier years when labour was expensive and on smaller and poorer farms. On most farms, they helped at peak times, especially during the harvest. In the war years, wives did tasks formerly done by their husbands overseas – everything from ploughing to stooking. Generally, they enjoyed this work, although it sometimes interfered with UFWA and youth club activities.[54] They also looked after the farms when their husbands were away hunting or fishing, or hauling coal, wood, or grain. Many men left home for weeks or months to work for wages, on contracts, or in small businesses. Sometimes they were away on UFA business: recruiting new members, organizing locals, attending conventions, establishing co-ops, or doing political work after the war.

By running the farm in the absence of their husbands, women made this movement activity possible. Moreover, their commodity production and domestic, subsistence, and field work made members' farms viable by producing needed cash, lowering costs of maintaining the family and farm, and freeing up men to generate off-farm income.[55] Without this work, there would have been fewer farms, fewer UFA/UFWA members, and a weaker movement; indeed, the movement might not have been formed, let alone built or politicized.

Farm women's work illustrates the difficulty of making a sharp distinction between market and non-market work. Which of the two was raising chickens? Many things – the farm and larger economies, the environment, the availability of wage work – might determine whether women ultimately would be raising those chickens mainly for the market or for home consumption. Yet even women's more purely non-market work, such as raising children or washing clothes, was essential to the operation of market-oriented farms, present and future.

Many farm men acknowledged the importance of farm women's market and non-market work. Rice Sheppard frankly stated that without farm wives, most successful male farmers, including himself, 'would have been utter failures.' Expressing a similar sentiment, W.J. Keen of the Society of Equity informed one local farmer that 'wives, mothers, sweethearts' were invited to the 1905 annual meeting, 'for the founders know only too well the part they play in our business.'[56] Such recognition of women's work was a reason why many male farmers supported the UFWA agenda and encouraged women to join the farm movement.

Census and qualitative data show that the Alberta farm economy and movement were not driven by a wheat economy before 1922. While wheat became increasingly important, it never became a dominant staple in the period under study. Non-wheat production and activity remained integral to the rural economy. Far from being based on the production and distribution of wheat for export markets, the early Alberta economy resembled many nineteenth-century rural economies, being based on a number of agricultural products and on local exchange, occupational pluralism, and subsistence work.

This multifaceted rural economy, which women's work supported, helped to form, build, and politicize the Alberta movement by enabling members to stay on the land and by moulding their sense of mutuality as it forced them to work together, at many levels, on a variety of projects. The diverse Alberta economy was a factor in the development of the provincial farm movement and its culture.

Chapter Four

Creating and Defining the Community

Our meeting together ... has tended ... to promote a community spirit.[1]
M. Shield, secretary of the Rathwell UFWA

'Community' was the foundation of the farm movement. Social activity, mutual aid, and local work gave rise to a community ethos – attachment to the people of a rural locality – that contained feelings of mutuality on which the forming, building, and politicizing of the movement depended. By fostering class consciousness and accommodating producers who differed in ideology, ethnicity, product specialization, economic status, and institutional affiliation, the United Farmers and Farm Women of Alberta (UFA/UFWA) strengthened this sense of community while expanding it to encompass the larger farm movement and even other classes with whom farmers felt a community of interest, especially political interest. At the same time, there were limits to their notion of community, particularly with other races and groups.

Farmers' feeling of rural community – which helped them to adapt to a frontier environment – began to emerge with the 'creation of a European landscape' of fields, roads, bridges, and towns that 'linked people's experience with a specific sense of place.'[2] It was reinforced by formal and informal economic exchange between farmers and between producers and townspeople and was intensified by a utopian faith in the agricultural potential of a district propagated by immigration literature and embraced by farmers to justify their choice of homestead. Their belief that monopolies, poor markets, and high tariffs and freight rates kept them from prospering in a rich land formed the movement before

1909 and led the UFA/UFWA to take action, ultimately political action, to channel back to farmers the wealth flowing from the soil.

UFA/UFWA locals built a sense of community. They helped frontier women and men to 'belong' by bringing them together to talk, work on community projects, strengthen their economic links, or simply enjoy themselves. Many farmers, especially women, joined the UFA/UFWA primarily for social contact and the locals' activities, including concerts, dinners, sporting events, plays, and even masquerades, where one might see a costume 'composed entirely of Grain Growers' Guides.' Roseview local put on a typical social in 1910:

> The first part of the program consisted of songs, recitations, duets, and comic dialogues, which brought forth roars of laughter, applause, and well-merited praise from the audience. A dialogue by the children entitled 'Little Grain Growers,' in which each child held a card with a letter of the two words 'Grain Growers' printed on it and recited a verse suitable to the letter and the occasion, caused much amusement and favorable comment.
>
> The [supper] boxes supplied by the ladies were then auctioned off ... [and] after the good things provided by the ladies had been done justice to, the floor was cleared so that all who wished might indulge in tripping the light fantastic to their hearts' content.[3]

Such activities, which usually pointed to the movement and its work, forged ties of mutuality from which the movement developed.

Locally written songs promoting community pride and agrarian loyalty were popular at union meetings and socials. One UFWA union sang, to the chorus of 'Yankee Doodle':

> Doondale, Doondale, that's our name;
> Protecting farmers' interests, that's our game.
> Co-operative efforts are our aim
> In sunny southern Alberta.

After the war, the UFA/UFWA sold over 1,000 copies of the song, 'Equal Rights for All,' written by a local UFA man. Alluding to the UFA/UFWA motto 'Equity' and seeking a community of interest with urban dwellers, it proclaimed:

> Steadily march along, the battle's just commencing;
> We fight for equal rights for one and all;

And if united there is nothing now preventing
The stronghold of the enemy shall fall.
Our city friends we gladly too will welcome,
Then join us in the fight both one and all.[4]

Annual UFA/UFWA picnics, with up to 3,000 participants, also formed bonds of community – and attracted new members as farmers and townspeople mingled and enjoyed activities such as baseball, football, tugs of war, races, and shooting and bucking contests. Picnics required much work and organization. At one locale, visitors were greeted by a 'race track with edges plowed, a football field, all nicely mown, heaps of hay for visitors, [and a] flag flying with Blackfoot U.F.A. in gold and blue.'[5] Organizing picnics trained UFA/UFWA members for other movement work and was a source of community pride as unions tried to outdo one another.

In building stronger communities, UFA/UFWA unions could break down cliques by bringing members of different clubs or factions into the movement. UFA/UFWA locals were not exclusive. All 'directly interested in farming,' including non-farmers, could join[6] and were invited to picnics and socials.

UFA/UFWA unions also built community spirit by mobilizing farmers to assist needy UFA/UFWA members and others in the district. Unions provided opportunities for farmers to practise the pioneer mutual-aid ethic and the golden rule – the 'Lord's "inasmuch."' While George Fisher was recovering from an illness in early 1919, a group of farmers under the direction of the local UFA secretary brought twenty-two plow teams to Fisher's farm and spent two days turning over, seeding, and harrowing fifty acres.[7] Such scenes were enacted in hundreds of communities, partly because the UFA constitution instructed members to 'extend fraternal care to one another in sickness, misfortune, or distress.' Following this precept, unions undertook various kinds of farm work, gave money and goods, built houses and barns, and sewed and cooked for persons who were ill, injured, burned out, or whose crops had failed. In response to an appeal from central office, some UFA/ UFWA members helped neighbours who were suffering from influenza in 1918–19.[8]

UFA/UFWA farmers believed that helping persons in the neighbourhood was a form of 'co-operation.' 'I was a victim of a broken ankle,' related one UFA man, 'and my crop would have been in the ground now, but the co-operation and true fellowship that exists in local 273 would not permit it.' 'True co-operation,' he concluded, 'is the only way to success.'[9] Such thinking and the practical aid supporting it created a foundation of reciprocity on which the forming, building, and politicizing of the movement rested.

The UFA/UFWA could even help to meet a community's spiritual needs. Because the main denominations were slow to adapt to frontier conditions, church organization lagged in rural Alberta. A survey by UFWA leader Leona Barritt in 1918 suggested that two-thirds of rural school districts had no church service and that most others had irregular service. The UFA/UFWA partly filled this gap by becoming a quasi-religious institution. 'We are trying to do the social work that the church has been unable to do,' Barritt explained, 'and to raise an ethical standard where the church has been unable to obtain a footing.'[10]

UFA/UFWA members prayed, sang hymns, and read Scripture in conventions and local meetings. Sometimes, like Christians sharing their personal testimonies, they gave their 'testimony' about what the organization had 'done for me.'[11] Biblical rhetoric infused their discourse. UFA Women's Auxiliary president Jean Reed admonished members to 'study to show thyself approved of God.' Because women were thought to be inherently spiritual and responsible for children's moral development, UFWA members set up Sunday schools and called for Bible readings in classrooms. One UFWA 'girls'' club studied the women of the Bible.[12]

UFA Sunday was a poignant expression of the UFA/UFWA Christian and community spirit. Started by the Roseview union in 1914, it became an annual event in many UFA/UFWA communities by the mid- to late-war years. Featuring a sermon on applied Christianity, the services celebrated the movement 'from a religious viewpoint.' At one UFA Sunday service,

Mr. Sheppard of Edmonton commenced with a service of song ... [It] was ... followed by an address on practical Christianity, which proved conclusively the U.F.A. was practically a Christian institution, its motto being Equity ... [T]he audience then sang the hymn poem, 'Stand up, stand up for freedom,' which contains the following noble lines: 'God gives to each a vision of purer, brighter days, when all our fair Dominion true Equity displays' ... President Speakman led in prayer, lifting us from earth into the presence of God. The sermon which followed was a powerful one, based on a verse from Ephesians 4 and 5 ... He traced co-operation ... in the community, the nation, and the whole earth ... Christ being the head we must all co-operate with each other in His spirit.[13]

Reflecting farmers' desire to unify the community, a UFA Sunday service often featured several ministers speaking against sectarianism. McCafferty union went further and started a non-denominational 'community church' to teach 'the life of Christ in a democratic age.'[14] By promoting Christian fellowship and weakening religious barriers in communities, the UFA/UFWA built bonds of 'oneness' that drew the movement together.

While reinforcing local and ultimately movement ties through religious and social activities and mutual aid, farmers sought to strengthen communities through practical work and improvements. The Patrons of Industry agitated for a bridge and a teacher-training school at Edmonton. The Alberta Farmers' Association was concerned with many local issues, from herd laws to drainage, which is one reason why it had greater success than the Society of Equity. UFA/UFWA conventions dealt extensively with questions that affected farmers locally, such as railway branch lines and fencing and fines for bulls running at large.

Unions made many demands about community matters. They pressed for school districts, irrigation, telephone and medical service, post and telegraph offices, and railway facilities. Their efforts sometimes bore fruit. Queenstown local convinced the government to let union members cut hay on the Blackfoot reserve after individual farmers had been denied the privilege. The local also obtained telephone service for the community and lobbied the province for a bridge, 'pestering them to death until we got the bridge,' John Glambeck boasted.[15] Such small triumphs built the confidence that made larger victories possible.

Unions themselves did much local work. They organized cemeteries; made local road improvements, for which they obtained grants; controlled pests, weeds, and stray livestock; and built and equipped schools, churches, and community halls. Planning and constructing halls, whether for mainly the UFA/UFWA or the larger community, was a communal event, involving local donations of labour and money. Halls facilitated the social, economic, and educational activities that fostered a sense of community. They had kitchens and auditoriums for meals and theatricals, and some had additional amenities such as libraries, games rooms, women's restrooms, co-operative trading rooms, and athletic and recreation equipment.

All this local work and activity strengthened farmers' community ethos and sense of mutuality. 'Our club has brought sunshine and happiness to many homes, and a more friendly feeling exists in the community,' noted one UFWA woman. Just meeting together, another testified, could create a 'real community spirit.'[16] That spirit contained notions of reciprocity on which the movement was formed, built, and politicized. Being and working together in the locals trained farmers to think collectively and work for the benefit of all.

Farmers' community ethos could form moral economy ideas about community rights. This was evident in a UFA convention resolution that argued, in effect, that local interests should prevail over a contractor's right to maximize his profits in a free market. It demanded that custom threshermen be compelled by law to offer their services to all farmers in an area before moving to another, 'as a great amount of hardship' was being 'experienced through threshers leaving a few men scattered throughout the district ... and not threshing their grain.' It concluded that because the law helped threshermen to obtain payment, 'it is equally right that the customers should have protection.' Farmers' community outlook also inclined them to favour local democratic control, which is partly why they endorsed the proposed Municipalities Act in 1911; it promised local 'self-government.'[17]

The UFA association assisted farmers with their district concerns. In 1910 members of several locals in southwestern Alberta were upset about fires that were consuming valuable pasture and timber, and about having to fight fires or put up fire crews without compensation. On their request, the UFA executive convinced the government to act on the matter.[18] The UFA also supported Gleichen and Strathmore area farmers who believed that their costly CPR land was unsuitable for irrigation. They lost a court case and a later appeal, but UFA president Wood helped to arbitrate a deal with the company in 1916 that generally satisfied the farmers. The UFA central assisted members and unions across the province in their efforts to obtain railway crossings, loading platforms, stockyards, weigh scales, and harvest workers. It resolved disputes between them and railway and machinery companies and provided advice on matters ranging from filling out petitions for telephone lines to organizing pound districts. In response to a convention request, it set up a livestock information bureau so that farmers could find their strays.[19]

The Alberta farm movement grew in stature and solidarity – was built and politicized – but only because it rested on this rockbed of community work. The UFA/UFWA's help with local issues fostered mass movement commitment because it met farmers' day-to-day needs. If the leaders had tried to steer the organization exclusively towards larger class issues, such as freight rates and the tariff, they would have failed and the UFA/UFWA would not have attracted the support it did. UFA general secretary E.J. Fream knew that there was no use 'trying to straighten out big things if one's own house is not in order first.'[20]

Especially in the UFA's earliest years, some unions did little besides community work. 'The matters dealt with have been purely local,' reported one secretary, 'principally dealing with binder twine, the formation of a Local Improvement District, the opening of roads, and getting the telephone line extended into the district.' Some farmers grew impatient with this emphasis. 'Now, while these subjects are of interest to the local union,' wrote another secretary, 'and will be of some profit thereby, it seems that the big problems which mean much to every farmer in the province do not create the amount of interest they should.' Then he mused, 'The change might, however, come at a later date.'[21]

Come, it did. Many unions broadened their perspectives. J. Darrough described this development in the Bowell union:

> Heretofore we have taken too narrow an outlook: we have been content as a union to consider only local affairs and have failed to grasp ... that we are part and parcel of an organization that is not bounded in its activities by prescribed lines ... but is as large as our province in extent, and by its influence reaches out to all parts of our broad Dominion where producers of the necessaries of life are exploited for the benefit of the few ... But ... we have waked up. We no longer see as through a glass darkly, but with a clearer vision and broader view.

A similar process was evident in the annual conventions. Over a third of the demands made by the 1909 convention related to local issues,[22] though this percentage declined as later conventions dealt, increasingly, with 'class' questions.

Education in the unions, the *Guide*, and the conventions helped farmers to build on their local sense of mutuality to develop class consciousness and a feeling of national agrarian 'community,' a feeling expressed in the UFA/UFWA's strong support for the Canadian Council of Agriculture and the Inter-Provincial Council of Farm Women, formed in 1909 and 1919, respectively. At UFA/UFWA conventions, delegates learned about this larger farm movement and considered resolutions about provincial, national, and international matters as well as local ones. Inspired and broadened in outlook, they imparted their enthusiasm, sense of agrarian solidarity, and vision to their unions. Farmers also caught wind of bigger movement issues as association officers toured the locals or spoke at UFA/UFWA picnics.

As farmers' class awareness peaked after the war, their community ties made the agrarian revolt possible. When the provincial Liberals unexpectedly issued writs on 23 June 1921 for an election on 18 July, the UFA/UFWA was organized for provincial politics in only sixteen constituencies. With lightning dispatch, it organized an additional two dozen on petition of 20 per cent of the locals in each constituency, as stipulated by the 1920 convention, and forty UFA candidates were placed in the field. Thousands of farmers attended political rallies, made campaign contributions, distributed literature, acted as scrutineers, and gave rides to the polls. All this was done with very little help from central office and could not have been accomplished without the social connections and organization of the UFA/UFWA locals. A wave of political excitement, based on community relations and events, engulfed the countryside. In the words of Barbara Cormack:

> The month ... leading up to the ... election was not so much a campaign as a crusade. Every little schoolhouse, every country store, every straggling fence across which neighbours talked became a rallying ground for the expression of political theories.
>
> The rural school, in particular, was the focal point of such gatherings. For miles and miles they came – people who had never attended public meetings in their lives, jolting over the rough trails in buggies, wagons, democrats – children and babies tucked in behind – wet days or dry – all to have a look at the candidate or special speaker and to thresh out the pros and cons with the neighbours. Far into the night they talked, the little building filling up with smoke, and the air so thick you could cut it with a knife
>
> To attract bigger crowds there were the picnics and celebrations. The crop was growing. It was not yet time for haying – all in all an excellent time for such get-togethers. There was the scent of battle in the air – but even more there was the fragrance of a new heaven and a new earth. With farmer representation in the Legislature anything could happen.[23]

The scene was repeated later that year during the federal campaign, when UFA/UFWA members helped non-British women to become naturalized and obtain voting certificates.

To take effective political and other action, the UFA/UFWA had to maintain a sense of community among farmers differing in ideology, race, ethnicity, product specialization, economic status, and institutional affiliation. Limits to their notion of community, however, became apparent. Still, because the movement generally accommodated, and often reconciled, different groups of farmers, its healthy development was assured.

Ideological differences were one of the earliest and most serious threats to movement unity. While sharing many movement culture notions, UFA/UFWA farmers did not have a more or less monolithic 'petit bourgeois' outlook. Some espoused a radical ideology, following the path of the Patrons of Industry, the Farmers' Association of Alberta, and the Society of Equity. Others – the majority – followed the liberal trail blazed by the Territorial Grain Growers' and the Alberta Farmers' associations.

Radical Alberta farmers, echoing a long-standing British and American radical tradition, castigated monopolies and demanded 'equal rights' – no special privileges for corporations from governments. Their notion that they and workers were exploited fellow producers who created all value was behind their desire for a farmer-labour political alliance to fight for a redistribution of wealth through drastic monetary reform and government ownership. More suspicious of corporate power and imperialism than liberals, they also were stronger supporters of civil and women's rights. Farmers of the liberal wing, on the other hand, believed in the benefits of competitive capitalism and, prompted by progressivism, Toryism, or the new liberalism, called for some state intervention to ensure equality of opportunity and greater economic equality. They were also thoroughly committed to self-help through improved farm production and especially co-operative enterprise, and before 1919 they shied away from independent political action, preferring that the UFA/UFWA act as a political pressure group.

These two outlooks and programs had the potential to split the UFA/UFWA, but the experience of a divided movement before 1909 convinced the two wings to get along, a task made easier by the compatibility of their agendas on key questions such as the tariff, freight rates, and direct legislation. On other issues, there was a measure of consensus with disagreement about how far to apply a principle. For example, both wings believed, as had the American Populists of the 1890s, in state ownership and control of utilities and major industries, although radicals wanted more government involvement in the economy than liberals did. On still other matters, ideology gave rise to conflicting views. Radicals wanted government banks or loans for farmers; during the war, liberals felt that co-operative credit was a better solution. There was never, however, a serious rift over this or any other issue; farmers were democrats and accepted the majority position in the conventions, knowing that strife in the movement would decrease their chances of getting any meaningful reform.

Only politics came near to wrecking the movement. Radicals believed that the UFA/UFWA should take direct political action; liberals did not concur until after the war. The resulting friction destroyed or weakened some unions, although most reached a decision one way or the other without serious divisions. As evidence of the importance of local leadership, many political activists convinced their locals to endorse independent action and other radical causes. Political activism was particularly strong in southern Alberta, owing to the region's fluctuating crop yields and the large number of American settlers who were familiar with radical agrarianism and had few ties to Canadian political parties.

After 1916 most radicals joined the Non-Partisan League, an independent agrarian political movement, while remaining in the UFA/UFWA. The UFA/UFWA avoided internal dissension and a mutually destructive fight with the League by endorsing direct political action in 1919. That move satisfied the radicals, who, although initially opposed to UFA president Wood's idea of political action by occupational groups, came to believe that it could achieve their agenda. Unity over politics – the movement's most divisive issue – had been realized, in both local communities and the larger UFA/UFWA movement.

Nationalism and racial, ethnic, and linguistic differences also challenged movement unity and revealed the limits of members' sense of community. Nativism was part of North American agrarian culture, and it had hurt the pre-UFA Alberta movement, but the UFA/UFWA weakened or dealt with prejudice, so that it did not seriously hamper the organization's growth. Historians have debated whether racism and ethnocentrism resulted mainly from structural factors, economic factors, psychological tensions, or from multifaceted causes.[24] The latter paradigm best explains the situation in rural Alberta.

Alberta farmers were quick to exhibit negative attitudes towards Amerindians. Rice Sheppard proclaimed that pioneers had converted an 'almost worthless land into golden wheat fields' and had built 'up a nation out of what a few years past was considered a worthless land of snow and wild bands of red Indians.'[25] By suggesting that settlers had entered an essentially unpeopled wasteland – a 'land of snow' – Sheppard was depicting unassimilated Amerindians as 'other': they were 'red,' not white; 'wild,' not civilized.

Such an image was a product of myth. The agrarian myth, which idealized agricultural development, marginalized Natives by implying that non-farming peoples wasted land and were degenerate. American literature about the frontier, including James Fenimore Cooper's well-known tales, portrayed Amerindians as children to be raised and civilized on reserves, as noble savages who were dying out, or as barbaric, devil-like savages to be cut down like the trees of Frederick Jackson Turner's forest. Many Albertans shared these views, seeing Indians, in the words of one contemporary, 'as a sort of pest to be exterminated.'[26]

Farmers' distorted images of Amerindians were reinforced by a need to justify their ownership of aboriginal land. There was more to this, however, than capitalistic acquisitiveness. Gerald Lively, the 'poet of the western farmers' and a socialist who foresaw the end of the 'cursed competitive system,' wrote:

> And the farmer's still forgotten when the rulers give a feast,
> He's not consulted if he'd come or not;
> For though he wins an empire from the savage and the beast,
> His payment's still the lowest of the lot.[27]

No less than Sheppard, Lively considered Amerindians 'savages' and was glad they had been shunted aside for white settlement. Economic self-interest and racist myths prompted most Alberta farmers to believe that whites were destined to take over the land: to build a socialistic society, as Lively envisioned, or a capitalistic one, as most farmers desired. This was the basis of their prejudice.

Farmers also gained psychological income from their racism. There was no little pride in Sheppard's and Lively's argument that farmers were transforming a wasteland of 'red' 'savages' into a 'civilized' nation. Additionally, farmers living near reserves had social and economic reasons for their prejudice. They wanted, or wanted other whites, to acquire reserve land[28] to develop the local economy and community.

There was little incentive for farmers to moderate their views. Reserve Indians could not become UFA/UFWA members, because they were not independent producers. Lacking the franchise, they could not politically support the organization. Moreover, they were isolated from whites. Ignorance about other races can breed bigotry, and farmers' ignorance about Natives was unchallenged by contact. Indians, therefore, were never part of a UFA/UFWA community. Economic interest, ignorance, and myth ensured their exclusion.

According to the frontier myth, the Métis possessed Indians' racial traits, and farmers tended, as a result, to have a negative view of 'half-breeds.' E.N. Barker, a prominent Alberta Farmers' Association and UFA man, joined a troop to put down the 1885 Rebellion and apparently had little concern for Métis grievances. He described the conflict rather nonchalantly as a 'difference of opinion' that 'did quite a little for Alberta and varied the monotony of life for a time.' He quipped, 'Nothing is quite so distressing as the commonplace when it's continuous.'[29]

Economic competition could bring farmers' racism to a boil. In 1918 one farmer was livid that 'Indian half-breeds' were undercutting 'our people ... American, Scotch, Irish, Russian, Ruthenian' in selling wood products. He appealed to UFA members to buy at a living price from whites who were building up the country rather than patronize the Métis who allegedly did 'little or nothing to advance civilization.'[30]

Some UFA/UFWA farmers, in contrast, accepted the Métis as part of their community. Revealing how personal contact can break down prejudice, Rice Sheppard wrote of his 'half-breed' neighbours: 'No pure white was ever more kind or ready to give a helping hand than Mr. or Mrs. Inkster and family.' There were even attempts to bring the Métis into the movement. In 1920 the Grand Prairie UFWA local took 'steps to do special work among the Cree people' and asked central office for literature in Cree or French. Moreover, the UFA protested a law that appeared to protect a rich citizen from prosecution for fraud in obtaining Métis script.[31] Farmers could see the Métis as fellow victims of plutocratic influence and sometimes as members of a UFA/UFWA community, although barriers to their acceptance remained. Class interest, local contact, Christian sensibilities, and a democratic ethos could mute, but not eliminate, prejudice.

The same can be said about the attitudes of some farmers towards African Americans, though the main reaction to this group was hostility. In the spring of 1911 the Edmonton Board of Trade protested, as it had the year before, the recent settlement near the city of several hundred Oklahoma Blacks and insisted that no more be allowed to come. Many UFA locals endorsed the board's demand – five sent resolutions to the government – and two locals proposed that 'negroes' already in the country be put on reserves to prevent them from coming into contact with whites.[32]

This prejudice had little to do with economic or structural factors. One local argued that another influx of Blacks would have a 'disastrous influence upon the welfare and development of this province,'[33] but this was less a sincere belief about the economic impact of Blacks than an attempt to justify excluding them. If any really believed that Blacks would hurt the economy, their conviction was based on non-economic racist assumptions that Blacks were inherently lazy. In no real way were Black settlers an economic threat to Alberta farmers. They were not like Asians in British Columbia who replaced white miners and lumber workers and lowered their wages. In fact, Alberta farmers usually favoured settlement, believing that it resulted in lower taxes and better services. For economic reasons, then, UFA locals should have viewed Black settlers as a benefit. Their problem was the skin colour of the newcomers.

Farmers' reaction to the Blacks was fundamentally a product of 'psychological tension.' The sudden influx of non-whites – combined with fears that thousands more were on their way – created the spectre of racial plurality. This was unacceptable to farmers; they 'yearned for a racially homogeneous society.' Declared one UFA secretary, 'This country should be wholly a white man's country.' Most farmers agreed. They feared that racial heterogeneity 'would destroy their capacity to perpetuate their values and traditions, their laws and institutions.'[34]

Furthermore, many farmers, particularly those from the United States, believed that Black immigration to Alberta would create a situation of racial conflict and violence like that experienced in the American South. They also adhered to a centuries-old American myth that Black men lusted uncontrollably after white women and frequently raped them. Isobel Graham, the women's editor of the *Guide*, revealed this mindset:

> Fireside would like to know what the people ... think about the negro invasion that is now pouring into the Canadian west ... and farming large settlements contiguous to and among the whites.
>
> There can scarcely be anyone who is not aware of the atrocities committed by members of these terrible communities, the only corresponding punishment for which is the lawless lynching ... Already it is reported that three white women in the Edmonton and Peace River districts have been victims of these outrages accomplished in peculiarly fiendish abandon.
>
> Where will the end be?

... Ottawa has done nothing so far. How many of these industrious, courageous, unprotected country women must be sacrificed to the horrors of a negro attack before the slow and rusty machinery that drives the engine of state can be induced to erect a barricade against so dreadful an evil?

The state was not as rusty as Graham thought. By rigorously enforcing immigration regulations, it soon halted Black immigration in response to the outcry of western boards of trade, the Edmonton Labour Council, women's organizations, and farmers.[35] Racism had united these groups as nothing else could have done. Psychological tension, ignited by a sudden influx of Blacks – the apparent vanguard of many more – had thrust racist ideas to the fore, fanning a flare-up of nativism that transcended class and other boundaries.

Gender inequality could reinforce racism. Women like Graham were angry that Blacks had the right to homestead, while British Canadian women did not. 'It should be possible,' she snapped indignantly, 'for Canadian women to secure from the government ... at least an equal share with the foreign negro in the rich heritage of the Dominion's homestead lands.'[36]

A few UFA locals did not fully support this anti-Black frenzy. One union did 'not agree with the Edmonton people in trying to stop' Blacks from entering the country. It did not 'believe in encouraging them to come,' but argued that 'unless undesirable as to character,' they 'should be given a chance in this fair country of ours.' It concluded, 'Color alone should not make any difference.'[37]

The UFA/UFWA could weaken nativism. As prejudice thrives on the unknown, getting to know other people can promote acceptance. UFA/UFWA locals often brought together persons of different backgrounds, and occasionally different races, to socialize and discuss mutual problems. The Poplar Ridge local, whose members were Black, held a dinner and dance in 1917, which some whites from the Colinton union attended. The Colinton secretary reported that the

members of the Colinton local had nothing to complain of about the excellence of the program or the treatment meted out to us. The tables were loaded with good things, and the address given ... had enough fire in it to make any slacker, colored or otherwise, line up and join the U.F.A. All went home well pleased with the entertainment, and when Poplar Ridge local again opens its hospitable doors, the white people will be well represented.[38]

One or two other Black locals were formed, but the ramparts of racism in the UFA/UFWA were never really broken down. Black and white unions were more or less racially exclusive,[39] and white UFA/UFWA members continued to hold stereotypical views of Blacks, which they perpetuated through their minstrel shows. Most farmers' concept of a UFA/UFWA community did not include Blacks.

Racial stereotypes and the prospect of Asian immigration during and after the war set off a new wave of racism. The topic of Asian labour was discussed at the 1918 UFA convention, where several speakers 'told of the experience of British Columbia, California, and South Africa with the Orientals.' Their racist ideas confirmed, the delegates decided, in spite of their great need for farm labour, 'to go on record as being absolutely opposed' to bringing in Asians, even as temporary workers. Prejudice had proved stronger than economic interest. Unlike some British Columbia farmers, UFA men were willing to forgo cheap and plentiful labour to save the country from an alleged racial menace. Drawing further on racial stereotypes, some UFWA women felt that Asians posed a moral or sexual danger. When the women of the Calgary UFWA local learned of the 'large number of girls – especially country girls – in the employ of Orientals in Calgary and other cities,' this knowledge lay 'heavily' on their hearts, and they consequently 'sought an avenue of service to these girls.' The 'service' they probably had in mind was pressing for legislation like that in Saskatchewan and Manitoba, which prohibited Asian men from hiring white females 'in places of business or amusement.'[40]

As more farmers became dependent on wage work after the war, owing to crop failure and falling commodity prices, the potential economic impact of Asians fostered nativism. Discussing possible irrigation jobs, L.H. Jelliff, a prominent UFA man, asserted that citizens did not want a 'bunch of Chinamen and Japs to do the work the farmers can do.' Radical UFA/UFWA farmers worried about the effect of Asian workers on white labour in general. One union viewed with consternation 'the ever increasing number of Chinamen' who were coming to Canada to compete with whites for jobs. It argued that because 'thousands of our boys' had fought 'to keep this a white man's country,' the minister of immigration should give the matter 'closer supervision' and grant no railway company 'permission to engage laborers in foreign countries under any conditions.'[41] Asians would never belong to a UFA/UFWA community.

Racism in the UFA/UFWA stemmed from several factors – economic, cultural, and psychological. Economic considerations informed perceptions about Amerindians, Métis, and Asians, but the prospect of racial plurality, and with it the apparent threat of cultural and moral degeneration – heightened by fears of further immigration – thrust farmers' racial animus and stereotypical thinking about Blacks and Asians to the front.

Racism did not, however, hurt the farm movement. With few non-white farmers in Alberta, white farmers could express prejudice without alienating many potential members. If anything, racism strengthened farmers' sense of community by creating a feeling of solidarity against a perceived social threat. Still, a few Black and possibly a few Métis UFA/UFWA unions were formed, and there was never any campaign to have them removed. Class interest, local contact, democratic ideals, and Christian notions of the oneness of humanity broadened some farmers' definition of their community beyond the strict limits of their racism.

Many UFA/UFWA communities contained non-Anglo-Celtic white minorities. The only opposition the organization officially expressed against such groups in the period under study was a request in 1919 for the cancellation of military exemptions and other privileges of pacifist groups like the Hutterites. At the local level, there were isolated wartime demands for measures such as a head tax on 'enemy aliens' and periodic outbursts about 'men of alien race' homesteading while British women could not. Moreover, prejudice within unions sometimes made it hard to maintain unity, and a few farmers would not join locals that had members of certain nationalities.[42] UFA/UFWA conventions refrained, however, from endorsing the Saskatchewan and Manitoba Grain Growers' demand that 'foreigners' be barred from homesteading during the war to keep the best land for returning soldiers. Nor did the UFA convention echo the Saskatchewan Grain Growers' call for 'desirable immigration' only. With more than half of Alberta farm operators in 1921 born outside the empire,[43] it was apparent to most Alberta farmers that the UFA/UFWA could not afford to exhibit such prejudice; it had to appeal to a variety of ethnic and national groups if it wanted to succeed.

Besides class and strategic considerations, ideology promoted acceptance of ethnic groups in the UFA/UFWA. At least some farmers felt that blood mixing of European 'races' produced not racial degeneration but racial improvement. They did not believe in Anglo-Celtic superiority, but in the melting-pot ideal of Crèvecoeur and F.J. Turner. A 'new man' with new principles would emerge from the blending of the races on the frontier. E.N. Barker argued that racial mixing resulted in 'activity and progress,' while Joshua Fletcher maintained that 'the mixed race is the most law abiding.'[44]

Community dynamics also promoted openness to minority groups. While some minorities were isolated in block settlements, which raised suspicions about them, most lived in ethnically diverse localities or had social or economic contact with other groups, often through the UFA/UFWA. This contact, which increased as more of the 'foreign born' joined the organization, weakened nativism.

Before the UFA was formed, anti-American nativism kept some Alberta farmers from joining the U.S.-based Society of Equity. As more Americans settled in the province, however, they joined UFA/UFWA communities and made the movement their own. By mid-war, they were overrepresented in the association leadership and shaped UFA/UFWA policies. Some 27 per cent of the farm population in Alberta in 1921 was American, compared with 16 per cent and 4 per cent in Saskatchewan and Manitoba,[45] and this American presence helps to explain the UFA's adoption of radical credit and political ideas. American settlers had no loyalty to the Canadian political parties, and some had supported soft-money doctrines and third parties in the United States.

About 27 per cent of Alberta's farm operators in 1921 were born outside the United States, Canada, or Britain. They included northern Europeans, who were well accepted in Alberta, and central and eastern Europeans, whom many British Canadians placed well down in the 'ethnic pecking order.' Although most successful in attracting Anglo-Celtic persons, the UFA/UFWA organized virtually all European groups. In many areas, it recruited them into ethnically mixed locals. In districts with large numbers of French, German, Dutch, Russian, Hungarian, Mormon, or other settlers, unions based on ethnicity, language, or occasionally religion were formed. Farmers' democratic ethos and desire to attract new members and growing minority influence in the UFA/UFWA ensured that xenophobia, while present, had no great effect on the movement's openness to minorities and support for their rights. UFA president Speakman addressed Germans in their own language during the war, and many UFA/UFWA members opposed the disfranchisement of Germans and central and eastern Europeans in 1917.[46]

This stance contributed to 'a groundswell of Ukrainian support for the UFA' from 1918 to 1921. By the latter year, an estimated 3,000 Ukrainians were UFA members in forty-seven locals. Dmytro Prystash, the principal Ukrainian UFA leader, persuaded the UFA association to donate $400 to assist with a pro-UFA Ukrainian newspaper. He also convinced the 1919 convention to demand that Ottawa remove all restrictions on Ukrainian newspapers and publications, reinstate the vote for Ukrainians, and officially recognize the Ukraine as an Allied nation. In addition, Ukrainian delegates, with the backing of other UFA/UFWA members, nominated two Ukrainian UFA candidates for the 1921 provincial election and a by-election held later, and both won.[47] Ukrainians and other central and eastern Europeans were active and fairly well-accepted members of UFA/UFWA communities.

Though some UFA/UFWA members hoped to assimilate minorities fully into the British-Canadian norm, this was not the official UFA/UFWA position. There was not even much support in the organization for an English-only school policy, albeit partly because the Alberta government had already taken a strong stand against bilingual education. Two resolutions demanding that English be the sole language of instruction in schools were presented to the 1919 UFA convention too late to be dealt with by the delegates and were therefore considered by the executive. It decided to take 'no action' on one while refusing to endorse the other because it contravened Quebec's constitutional right to use French.[48]

While UFA/UFWA farmers wanted to 'Canadianize' 'foreigners' by having them learn English and be active citizens, at least a few in the movement felt that all groups had something to offer Canada. UFA general secretary H. Higginbotham wrote:

Have we not as individuals and communities a duty toward these new Cana dians? Their traditions, their customs, are different from those of the British born, but can we not appreciate the fact that while we may have something of value for them, they in turn have much to enrich our civilization? Let us become familiar with the history and customs of their native land, so we may better understand their position in this new land and give them encouragement and assistance to become Canadian citizens in the truest sense ... Break down the racial feeling.[49]

After the war, the UFA/UFWA stepped up its recruitment of minorities, hoping that they would vote UFA if brought into the movement. To this end, it distributed literature in French, German, and Ukrainian. One pamphlet appealed specifically to minority groups, claiming that the UFA provided 'an organization from which our foreign population who have been betrayed and manipulated for the advancement of politicians' schemes may expect the same fair and just treatment as is extended to all other classes of Canadians.' It assured them 'that our organization is anxious to co-operate with them and have them co-operate with us for the advancement of our mutual interests.'[50] In 1921 a UFA/UFWA 'foreign born' committee was formed, consisting mainly of local members who, between them, spoke a dozen languages and acted as organizers. Thanks partly to their work, the movement had notable success in recruiting minorities.

The result, very often, was stronger local communities. 'This neighborhood being made up of different nationalities, we seldom saw much of one another,' explained Mrs Frank James, 'and we felt the need of something to draw us together in a more neighborly manner. The organizing of the U.F.W. has solved our problem.' Such unity between groups could foster pride in the movement. UFA director F.W. Smith boasted at a local meeting that 'the different nationalities represented here truly show that the U.F.A. ... can unite all men into a common brotherhood.'[51]

By organizing most groups of farmers, the UFA/UFWA built community, class, and movement solidarity. Yet minorities were underrepresented in the association leadership; there was no 'foreign' officer in 1918 and only one in 1916 and 1920.[52] Ethnic barriers were weakened in the UFA/UFWA, but were not obliterated. There were limits to the concept of a multicultural UFA/UFWA community.

Within its local communities and the larger UFA/UFWA community, the organization had to deal with tensions between grain growers and livestock raisers. Most early UFA members were small ranchers or mixed farmers who believed that big cattlemen monopolized land. Such members were therefore hostile to the idea of closed leases, which would 'keep out the small farmers and ranchers.' By 1912, however, the UFA recognized that farming was not feasible on some land and proposed that it be leased, with settlers having the first chance to secure leaseholds or permits.[53]

Opposition to the big ranchers continued during the war, which prompted the UFA to demand that large leases be taxed. Members were also upset that riparian rights in the province were largely in private hands; they believed that the entire community should have access to lakes and rivers for watering. Accordingly, UFA officers endorsed requests for public livestock approaches. In southwestern Alberta, farmers were angry with sheep ranchers whose animals damaged their crops and ate their pasture. At the UFA's request, the province provided legal protection for farmers from this depredation.[54] After the war, farmers argued that large leases obstructed road development and made it hard to locate schools in convenient places. They wanted this land kept open for farming or reserved for public grazing. In 1920 the UFA executive asked the government to allow settlers adjacent to livestock leases to form community lease districts.[55]

While opposing large cattle and sheep ranchers, the UFA/UFWA had to accommodate tensions within its ranks between grain and livestock specialists. Grain farmers wanted a compulsory hail insurance acreage tax to spread the costs of coverage over a larger area. Livestock producers, who were less affected by hail, successfully blocked this suggestion at the 1909 convention. Something of a compromise between the two groups was reached when the 1912 convention instructed the executive to press the government for a compulsory scheme and, if unsuccessful, to propose that each municipality under the new act administer a hail tax if a majority of its ratepayers approved the idea. The latter proposition, which the province essentially implemented, ensured that municipalities dominated by livestock producers would not impose a tax. Partly for the sake of stockmen in municipalities favouring the tax, the 1918 convention endorsed a new scheme that would tax crop land only while providing better service to grain growers.[56] A solution acceptable to grain and livestock producers had been found.

Friction between grain specialists and stockmen also arose over the free range. Livestock raisers opposed 'any legislation which will tend to curtail the running at large of stock.' Grain growers naturally wanted laws to protect crops from livestock and to provide adequate compensation for damages. Seeking to accommodate these divergent interests, the 1912 convention asked for an amendment to the pound ordinance to establish 'a means of settling, with the minimum of expense and ill feeling, all claims for damages done by stock, without restricting the range of domestic cattle and horses.'[57]

As settlement proceeded, the UFA spoke more for mixed producers and less for ranchers. The 1913 convention asked the government to consider 'the claims of the real backbone of the stock industry, the mixed farmers, when making rules in regard to the grazing of lands.' At the same time, the ranchers' influence was evident in the tabling of another resolution demanding that they pay 'their full share of school taxes.' Three years later, however, the convention requested a school tax on ranch as well as on farm land.[58]

Thus, the UFA represented grain specialists, mixed farmers, and small ranchers, and it opposed large cattle and sheep ranchers. When the interests of its livestock and grain producers conflicted, the organization sought a mutually acceptable solution. The UFA/UFWA sense of community, both at the conventions and locally, was maintained, facilitating the building and politicizing of the movement.

While accommodating different kinds of producers, the UFA/UFWA represented and worked for farmers of all economic 'classes.' Much movement work, including agitating for lower tariffs and freight rates, was for rich and poor members alike. Other work helped well-off farmers, such as fighting for producers' right to reserve railway cars to ship grain directly to market. Without enough grain to fill a car, struggling farmers could not benefit from this privilege. Yet the UFA sought to make direct shipping feasible for many members. In 1910–11 it demanded smaller railway cars and lower minimum car weights to assist 'medium- and small-sized farmers' unable to fill and bear the expense of larger cars. A few unions set up co-operative weigh scales, allowing small-scale producers to pool their grain to fill a car. In 1909 the UFA tried to get the railways to supply partitions in livestock cars so that shippers with only a few animals could keep them separate when combining with others to make a car load.[59]

The UFA/UFWA also worked for down-and-out members. It collected thousands of dollars and items of clothing for crop failure victims, asked for protection for them against seizure or foreclosure, requested special provisions for homesteaders in marginal areas,[60] tried to procure good-quality seed grain for needy producers, arranged for unions to issue certificates for reduced freight rates on seed,[61] and persuaded the government to distribute seed and food more widely in 1915 and to provide a fairer means of collecting for them. Five years later, the UFA proposed a lower price for seed wheat; vice-president Baker explained that farmers with a crop 'were willing to make a little sacrifice for the benefit of those who were less fortunate.'[62]

Officers like Baker encouraged the UFA/UFWA to help less well-off farmers because they needed their support to stay in office and knew that a crop failure or collapse in commodity prices could put them in need of the organization's help. Therefore, the UFA/UFWA did not serve simply an elite leadership or well-to-do farmers. As it successfully accommodated different ethnic groups and product specialists, it worked for all classes of the farm community. In so doing, it avoided internal divisions and promoted the building and politicizing of the movement.

While preserving a sense of community between 'classes' of farmers, the UFA/UFWA had to maintain harmony with the Women's Institutes. The Institutes and the UFWA collaborated on projects in many communities, but there were differences between them: the UFWA was more agrarian, class conscious, and independent than the government-funded Institutes, which included both town and country women. As a result, and because of personality clashes, friction sometimes occurred between the two organizations. Mrs J.E. Rosebrough of the Gem UFWA union related that

> in our midst we have ... a Women's Institute ... which, I believe through no fault of our own, is threatening to split our community ... During the past year, we have tried working ... in their organization ... for the purpose of avoiding this rift. But we didn't seem to be doing any good ... Since we honestly and sincerely tried working [with them] ... and [are] getting no ... return for our trouble besides dividing our time and strength between the two, we feel that the course we have taken is the only one possible. We would like, and in the future intend, to centre our efforts in the U.F.W.[63]

Fortunately, such scenarios were not too common. Just as it accommodated farmers differing in ethnicity, economic status, and agricultural specialization, the UFA/UFWA generally got along with the Institutes, thus preserving the sense of rural community that made the movement possible.

Relations between farmers and other local and regional groups also were generally good, and much interclass co-operation occurred. Tensions sometimes arose, however, especially between farmers and retailers as UFA/UFWA co-operative buying increased. Still, farmers experienced less friction with merchants than some literature suggests.[64] Farmers' sense of community included other classes, although there were limits to their willingness to work with them.

Many locals sought to maintain cordial relations with area merchants by dealing with them rather than shipping in food and dry goods co-operatively. One union explained that 'while we are not averse to wholesale buying by farmers, we urge it only when the dealer puts too wide a margin of profit between himself and the consumer.' UFA general secretary P.P. Woodbridge similarly advised locals to avoid interfering with merchants by confining their co-operative purchases, where possible, to goods normally handled from manufacturers to farmers by commission agents.[65]

One woman from the Doonsdale UFWA described how merchants and the local UFA worked out a mutually agreeable arrangement:

> At our last meeting we had two of our merchants. It seems there has been some ill feeling between the merchants and the U.F.A., the former claiming that the U.F.A. were fighting the town, and the latter, vice versa. The U.F.A. local had a man to present their side, and the merchants very ably presented theirs, with the result that we came to the conclusion that the only remedy would be co-operation.

With a similar end in view, Alliance union appointed a 'Local Trade Committee' to confer with shopkeepers.[66]

Most locals avoided conflict with merchants because they did not want to be called town wreckers; they liked to believe that they were building up their communities. Concerned that some thought 'we were trying to run the local store prices down,' Clark union adopted a by-law prohibiting it from selling to non-members for less than regular store prices.[67] Farmers were reluctant to alienate merchants who provided credit and goods that locals could not buy co-operatively. The presence of retailers in UFA/UFWA unions, the threat of social alienation from the larger rural community, and the possibility of working on mutually beneficial projects were additional reasons for farmers to preserve workable relations with dealers.

Notwithstanding, locals could take a hard line. Olds union bought direct from processors and manufacturers to force merchants to drop their prices. 'In every case we give the home dealers a chance to serve the union,' explained J. Stauffer. 'They thought the farmers would not dare to ship in anything themselves. They were ... shown that unless they give the farmer a square deal they will lose their best trade.' Despite this run-in, the strength of community ties were such that in the following year the union worked with the Olds Board of Trade.[68]

Merchant resentment must have been particularly keen at Gleichen, where the UFA local 'distributed about 60,000 lbs. of flour and other mill stuff, 44,000 lbs. of binder twine, 367 cases of fresh fruit, and 1,800 boxes of apples, besides quite a quantity of dried fruit,' on which farmers had saved about $4,000. It must have been small comfort to Gleichen dealers that the union's motto was 'live and let live.'[69]

In some locales, conflict between retailers and farmers escalated during and after the war, as UFA/UFWA co-operative buying increased and cut into merchants' profits, sometimes jeopardizing their livelihood.

'The Popular June Wedding,' by Arch Dale. *Grain Growers' Guide,* 31 May 1916, 6.
The marriage of 'rural community' and 'co-operation' created tensions between
farmers and dealers in some localities.

Merchants occasionally reacted by threatening to stop farmers' credit or
by influencing companies not to sell to UFA unions. They argued that
farmers should buy locally to build up the towns and should make paying their store debts a priority, since merchants had generously given
them credit. Farmers replied that they paid for this credit in high interest rates and prices and became indebted to storekeepers only because
they could not borrow enough money from the banks.[70] There were definite limits to farmers' sense of community with merchants.

Tension between farmers and other local groups usually stemmed
from passing issues. In 1913 farmers were angry that money was spent
on highways for the 'idle rich,' while rural roads were often impassable.
Two years before, the UFA and several boards of trade were at odds over
minimum railway car weights. In 1915 the UFA opposed an Edmonton
Board of Trade application for a freight rate classification change, and
in 1921 it protested a Red Deer Board of Trade request for an increase
in the business needed for a station agent.[71]

Despite such episodes, farmers generally saw local urban groups as members of their community with whom they could co-operate. In 1894 the Patrons of Industry and Edmonton citizens joined to agitate for a bridge across the North Saskatchewan River. In 1901 businessmen, grain dealers, and farmers met to protest the grading of Alberta oats by the Grain Standards Board. Six years later, the Alberta Farmers' Association convention endorsed resolutions submitted by boards of trade calling for reduced railway rates and an end to railway bonusing by urban centres.[72]

UFA/UFWA unions commonly co-operated with local groups. The Granum Board of Trade, merchants, and farmers jointly sought extended telephone service; the Clairemont townspeople and UFA union formed an association to improve local roads; and two UFWA unions worked with Calgary women's clubs, the Board of Trade, and city council to establish a women's restroom and crèche.[73] Across the province, UFA unions worked with boards of trade to encourage local railway construction.

Considerable collaboration occurred between the central association and urban groups. The Calgary Board of Trade endorsed the UFA stand on reciprocity and its demands for freight rate reductions; the UFA/UFWA approved a Calgary Board of Trade plan for a public health department; and the UFA supported the efforts of the Calgary Consumers' League to establish a public market. It also seconded an Associated Boards of Trade request for the appointment of a freight rates expert to help with submissions to the Railway Board.[74]

UFA representation on many boards of trade, including the Calgary Board, promoted this co-operation, but its motivating force was mutual self-interest. Town and country alike would benefit from new infrastructure, utilities, and restrooms, as well as public markets, freer trade, and lower freight rates. Believing that their own prosperity depended on agriculture, businessmen could go to great lengths to help farmers. During the war, several dozen Lethbridge 'citizens' guaranteed loans for farmers so they could buy livestock, and the city's Board of Trade called a water conference for farmers and lobbied with the UFA for government aid to drill wells.[75]

Through such work, the UFA/UFWA formed a sense of interclass community, a notion that included much of the prairie and far West. Regional co-operation began in 1909 with a conference called by the Alberta premier, A.C. Rutherford, involving the UFA, elevator companies, banks, railways, Alberta and British Columbia boards of trade, and the Alberta government. The purpose of the conference was to promote the development of a Pacific outlet for grain; to that end it called for dominion-owned coastal grain terminals, measures to facilitate the western movement of grain, and a new Alberta and British Columbia inspectorate.[76]

There were limits, however, to the sense of community shown at the conference. Under pressure, the farmer delegates compromised their request for government terminals by conceding that the CPR should be allowed to build them if Ottawa did not soon do so. Moreover, the farmers were induced to endorse a motion asking for a change to the Manitoba Grain Act to enable producers 'to get cars at the elevators in the same proportion as though they loaded them from the platform.' An angry *Guide* pointed out that this would 'make it easier for the elevator companies to secure control of a much larger portion of the wheat' and make it harder for farmers to get cars to ship directly. In the end, the government did not meddle with the act and UFA spokesmen learned their lesson. In future they would not countenance any changes to the car-order provisions of the act, and they 'stuck steadfast' to the principle of state-owned terminals.[77]

Farmers' interest in shipping to the west coast was rekindled in 1912, when the opening of the Panama Canal was imminent. To consider the canal's advantages for western Canada, the Calgary Development Bureau and the Calgary Board of Trade organized a conference of western politicians and farm and business delegates. The conference approved resolutions presented by UFA secretary E.J. Fream favouring reduced western freight rates and a government grain terminal. It also formed an association to promote its agenda and the western shipping route, and it elected UFA representative James Bower as the association's Alberta vice-president.[78]

In 1910 British Columbia businessmen and UFA and provincial government representatives met in Vancouver to consider Alberta-B.C. trade relations. Here, too, a degree of regional interclass 'community' was realized, since all the resolutions proposed were adopted, including UFA demands for state abattoirs, a suitable hay inspection system, a merchant licensing and bonding law, and lower freight rates. At the same time, the conference created intraregional tensions, since Alberta boards of trade dominated by businessmen with eastern interests opposed, or were indifferent to, some of the conference recommendations.[79] The limits of a western sense of community again were apparent.

Such limits were further evident as farmers tried to co-operate with labour. The Society of Equity had linked up with the Trades and Labour Council (TLC) in 1907, though little came of it. A renewed initiative came at the 1911 convention, when the Wheatland Centre local proposed that the UFA talk with the labour movement about affiliation. This was too radical a move for most delegates, but they later approved a recommendation that the executive appoint a committee to 'confer with the organized workers of the province to ascertain if there be any neutral ground on which to work our common interest.' This committee was struck, and it found that it shared ideas with the TLC executive about issues such as direct legislation. The two parties suggested that each of their organizations appoint a committee to periodically take up questions of mutual interest. The UFA convention appointed its committee in 1912.[80]

Shortly after the convention, W.R. Ball's West Salisbury union passed a strong resolution calling for a meeting in June with the 'trades and labor unions of Edmonton and Calgary' to form an agrarian-worker political alliance that would secure legislation for the 'wealth producers' and 'protect them from the grasp of corporate greed.' It was 'hopeless,' the resolution asserted in true anti-monopoly fashion, 'to pin our faith to either of the old parties'; they were 'in the mighty grip of railroads and other combines and monopolies.'[81]

Most unions were prepared to send a delegate to the proposed meeting. Radicals were especially enthusiastic and hoped it might lead to a farmer-labour party, while liberals generally believed 'it would result in good if they did not go the length of forming a third party.' Only a few unions, such as Table Butte, decided 'not to have anything to do' with the convention. The local felt that the sympathies of labour unions did 'not run with the farmers, an instance of this being the coal strike of last year.'[82]

In spite of such opposition, a joint meeting was held that formed the Alberta Federation of Labour (AFL), which would include labour organizations and the UFA. Those attending called for direct legislation, a parcel post system, and an extension of workers' political and other rights. At one point, however, the shoe began to pinch for the farmer representatives. At their request, resolutions were amended to say that farmers' employees should remain exempt from the Workmen's Compensation Act and that the Federation executive should 'consider the position of the farmers' when requesting legislation to compel fortnightly payment of wages.[83] There were limits to farmers' sense of community with workers.

UFA vice-president J. Quinsey and UFA president W.J. Tregillus were elected vice-presidents of the AFL. Despite Tregillus' endorsement of this new farmer-labour body, however, the UFA soon distanced itself from it – to the consternation of the AFL labour leaders. All the UFA board was prepared to do was pass a 'sympathetic but non-committal' resolution that expressed support for the AFL's objectives and promised the UFA's assistance 'when any common ground arises.' The directors realized that allying the UFA in a definite way with labour would split the farm movement. They knew that many liberal members felt that 'when we have succeeded in reaching the majority of the farmers in the province, we shall find there is no need of ... alliances with other labor organizations.' That the directors had struck the right chord with most members is suggested by the passage of a motion at the 1913 convention that endorsed the board's declaration of sympathy with labour and its vague promise of co-operation in matters of common interest.[84] The resolution expressed the limits of the sense of community most farmers felt with the local and provincial working class.

In the period under study, the UFA/UFWA never again considered a formal affiliation with labour, although some locals, especially radical unions, passed resolutions supporting workers' rights, sided with labour during the Winnipeg General Strike, and continued to seek a rapprochement with the labour movement. The UFA Political Association, the political arm of the UFA/UFWA after the war, sought an alliance, while the Edmonton and Strathcona UFA/UFWA constituency associations drafted a joint political platform with the Dominion Labour party and veterans in 1921,[85] though with little result.

The high point of political and 'community' collaboration with labour came in 1921 in the Calgary and Medicine Hat federal and provincial constituencies, where farmers and workers co-operated in voting without alliances or joint platforms. Where one group was in a minority in a constituency, it supported the other group's candidate rather than split the reform vote by running its own candidate. Even liberal farmers endorsed this plan because they secured workers' votes without affiliating with them or endorsing their program.

The strategy was first used during the Medicine Hat federal by-election, when labour voted for the UFA candidate running on the Farmers' Platform. For the provincial election of 1921, the UFA/UFWA supported the labour candidates in the Calgary constituency, who ran on a labour platform. In the Medicine Hat provincial constituency, the UFA and labour each nominated one candidate, who campaigned on his group's program while receiving both groups' electoral support. There was an analogous agreement for the federal election in the East and West Calgary constituencies. The farmers endorsed the labour candidate in East Calgary, and labour backed the candidate favoured by the farmers in West Calgary. These and similar arrangements in a few other Alberta ridings – and there was more farmer-labour political co-operation in Alberta than elsewhere in the prairies – helped the UFA and labour to win more seats than they otherwise would have won. A strange anomoly occurred in Strathcona, however, where Rice Sheppard, that stormy movement pioneer, became a federal labour candidate after failing to gain the UFA nomination. He lost the election to the UFA candidate, D.W. Warner, who had been president of the Alberta Farmers' Association when Sheppard was secretary. In Lethbridge, another farmer-labour battle broke out: M.F. Finn, representing labour, and L.H. Jelliff, the UFA standard-bearer, locked horns, and the UFA emerged victorious.[86] The tenuous bonds of community of interest between the UFA and labour had been broken.

Yet in many towns, especially smaller centres, workers, women, and businessmen often voted UFA. There was a strong negative correlation between town size and electoral support for the UFA in the 1921 elections. People in towns considered themselves part of the rural community; they relied on the farm economy, had considerable contact with farmers, sometimes through the UFA/UFWA, and therefore tended to identify with rural interests and UFA candidates. Indicative of this inter-group community support was a UFA political convention held in Etzikom for the Medicine Hat riding:

> In some respects, it was an extraordinary gathering. Grit and Tory, farmer and businessman, lawyer and mechanic occupied seats side by side ... Every portion of the western part of the district was represented ... It was unanimously resolved to participate in provincial as well as federal politics ... [A]n onlooker could readily see that the farmers and the businessmen in smaller towns meant to pull together and work in harmony.[87]

Not only did businessmen, professionals, and workers vote UFA; some were UFA/UFWA members, and some UFA/UFWA political constituency associations permitted non-farmers to run as UFA candidates.[88]

Thus, there was much co-operation in political and especially social and economic matters between the UFA/UFWA and urban dwellers. They felt a certain sense of community and believed that they had common local and regional interests and grievances. Their co-operation reinforced the UFA's co-operative ethos; farmers argued that their working together built a 'spirit of co-operation.' Their collaboration also assisted the movement: without the social, economic, and political support that other groups provided, the UFA/UFWA would have been less successful. In local trading areas, intergroup co-operation flowed naturally from town and country ties based on occupational pluralism, local exchange, and social activity, which the UFA/UFWA facilitated. Working together reinforced those ties and farmers' sense of community, because they believed that their collaboration fostered 'the neighborly spirit,'[89] a feeling of reciprocity that promoted movement development.

Social activity, mutual aid, and local work built a sense of community that contained feelings of mutuality on which the movement relied. A community perspective and common interests fostered co-operation between the UFA/UFWA and other local and regional groups. Although there were limits to this collaboration, it expanded the UFA/UFWA's notion of community and furthered its work. As well, the movement accommodated – again within limits – different groups of farmers. In so doing, it strengthened local communities, developed a movement feeling of community, and avoided the splintering that had plagued the pre-UFA movement, making possible the building and politicizing of the UFA/UFWA.

Chapter Five

The Building of the Movement, 1914–1918

Civilization ... is standing at the crossroads; in every heart there is a barely conscious feeling of expectancy. In the silences it seems to us as though great things were stirring in the womb of time; we almost seem to hear the rustle of great events rushing to us through space. What is this old world about to bring forth?[1]

UFWA president, Irene Parlby

During the three decades prior to 1909 the Alberta farm movement was formed, a process culminating in the birth of the United Farmers of Alberta (UFA). From 1909 to 1913 the UFA was partially built; it grew rapidly and developed aspects of its culture, especially its self-respect. Shaped by the war, the organization completed its movement building from 1914 to 1918. It doubled its membership, created a women's section, and moulded a social ethic – a belief in reform through state action – that was informed by wartime sacrifices and work, maternal ideology, the social gospel, and recent government intervention. Farmers' belief in democracy, based on their control of the association, and their feeling of class opposition also were strengthened by war-related experiences. These sentiments and beliefs, reinforced by collective self-confidence and a sense of citizenship responsibility, prompted farmers to build the movement and to consider entering politics directly.

From 1914 to 1918 the movement gained the membership base from which its post-war expansion and political action would spring. Though the directors officially oversaw recruitment and a 1918 membership drive directed by central office had some success, the unions did most of the organization work independently. They were inspired to do so by the achievements of the UFA and the United Farm Women of Alberta (UFWA). Discussing the association's history at a local meeting, future UFA member of Parliament Henry Spencer described 'the influence exerted by such a powerful organization.' He boasted that a government representative had asked the last convention for its views on a proposed credit bill before it was brought before the legislature, and he concluded that the movement 'could be made still more powerful and beneficial by all farmers becoming members.'[2]

The war also underscored the effectiveness of organization. Spencer pointed out that 'Germany would have been beaten long ago had she not been so thoroughly organized.' Towards the end of the war, UFA/UFWA leaders noted that other classes were organizing and warned farmers that if they did not follow suit government policies would not reflect their interests.[3]

Farmers responded to such appeals. Though the growth rate was uneven, paid membership swelled from over 9,000 at the end of 1913 to upwards of 18,000 men, women, and youth by the end of 1918. In 1914 membership increased by about 1,600, despite losses in the older unions, particularly in the south, where drought left some unable to pay their UFA dues and forced others to resettle or temporarily work elsewhere. Overall losses in the south continued in 1915, since farmers were too busy with a record crop to do organization work. This and overseas enlistment kept male membership from growing during that year, but the women's section, created in January, formed twenty-three auxiliaries with some 325 members, and about 250 women joined UFA locals. By the end of 1916 there were fifty women's locals with about 900 members; two years later, there were some 1,400 on the rolls. In 1916 UFA membership also rose solidly, by 1,500 or more, and in the following year the UFA gained almost 3,000 new members, although growth was slow in the deep south as a decade of drought began. That drought, combined in 1918 with frozen crops in the north and the outbreak of influenza, checked the movement's increase.[4] But with a large membership and corpus of experienced local organizers, the UFA/UFWA was poised for the post-war era.

The creation of the Women's Auxiliary in 1915 was a major moment of movement building. The 1913 UFA convention had called for an affiliation of women to the movement and instructed the board to help to organize a women's convention in the next year. A few women's clubs linked themselves to UFA unions and some women held a convention, but they neither appointed a secretary to handle mail nor planned another convention. Meanwhile, the 1914 UFA convention amended the constitution to allow daughters and wives of members to join the association on a family fee basis. A year later, fifty-eight women, including some from local clubs and the Women's Institutes, responded to an invitation from UFA secretary P.P. Woodbridge to all women, organized or not, to meet during the 1915 UFA convention to consider forming a UFA auxiliary. They voted for an auxiliary, elected provisional officers, and endorsed the UFA constitution, which was amended the following year to recognize the women's section. The UFA gave $100 for the Auxiliary's work in 1915 and $500 in the next year.[5]

A majority of women at the 1916 convention voted to change the name of their section to the United Farm Women of Alberta. They apparently wanted greater autonomy and a name that indicated they were an integral part of the farm movement rather than a mere 'auxiliary.' Some UFA men resisted the change, but after 'a great deal of insistence' by the women, the UFWA was created. Later, the UFWA president was put on the UFA executive and the UFWA executive became part of the UFA board.[6]

While desiring autonomy and recognition in the movement, the women did not want to be separate from the UFA. UFWA president Irene Parlby later clarified: 'There are not two organizations. We are one organization ... We are the women's section of the U.F.A. organization. Personally, I think we made a mistake in taking a separate name. It has often occurred to me that we would have done better to have called ourselves the "Women's Section" because it puts us right where we belong. It is one organization.'[7]

Until the 1980s historians argued that the pioneering partnership weakened patriarchy. Recognizing their wives' contributions to the farm and community, farm men gave them greater equality and supported their agenda. These scholars also tended to be critical of farm women for espousing social feminism rather than pursuing an equal rights program. More recent work denies that farm men were less patriarchal than other men, highlights their opposition to farm women, and is more sympathetic to the latter, since it focuses on their equal rights work and downplays or reinterprets their social feminism.[8]

Both views have merit and weaknesses. As the newer studies show, the UFA did not grant women equality in the organization, but as the older literature argues, the UFA supported the UFWA agenda. The older school inaccurately portrays women as more or less content with their status, while the newer school sometimes exaggerates by depicting them as strongly challenging prevailing notions about gender. These polar images reveal, at best, the mindsets of only the most traditional or most radically 'feminist' farm women.

Most women were concerned about gender issues, as the newer scholarship contends, but, as the older writing stresses, they also believed in inherent gender differences and felt that their main role was motherhood. They did not use maternal discourse primarily to gain acceptance for women's rights.[9] They knew how to garner support for their agenda by appealing to traditional values, but they also espoused those values. Either downplaying women's conservatism and belief in domestic ideals while emphasizing their commitment to female autonomy and rights or understating their pursuit of greater gender equality misrepresents their outlook. Farm women saw no contradition between their equal rights and traditional causes. Moreover, although their class identification was usually primary and their gender allegiance secondary,[10] no rigid ranking can be posited for these or other priorities; their relative importance varied according to the issue and context and women's personal desires. Some women were part of the movement mainly for fellowship or to improve their communities.

In the earliest UFA days, women sometimes attended local meetings, occasionally participated in discussions, and often helped with social activities. By 1914 a few women were UFA members. Some women joined the UFA even after the UFWA was formed, often intending to start a UFWA union later. Membership in many UFA locals, however, remained all male, and the number of women in mixed-sex unions was usually a quarter or less of the total. Nevertheless, many mixed-sex UFA locals elected at least one woman officer or convention delegate.[11]

Most men appreciated women's contributions. 'The union is so deeply indebted to them,' one farmer commented. UFA president James Speakman knew the value and hardship of domestic work. Noting that housekeeping made his 'back ache worse than a day's hoeing,' he encouraged men to buy more household labour-saving devices. The UFA later endorsed a UFWA demand for the removal of duties on such appliances. Farmers were also aware of the importance of women's outdoor work. Rice Sheppard acknowledged that without women's unpaid assistance most successful male farmers would have failed, which is why he seconded the motion that carried at the 1912 convention calling for a women's section. The resolution stated that farm women were 'sharing with the men the burden of the struggle for better conditions.'[12]

Such recognition of wives' work in the UFA, home, and field inclined some men to support women in the movement and their demands. Their motivation was not only fairmindedness, although this was not absent. Nor was it the case that men simply could no longer justify inequality by appealing to separate spheres, since women had blurred those spheres by doing 'men's work' on the farm. It was a matter of self-interest. Men knew that if they did not welcome women and back their agenda, they would not have their wholehearted help in the movement. Furthermore, Christian and democratic ideals about social justice and the equality of all persons influenced farmers' attitudes, as did ideology. Though left-wing organizations were less supportive of women's rights than scholars used to think,[13] UFA radicals were generally more sympathetic than other males. Women's arguments also won over UFA men. Direct exposure to women's claims helped UFA men to adopt more positive views than they otherwise would have done.

Assumptions about gender further prodded UFA men to support women. Both sexes felt that organized women would have a beneficial moral influence in a frontier society. They also believed that women, if enfranchised, would protect the home, houseclean politics, and be nonpartisan because of their lack of political entanglement and their ethical superiority. A number thought it only just that women have the vote;[14] many hoped that enfranchised rural women would bolster agrarian political power. For these reasons, Alberta farmers, like their prairie counterparts, were on the vanguard of support for female suffrage. The UFA called for the measure from 1914 until it was granted provincially in 1916 and federally in 1918.

UFA men also supported women's other demands, including those for property rights. Women's right to dower – their legal claim to a lifetime interest in a third of their husbands' property – was abolished in the West in 1885–6; and shortly after the birth of the new provinces in 1905, prairie women began fighting for legislation that would guarantee them a portion of their husbands' estate and the right to a say in the disposition of family property they had jointly obtained or developed. In 1915 the Saskatchewan Grain Growers' Association and the UFA took up this cause; the UFA convention asked for legislation to provide 'a legal share to every married woman in the division of the estate' and to ensure 'that no deed or mortgage be legal without the wife's signature.' The province responded that year with a flawed act, which UFA general secretary Woodbridge described as not in 'the form ... we asked for'; it required a woman to file a caveat against her husband's homestead if she wished to prevent him from selling or mortgaging it against her

'The Door Steadily Opens,' by Dick Hartley. *Grain Growers' Guide*, 21 Sept. 1910, 21. Class interests and assumptions about gender led organized farmers to support women's suffrage. This cartoon suggests that, because of their virtue and domestic instincts, women would, if enfranchised, sweep away 'monopoly,' 'special privilege,' the liquor trade, and other social ills. To protect the home and promote agrarian causes, women must be allowed to clean society with the vote.

will – an obvious impracticality for most women. Two years later, the government passed a better act, which gave every wife a life estate in the homestead while barring her husband from disposing of it without her agreement in writing.[15] Unsatisfied, the UFWA demanded a law in 1918 to make the wife's signature necessary for all land transfers, a request the UFA made to the government. The UFA also endorsed women's calls for the municipal vote and equal parental rights in the control and custody of children.[16] In fact, while the UFWA may have at times tempered its agenda because of potential UFA opposition, the UFA adopted all the resolutions the women's section presented for its approval during the war. The only partial exception involved a UFWA motion favouring legislation to protect a wife from being denied 'a larger share by will than she would have been deprived of had her husband died intestate.' This resolution elicited 'considerable discussion' in the UFA convention, and the delegates instructed the board to 'adjust' it with the UFWA executive. This demand was apparently met; the resolution was amended to request legislation to guarantee a wife 'a third of the property by will.'[17]

Despite the UFA's general support for the farm women's program, women did not find equality in the organization. Though UFWA women could vote in UFA conventions and the UFWA organized its own locals and conventions, the UFA controlled what the women's section demanded of governments by screening its resolutions and lobbying on its behalf. There was also no pay equity. From 1917 the UFA president received a salary, but the the UFWA president did not; the UFWA secretary was paid less than her UFA counterpart; and UFWA officers received less for their expenses than UFA officers, at least before 1918.[18]

Women rarely protested these inequalities; they were used to such treatment elsewhere and wanted to maintain class solidarity. They felt that 'the farmer's battles are the battles of the farmer's wife.' Adhering to this tenet, Irene Parlby recoiled when she learned of the upper-middle-class Toronto-based Women's party formed in 1918. Irene, née Marryat, came to Alberta from England in 1896 and married Walter Parlby, a local rancher, in the following year. She was secretary of the Alix Country Women's Club in 1914, which became the first UFA Women's Auxiliary local; UFWA president, with a brief interruption, from 1916 to 1920; and minister without portfolio in the UFA government from 1921 to 1935. She also was one of the five women involved in the famous Persons Case. Parlby believed that the tariff and other policies supported by the Women's party had caused farm women's hardship. Beyond this, the idea of a party based on gender offended her conviction that the sexes should work together because of their complementary traits. 'We value the privilege of working on equal terms with the men of our organization,' she insisted. 'We have heard so much of the horrors of a man-governed world ... but heaven defend us from a world governed solely by women. "Man and woman He created them," not to work in isolated groups, but as the helpmate of one another, and the two points of view are necessary for sanity and wisdom.'[19]

This class focus did not weaken women's equal rights agitation. Fully a third of the UFWA convention resolutions during the war were about women's rights.[20] Women saw no contradiction in working for their class and sex, especially since the UFA endorsed their equal rights demands.

They also felt no inconsistency in agitating for greater gender equality and believing in the primacy of motherhood. Irene Parlby reflected this equal rights and maternal feminist outlook. Though an ardent women's rights activist and critic of sexist attitudes, she always believed that 'women's most important place' was 'not in the polling booth or in the legislature, but in the home, as mother of the race.' Feeling that social problems would be solved only if women instilled ideals and integrity in their children, she was 'forcibly against women with young children running for public office.'[21]

Leona Barritt, first Auxiliary and UFWA secretary, was of like mind. Born in Nova Scotia, Barritt was a teacher and convenor of the UFWA school committee. Like Parlby, she insisted more than once that 'we are first and last homemakers ... The future citizens are being molded in our homes.'[22] Barritt and Parlby used this discourse mainly with other women; it was not a ploy to soften men up for equal rights demands. They used it because they believed it and because it encouraged other women to join and work for the UFWA.

Farm women's maternal ideology led them to organize and oversee youth clubs and the junior UFA/UFWA and to monitor teens closely. More than farm men did, they sought to control and protect young people, especially females, morally and sexually. They acted as chaperones at the rural youth conferences for 'girls' age sixteen and over and requested supervised dormitories at the agricultural schools. Moreover, the 1918 UFWA convention demanded stiff punishment for abduction of girls 'for immoral purposes,' and Irene Parlby called on unions to donate to the Travellers' Aid, which saved country girls visiting cities from 'horrible fates.'[23]

Maternal ideology also told women that, as family managers, they knew how to conserve food. Because of this skill, some felt that a woman should be appointed to assist W.J. Hanna, the government food controller responsible for promoting food conservation for the war effort. In 1917 Hanna asked women to sign pledge cards to restrict food consumption. Parlby mildly endorsed the idea, but most farm women were indignant and opposed signing until food profiteering and liquor distilling were stopped.[24]

Women also took a leading interest in world peace, supposedly because of their maternal instinct to preserve life. Barritt described a UFA resolution on peace as 'perhaps ... nearer to our hearts' than requests for suffrage and women's property rights. Like their American counterparts, most prairie farm people opposed militarism, believing that they were isolated from danger and that war stemmed from international trade competition brought on by high tariffs. They described the pre-war arms race as unchristian, a project of armament trusts, and a waste of tax dollars. Some argued, with breathtaking naïvety, that preparing for war invited hostility and that nations with few defences were safe from attack.[25] Farmers in Alberta, Manitoba, and Ontario condemned the naval policies of both political parties and demanded that the whole question be put to a referendum. Despite this stance, they generally supported the war effort once hostilities had broken out, though the UFA/UFWA never adopted a crude jingoism; it called for a peace to satisfy 'all legitimate national aspirations.'[26]

Alberta farmers of both sexes believed that women's influence could help to make a lasting peace; they were more peace loving than men whose 'brute instinct' and 'combativeness' had led to war. In 1918 Barritt argued that women should be represented at the peace conference and should hold international meetings to foster public distaste for militarism. Women did not, however, think that all male traits were bad. Well-known author, women's rights activist, and former Manitoba farm woman, Nellie McClung, told the 1917 UFA convention that men's destructive element made them pioneers and enabled them to overcome adversity.[27] What was needed, farmers believed, was that women's peacemaking, moral, and constructive tendencies be more strongly felt in the world to balance male influences.

Such expressions of maternal ideology built the movement by attracting women to it and encouraging the support of men who were assured that organized women aimed to protect the home and 'mother' a war-torn world. Women suggested that even gender causes, such as suffrage and the dower, would promote these ends.[28]

Women's maternal ideology contributed to their promotion of causes that developed and reflected a social ethic – a commitment to reform through state action – which grew out of the war. Fearing that the soldiers' sacrifices might be in vain, farmers concluded that governments must create a new society through prohibition, health care, eugenics, social welfare, and progressive taxation. Farmers built the movement to press governments to implement these measures. Moreover, the UFA appreciated women's work in this area and reciprocated by supporting the UFWA and its agenda, including its equal rights demands.

Like most organized farmers, UFA/UFWA members believed that prohibition, which the UFA first endorsed in 1913, would justify the war by regenerating social morals. Other war-inspired motives included fear that young soldiers, out of their mothers' sight, might succumb to the demon rum; a desire for an efficient war effort without the waste of alcohol production; and a desire to control 'enemy aliens' and to share, if only in a small way, in the sacrifices of the war. Some women supported prohibition because they had been abused or had seen resources squandered by inebriated husbands. Religious beliefs and the high frequency of drunkenness on the frontier further reinforced prohibition sentiment. Believing in the virtue of their cause and sex, women played a key role in the UFA and in temperance organizations by collecting signatures for a petition that led to a 1915 provincial referendum on the sale of liquor in which prohibition won.[29] Referenda were also held in Saskatchewan and Manitoba, and by 1916 all three prairie provinces had enacted prohibition legislation. Subsequently, the UFA/UFWA and other farm and temperance organizations across the country called for a national ban on the manufacture and importation of alcohol, which Ottawa effectively imposed in 1917–18 for the duration of the war.

Farmers felt that the new society that would emerge from the war must provide better health care. Wartime casualties highlighted the need to preserve life. Convinced that they were healers by nature and that the 'care of the race' was their 'job,' and prompted by a lack of rural medical service, women took the initiative. At Irene Parlby's suggestion, the executives of the rural municipalities and the UFA/UFWA together drafted a plan for rural districts to build and operate hospitals that would be financed by local taxes. The 1917 UFA convention approved the plan, the government passed an act based on it, and hospitals were soon organized. The UFWA also asked for rural medical inspection, and in 1918 the UFA/UFWA conventions endorsed a proposal for a provincial health department. The province created a department in that year and hired public nurses,[30] thanks partly to UFWA requests. Farmers' social ethic, a product of the Great War, had helped to establish Alberta's health care system.

Farmers feared that because of the war the 'race' was losing 'its strongest and most physically fit,' and they endorsed eugenics solutions to keep Canada racially virile. This was the dark side of their social ethic – their desire for social improvement through state action. A pseudoscience, eugenics posited that mental illness and retardation, social problems, and racial degeneration stemmed primarily from defective genes.[31] Seeing this as another 'phase of public health' for which they were responsible, western farm women demanded that the 'feeble minded' be segregated and that health certificates be required to prove fitness for marriage. The UFA gladly endorsed these requests.[32] To control the number of 'mental defectives,' the UFWA later called for sterilization.

Angus McLaren contends that most Canadian eugenicists were health professionals and that class fears largely explain the popularity of eugenics. Class concerns were certainly present in farmers' belief that 'mental deficiency' caused 'drunkenness, criminality, pauperism, prostitution, and illegitimacy.' Some farm women also believed that eugenics measures would protect mentally handicapped girls from exploitation.[33] Ignorance about mental illness fuelled eugenics hysteria.

Support for eugenics also flowed from trepidation about the consequences of immigration. Farmers believed that thousands of immigrants with 'congenital defects' had slipped by medical examiners and were a 'detriment to our nationhood.' There was surprisingly little Anglo-Celtic nativism in such outbursts: farmers did not think that any one ethnic group was more prone than others to hereditary defects or was more responsible for Canada's problems – unless it was the British, who, it was suspected, had dumped their undesirables at Canada's gate.[34]

Farmers' belief in eugenics was based on an ill-defined fear that Canada would degenerate in physical strength and mental and moral vitality if more 'misfits' were allowed into the country and if those present were allowed to propagate. Civilization might decline, and progress – social, economic, political, and cultural – might be arrested, especially since the nation's fittest were dying overseas. There was a class bias in this fear, because the 'mentally deficient' were often from the lower orders, but farmers were less focused than the urban middle class on how these 'undesirables' created an underclass with its attendant social problems; they concentrated more on the racial implications of hereditary defects: how those defects might drag all classes, including farmers, down.

Leading the prohibition, health, and eugenics campaigns, women also developed the movement's social ethic – its belief in reform though state action – through their war-related charity work. Viewing such work as social 'mothering,' they made packages for soldiers, bandages and garments for the Red Cross, and sent goods to convalescent homes. Starting in late 1914, women and men gave generously to several war funds; by September 1918 UFA/UFWA locals had donated almost $22,000.[35] Much of this money was raised at dances, socials, concerts, auctions, and from the sale of farm products. Collections were also taken at UFA Sundays for the YMCA military fund.

This war relief work built farmers' social ethic by making them aware

'Nothing But His Life,' by Arch Dale. *Grain Growers' Guide*, 18 July 1917, 6. Farmers from Ontario to Alberta insisted that if men were to be conscripted, wealth must also be conscripted through implementation of the taxation planks of the Farmers' Platform.

of widespread distress and the inadequacy of volunteer effort for dealing with the problem. Prairie farmers thought it unjust that the wealthy did not have to make financial sacrifices, while farmers 'did their bit' and 'worthy' families of soldiers were reduced to charity. The UFA and the Manitoba and Saskatchewan Grain Growers proposed a welfare measure – that the Patriotic Fund be raised by a tax – to make sure that all paid their share.[36]

Imbued with a social ethic and convinced that industrialists and other 'profiteers' were growing wealthy from war production, western and Ontario farmers demanded that if men were to be conscripted, wealth must also be conscripted through land value, graduated income, corporate profit, and inheritance taxes. To further control profiteering, they called for public ownership of railways and other industries.[37] Pragmatism, radical ideology, Toryism, American progressivism, and the new liberalism shaped these requests.

To ensure, then, that the war was not in vain, Alberta farmers, led by women seeking to 'mother' society, developed a social ethic, a belief that governments should reform society through prohibition, health care, welfare and eugenics legislation, progressive taxation, and other policies. The movement was built as farmers joined the organization, recruited others, and otherwise worked to see these measures implemented. Moreover, women's agitation in these areas promoted their acceptance in the movement and inclined men to support their whole agenda.

Believing that social redemption could atone for the shedding of blood overseas, prairie farmers embraced the social gospel, which promised to realize 'the Kingdom of God in the very fabric of society.' As a social religion, it was consistent with the UFA/UFWA's co-operative ethos. Still prevalent in the Alberta movement, however, was the evangelical notion that character development and moral improvement were crucial for social regeneration. Farm women sought to instil these virtues in youth, partly through organized play and field days.[38]

Nevertheless, the social gospel was coming to the fore. Relatively weak in the UFA before the war, it expressed farmers' yearning for a new heaven and earth to emerge out of the Armageddon in Europe. Henry Wise Wood, UFA president starting in 1916, popularized this vision. Formally of the Campbellite sect, Wood rejected his evangelical roots and imposed his own meaning on the Gospels and book of Revelation. These books, he argued, were not about personal salvation and the final judgment, but about the creation of a true democracy on earth. Like Hegel, Wood believed that the essence of the universe was spiritual and that the solution to social problems was 'spiritual rather than intellectual.' To bring about a perfect society, he felt that the church must infuse a 'spirit of unselfishness' into all relations, especially trade relations, replacing the spirit of selfishness, which then reigned in the world. To ministers preaching on UFA Sunday, he advised:

> Don't be afraid to enter into a frank discussion of trade, politics, social affairs in all their aspects. Tell them how the world has persistently refused to recognize the spirit element in trade, political, and all other reforms. That all real human reform is a matter of substituting the spirit of unselfishness for the spirit of selfishness ... Tell them that the only real thing Jesus ever taught us to pray for was this reorganized, regenerated, perfected civilization. Tell them how this regeneration deals with every element of civilization, trade, politics, labor.[39]

Partly influenced by Wood, other farmers increasingly used social gospel rhetoric. Irene Parlby declared that co-operation was 'a thing of the spirit of unselfishness.' Parlby, Wood, and UFA general secretary P.P. Woodbridge also articulated a popularized idealism that was part of the social gospel, arguing that farmers must visualize 'the perfect ideal, the city on the hill' to motivate them to attain their goals.[40]

The social gospel built the movement and its social ethic by attracting farmers and inspiring them to work for the UFA/UFWA to create, partly through state action, the society they envisaged – the kind of nation and world the soldiers had died for. Though a few social gospellers such as Wood were suspicious of government intervention, most believed it could inaugurate the 'city on the hill.'

Forged by the social gospel and a need to make good the soldiers' sacrifices, the UFA/UFWA's social ethic also evolved from war-related state intervention. As Ottawa supervised war production, imposed direct taxes, controlled fuel and food, and nationalized railways, farmers perceived that the state could benefit society. Their experience with government handling of the wheat market confirmed this conviction and, according to Paul Sharp, weakened their 'faith in the laissez-faire doctrine.'[41] It is hard to see how the UFA's pre-war demands for a government pork plant and chilled-meat system and for government grain elevators, terminals, banks, hail insurance, and abattoirs constituted faith in laissez-faire; nevertheless, farmers came to support a more activist state during the war, partly because of the government's control of wheat marketing.

Events leading to that control began in 1917, when the government permitted free trade in wheat between Canada and the United States, thus equalizing wheat prices between the two countries.[42] Soon after, grain prices rose sharply as it became apparent that there was not enough good-quality wheat to meet the futures contracts bought by the Allies. To prevent subsequent price disruptions, in June Ottawa created the Board of Grain Supervisors to control grain prices and the industry. The Board – which consisted of grain trade, labour, and farmer members, including UFA president Wood – fixed the price of wheat at $2.40 and, with an American price-controlling body, set uniform prices in the two countries for the 1917 and 1918 crops.

Many Alberta farmers were initially upset about price fixing and argued that if the board set a maximum price on wheat, the government should also control the prices of other goods, especially those used in grain production. Farmers soon accepted price fixing for its price predictability, however, and requested a minimum price for hogs. They also asked the government to organize the country's labour power and to help them increase grain production by financing, organizing, and buying machinery and providing seed. A conference of UFA and livestock producers proposed state-aided marketing and the conscription of vacant land for grazing.[43] Wartime experience had clearly expanded farmers' belief in state intervention and, by extension, their social ethic.

Farmers' belief that the single tax would redistribute wealth was a casualty of the war. In response to a 1913 *Guide* survey, 90 per cent of Albertans favoured raising all state revenues by a land value tax and land surtaxes – single-tax-inspired measures; the 1915 UFA convention defeated a resolution making almost identical single-tax demands. Farmers realized that the Henry George elixir would do little to attack corporate war profits. Moreover, the war and the recession that had preceded it made land speculation, a key reason for a single tax, less profitable. Farmers also discovered that absentee land owners could be beneficial: their land was free range, and they paid a large percentage of the local taxes.[44] As well, farmers feared that a single tax might increase their tax liability, since they were the major land owners.

Political reform seemed a more promising avenue to pursue. The dominion government's frequent use of the Order-in-Council to prosecute the war effort offended farmers' democratic culture,[45] a culture rooted in the democratic structure and reality of the UFA/UFWA. Despite greater executive influence in the organization owing to its growth, the number and complexity of war-related issues it faced, leadership, and sometimes apathy, the UFA/UFWA remained a grassroots-controlled movement.

Apathy was occasionally evident when the UFA convention gave resolutions it might have dealt with to the officers to handle. During the war, delegates turned a quarter of the resolutions over to the officers. Usually this practice was acceptable, since the delegates did not have the expertise or necessary information to pass on the questions at hand, although when the 1914 convention referred resolutions on credit, hail insurance, and a pork plant to the directors, it might have provided more direction. A couple of times, liberals referred resolutions to the officers so that radicals could not gain support on the floor for their views.[46] In such cases, democracy suffered.

Another possible complication for democracy was the number of resolutions submitted by the officers to the conventions. In 1918 twelve of the first fourteen resolutions on the UFA program were from the board.[47] This did not, however, indicate executive control of the agenda; the officers had been working on key issues, and many of their resolutions simply sought delegate direction – which was the democratic thing to do.

It has been argued that executive control was evident in the UFA officers' initiation of major policies. UFA/UFWA leaders spearheaded initiatives such as rural hospitals, a new hail insurance plan, and the amalgamation of the farmer elevator companies. It is difficult to see, however, how this constituted executive control. No mass hypnosis was used to get the 1917 convention to agree unanimously to the elevator companies' merger. The hail insurance scheme recommended by the directors was debated at great length before the 1918 convention approved it; it was not rubber-stamped by a dupable rank and file.[48] The same can be said about the UFA/UFWA's other major policies.

Notwithstanding, officers could affect convention decisions. President Wood convinced the 1918 convention that it was a bad time to provoke the banks by calling for a usury law. At the same time, there were limits to officers' influence, because most unions told their delegates in advance how to vote on the issues to be considered by the convention. Moreover, delegates sometimes defied the leadership. The 1915 convention refused to support a leader's amendment that would have annulled a resolution it had passed that implicitly criticized UFA officers for holding office in the Alberta Farmers' Co-operative Elevator Company.[49]

Furthermore, delegates did not blindly endorse officers' reports. The 1916 convention rejected the legislative committee's report as inadequate and instructed the committee to meet again and draft a definite credit proposal, which it did. In 1918 the convention told the committee to report on the provincial government's response to all UFA/UFWA resolutions, which it also did.[50]

Despite this grassroots control, the officers' authority increased during the war because of the organization's growth and the complexity and number of issues it had to deal with. In 1916 the board of directors gave the executive the right to pass on any matter if it did so unanimously, subject to the directors' review. The 1917 constitution empowered the executive to sort resolutions according to their importance and to consolidate similar ones for the conventions. The executive could also make any rules, consistent with the constitution, to manage the association's affairs and could delegate powers and duties to local boards. The following year, the executive appointed a committee to influence locals to amend resolutions it felt were inappropriate.[51] Moreover, the executive and board continued to appoint the general secretary and important committees and supervised the general office and district associations.

Farmers made constitutional changes that restrained this centralization of power and strengthened UFA/UFWA democracy. These amendments required the general secretary to send to the locals by specific dates all resolutions to come before the convention, so that members would have ample time to discuss them and instruct their delegates accordingly. Members also made sure that the officers followed convention instructions[52] and acted responsibly on resolutions the delegates did not have time to discuss. Locals whose resolutions were crowded out of the 1914 convention ensured that theirs were the first considered by the 1915 convention.[53]

Thus, in spite of executive power in the organization, the movement remained grassroots controlled, a contrast, farmers felt, to Ottawa's rule under the War Measures Act. Seeking to weaken that rule, the 1916 Farmers' Platform, which was endorsed by organized farmers in the prairies and Ontario, demanded an immediate end to 'the growth of government by order-in-council.' To break the hold of corporations and party hacks over the party system, the Platform called for the abolition of patronage and the introduction of exams for civil service appointments.[54]

Alberta farmers continued to believe that direct legislation would create a direct democracy like the UFA/UFWA, but their ardour for this measure was waning. The province's Direct Legislation Act was usable only when there was overwhelming support for an issue. Only prohibition, thanks to wartime idealism, attracted such support. Under the provisions of the Direct Legislation Act, a petition was circulated in 1915 for a referendum on the sale of liquor. The referendum was held and prohibition won, although this 'outburst of popular liberty' cooled some farmers' enthusiasm for direct legislation, since they thought it had served its purpose in banishing the bar. Consequently, they lost their sense of urgency to have the act improved. Since 1913 the UFA board had pressed for amendments, but unions had failed to respond to a post-prohibition appeal to endorse the directors' proposed changes.[55] The government, as a result, did nothing and the act remained essentially unworkable. The UFA/UFWA still officially supported direct legislation, but less fervently; farmers no longer saw it as a panacea.

This was partly because many became interested in proportional representation, a reform that promised to ensure the representation of parties and groups in government in proportion to their electoral support.

UFA general secretary Woodbridge popularized this measure in the *Guide* in 1916, many locals studied it, and the UFA began to use the system in 1917 to elect its officers. The UFA also asked that it be adopted for provincial elections.[56]

In trying to create a more democratic political system, the UFA/UFWA built its culture of opposition in the context of war-related challenges. This culture was grounded in a belief that farmers' woes stemmed from 'legislation which is the achievement of privilege,'[57] a conviction that grew with revelations and rumours of graft and as governments, especially Ottawa, argued that they could not meet 'contentious' farmer demands in a time of national crisis or spend on agrarian proposals that did not help the war effort. Farmers concluded that governments were using the war as a pretext to favour big business at their expense.

Farmers' failures as a political pressure group confirmed this suspicion. They were particularly frustrated when the wartime collapse of railway construction left branch lines unfinished and settlers' requests for extensions unmet. Farmers on the Canadian Northern system faced car shortages from 1915 to 1917, prompting the UFA to call for improved car availability. Freight rates were a central issue for all western producers; they were bitterly disappointed with a Railway Board ruling against equalized freight rates in 1914 and incensed with a 15 per cent increase it approved in 1917.[58]

The war also boosted Alberta farmers' anti-tariff campaign. Combining patriotism with self-interest, they argued that free trade with Britain would be 'a fitting expression of imperial unity' and asked that duties be removed from farm machinery so that they could produce more food for the Allies. Believing that the tariff had been raised 'under cover of the necessity of war,'[59] the UFA and the Saskatchewan Grain Growers endorsed a Free Trade League organized by the *Guide* editor, George Chipman. The League aimed to counter protectionist propaganda and support political candidates pledged to 'fiscal reform,' revealing to the old parties farmers' resolve to see tariffs reduced.[60]

Reflecting their social ethic, farmers believed that the tariff caused poverty and rural depopulation. As always, they opposed bonusing, especially when Ottawa appeared willing to support the Canadian Northern and Grand Trunk railways. UFA unions condemned a federal proposal 'to give to Mssrs. Mackenzie and Mann a free gift of $25,000,000.'[61]

Though frustrated over such matters, western farmers had some federal political successes during the war. Agrarian opinion was partly responsible for the elimination of tariffs on wheat, the reduction of patronage, and the enactment of prohibition and women's suffrage. Apart from these and a few minor achievements, however, farmers had little success with a federal government focused on winning the war.

More surprising was the UFA/UFWA's record with the Alberta Liberals. Although the organization helped to bring about health and women's property rights legislation, provincial prohibition and suffrage, and, in 1918, mothers' pensions,[62] there were limits to the government's responsiveness because of wartime fiscal restraints, its members' business background, its link to the federal party, and the influence of non-agrarian groups. The results of the 1916 legislative sessions challenge the notion of some scholars that the Liberals bent over backward to accommodate the UFA. Of the twenty-three UFA convention demands, the government met only two: one on the sale of gopher poison by UFA locals and another on brand inspection. Nothing was done about resolutions on matters such as co-operative credit and hail insurance, and, adding insult to injury, the government amended the Co-operative Societies Act against UFA wishes. The UFA/UFWA fared better in subsequent years, but the legislative report to the 1919 convention shows that the province effectively acted on only three of the 1918 convention resolutions presented to it. Not one UFWA demand was met.[63]

Believing, as the agrarian myth declared, that they were the 'backbone of the nation,' farmers felt they deserved better, and this attitude strengthened their antagonism to the groups behind their legislative disappointments. In 1918 some of those interests played on wartime stress to put down farmers. UFA president Wood expressed considerable truth when he commented:

I have just read in the Financial Times ... a tirade against the Canadian farmers which for ... false malediction certainly reaches down to the very depths ... This editorial is entitled, 'Still he wants more':

'The ... farmer has just put over 75 percent of the world's war profits into his jeans – pardon, into the pockets of his dress pants; he spends his winters abroad, lets the other fellow pay his war taxes, pensions, Red Cross and Patriotic Funds, etc. ... wants government ownership of railways so that the taxpayer will provide lower freight rates for crop moving; wants everything he consumes ... put on the free list ...

'The farmer is the most prosperous individual on the face of the Dominion ... But he is not satisfied.'[64]

Such comments, written in the context of a crop failure and the banks' reluctance to lend to producers, raised farmers' class consciousness to a fever pitch.

Fortunately, they had a culture to support them. The agrarian myth assured them that, whatever others said, the nation depended on them 'for its greatness.' Other aspects of their movement-sustaining culture were celebrated in a June 1918 issue of the *Guide* and especially in Hopkins Moorhouse's *Deep Furrows*, a book that was widely discussed throughout the rural West. These and other texts spun a tale of the origins and growth of the prairie farm movement, which instilled class solidarity and pride and a sense of historical legitimacy that movements crave. 'Read "Deep Furrows,"' one local UFA secretary advised, and 'look back at our past experience, and now look into our future.'[65]

Alberta farmers' culture did not tell them that politicians were ultimately to blame for producers' ills; their notion of citizenship told them that they could improve their situation and society by getting involved in politics. They believed that 'the people will have just as good a government as they are entitled to' and that the character of a democracy depended on 'the citizenship standard of the people.' Before the war, liberals felt that citizenship was best practised by nominating and electing good candidates in the old parties and building the UFA/UFWA into an effective political pressure organization.[66] Women as well as men were feeling 'the surge of desire ... to grow out into the larger life of citizenship,' especially after the federal franchise 'awakened' them 'to a realization of their civic responsibilities.'[67]

This belief in citizenship, along with the movement's successes and growth, fostered a collective sense of confidence and possibility, rooted in a feeling that the war was paving the way for a new era. At the 1918 convention, Irene Parlby proclaimed that civilization was 'standing at the crossroads; in every heart there is a barely conscious feeling of expectancy.' 'What,' she pondered, 'is this old world about to bring forth?'[68]

At this and other conventions, both sexes caught a 'vision' of the movement's 'possibilities for usefulness and service.' The 1916 convention was particularly uplifting. UFA vice-president S.S. Dunham exhorted the delegates to work 'with a new zeal,' calling them 'the veritable rocks composing the foundation of this new Canada.'[69] The women heard equally engaging addresses. Several wrote that 'the inspiration of that gathering kept their souls warm.' Many men similarly described the energizing effect of the convention, right down to the work of the locals.[70]

What energized farmers was that the UFA/UFWA helped them to feel good about themselves. To a people who thought others saw them as helpless hicks, it was intoxicating to believe they were 'part and parcel of one of the greatest organizations the world has ever seen,' a movement committed, not only to class betterment, but to national regeneration:

> To be a U.F.A. member is to belong to a movement which is rapidly making Canadian history. Every member has a right to a thrill of justifiable pride ... for the story of the organized farmers is one of the brightest pages in our national record – the abolition of the liquor traffic and of the patronage evil in public affairs, the enfranchisement of women, the agitation for a more equitable distribution of the burden of taxation, the growth of co-operation in the community and business life – these are some of the out-growths of the activities of our ... organization.[71]

Farmers built the movement as they gained a sense of 'the strength of our organization,' 'a power which if rightly directed must mean the dawn of a brighter tomorrow ... when the social evils under which we writhe ... are banished.' This utopian vision often had social gospel overtones. Henry Wise Wood concluded a UFA Sunday sermon 'with a description of the New Jerusalem, a picture of the world as it will be when his Kingdom had come.' Irene Parlby's concept of the good society revealed her class and gender concerns. Farm women, she mused,

> look forward to the day when no farm woman or man or child will call in vain for nursing or medical aid; when all farm boys and girls will continue their education until at least 16, with some possibility of continuing their studies after that; when every district will have its community hall and a possibility of good entertainments ... They look forward to the time when the tariff walls will cease to deprive them of so many things ... when co-operation will bring them the just fruits of their toil.[72]

Before the war, farmers had gained self-respect. Now they were confident they could inaugurate a new society to justify the soldiers' sacrifices.

Increasingly, Alberta farmers, like many other Canadian farmers, felt that direct political action was needed to create this society. Their oppositional culture and growing anti-partyism, fuelled by scandals and allegations of graft in Ottawa and in the three prairie governments, led to their conclusion that only non-party candidates – nominated, financed,

'One by One He Is Breaking His Bonds,' by Arch Dale. *Grain Growers' Guide,* 25 Oct. 1916, 6. This cartoon exudes the movement self-confidence felt by western farmers during the war.

and controlled like convention delegates – would support farm interests and be free from corruption. They advocated running independents or forming a new party or movement to gain a balance of power. As before, most political activists were radicals, seeking a farmer-labour political alliance based on the alleged common interests of the two groups as victims of plutocracy. Only direct politics could 'emancipate' producers from the 'bondage of trusts,' making them 'free men.'[73]

The wartime UFA political movement began with a 1915 convention debate on a motion proposing that the organization nominate political candidates. After heated debate, the delegates instructed the directors to ascertain the locals' views. The few unions that replied generally favoured the idea of UFA candidates. At the same time, the locals were seeking guidance about what to do for the next election. In response, the executive threw the whole question back to the unions, asking them to elect representatives for district conventions to be called by central office if enough locals appointed delegates. Each convention would decide what form of political action, if any, that members in its constituency would take. The executive stipulated that if members did not make the effort to hold conventions, it would 'conclude that the U.F.A. is not ripe for ... political action.' Few locals responded, and the 1916 annual convention settled the matter by defeating a resolution favouring independent politics.[74]

Most UFA leaders breathed a sigh of relief. Henry Wise Wood was convinced, based on his study of American farm associations, that direct politics would destroy the UFA. General secretary P.P. Woodbridge, who believed that farmers' salvation lay in co-operative enterprise, agreed.[75] Their arguments influenced some members, although a number of UFA officers, such as Rice Sheppard, favoured independent action. President James Speakman, who died in 1915, may have sided with Sheppard, but publicly he was non-committal.

Even liberal UFA/UFWA farmers, however, soon began to consider the possibility of UFA political action, especially after the old parties refused to endorse the revised Farmers' Platform of 1916, and after the agrarian Non-Partisan League stormed to power in North Dakota in the same year. The *Guide* rejoiced in this victory and admonished western farmers to take independent action themselves. Such a stance by the movement's official organ – it had broached the idea of third-party politics since 1910[76] – could not help but affect the UFA/UFWA.

The League would be more than a distant example of what farmers could accomplish politically. Shortly after its win in North Dakota, it was organized in Saskatchewan; in late 1916 it appeared in Alberta. In the following year, the Alberta League obtained its own organ, the *Non-Partisan*, edited by William Irvine. The League quickly became the voice of radical Alberta agrarianism; most radical UFA/UFWA farmers joined it while retaining their membership in the older organization. They were drawn to the League's platform, which was 'practically the same' north and south of the border and reflected the North Dakota League's socialist background. It called for government ownership of banks, utilities, and major industries, and compulsory insurance for health care.[77] The League's great attraction, however, was its commitment to political reform and independent politics.

The victory of two Alberta League candidates in the June 1917 provincial election sent shock waves across the province. One winner was temperance leader Louise McKinney; the other was UFA vice-president James Weir, an ex-Conservative and ex-newspaper man with a chip on his shoulder the size of a railway tie. Their success stemmed from their qualities as candidates, dissatisfaction with the Liberals' record, strong

Alberta League leadership, and farmers' growing class consciousness and confidence. The League was quickening the agitation for direct action, even in the UFA/UFWA. Might not this newly lit prairie fire consume the whole province in the next election?

The breakdown of the party system under the stress of the Great War appeared to open the door to federal politics for the League, and in the long run it did much to aid the agrarian political movement. Cultural tensions about French-Canadian participation in the war, evident in disputes about Ontario's Regulation 17 and the abolition of bilingualism in Manitoba, cracked the Liberal party; conscription completed the rupture as prominent Liberals, including the Alberta premier, Arthur Sifton, formed the Union government with the Conservatives in late 1917 to impose compulsory military service.

The apparent death of the old party structure, however, did not provide the opening for the League that might have been expected. The Union government convinced most farmers that it was the long-awaited 'non-partisan' administration that would purify politics. The West, therefore, with a promise of exemption from consription for farmers and with United Grain Growers president T.A. Crerar in the cabinet, went solidly Unionist in the 1917 election. The four Alberta League candidates were annihilated. Their criticisms of the Union government as a 'union of a pack of timber wolves' and their shrill demands for the conscription of wealth had provoked suspicions of disloyalty.[78]

Thus was the League fire dampened, though not put out; the agrarian political movement in Alberta checked, though not stopped. But ironically, the Union government, having headed off the independent political movement, would be a major catalyst of the post-war political revolt.

Although farmers' wartime idealism attracted them to the Union party, they also voted for it because they wanted a government of the best talent in order to win the war. Their patriotism was displayed by the 3,000 or more UFA men who volunteered for overseas service[79] and by the thousands of dollars and tons of clothing and other items that UFA/UFWA locals made and donated for war relief. In addition, a number of northern locals formed units of a 'U.F.A. Home Guard,' which Rice Sheppard organized for home defence and to free up soldiers stationed in Canada for overseas service.[80]

Farmers thus felt that they were 'doing their bit' to win the war, but was Unionism, which had risen from the ashes of partyism to win the war and launch a new era of clean politics, fulfilling its promise? At first,

'Union Rising, Like Phoenix, from the Ashes of Party Politics,' by Arch Dale.
Grain Growers' Guide, 31 Oct. 1917, 6. Farmers initially believed that the Union
government was the long-awaited non-partisan government that would purify
politics and end partyism. Political purity, which the Union government embod-
ies in this cartoon, is depicted as a female figure because women were thought
to be inherently virtuous.

it seemed that it was. The government quickly implemented conscription, direct taxation, and national prohibition and women's suffrage, while eliminating the worst forms of patronage. But was it enough to satisfy the UFA/UFWA? Many farmers believed that the Wartime Elections Act, which disfranchised certain immigrants, violated 'British justice,' and they were angry that the government did not conscript wealth by enacting the taxation planks of the Farmers' Platform.[81]

One act, in particular, convinced most Canadian farmers that Unionism was not what it was supposed to be. In May 1918 military events prompted the government to draft farmers age twenty to twenty-two. Producers considered this a breach of faith; having been promised exemption from military service, they had bought more equipment, land, and livestock to increase production. Now that their sons were going to be conscripted, where would they find the necessary labour for their expanded operations? Ontario and Quebec farmers – 5,000 strong – 'swept down upon the capital and used every political and personal effort to compel a change of government policy.' In Alberta, mass protest rallies were held, and the UFA central office was flooded with letters and resolutions from members and locals condemning the government's action. In a resolution sent to Ottawa, the executive recognized that the order would not have been issued 'had not the need for men been imperative,' but it held the government responsible for any resulting loss of food production.[82]

Many Alberta farmers, including two UFA board members, were incensed with this resolution, believing that it let the government off the hook. To avoid a split in the organization, the board endorsed a memorial that more effectively expressed farmers' sense of grievance. It asserted that 'the government cannot have fully appreciated the far-reaching effects of the measures taken' and warned that the situation called 'for the greatest possible wisdom in council ... to maintain that hearty support that a loyal people owe to a government in a time such as this.'[83]

That done, the potential rupture in the UFA/UFWA was averted. But the breach between farmers, especially western farmers, and the Union government never healed. James Miner, a Non-Partisan League and UFA member, declared ominously: 'It is now known what they can expect from us next election time.'[84] The agrarian revolt was about to begin.

Yet a number of liberals, including UFA president Wood, still believed that direct politics would kill the UFA/UFWA and that the movement

'The Silent Witness,' by Arch Dale. *Grain Growers' Guide*, 22 May 1918, 6. This ominous scene hints at the irreparable breach the Union government caused between itself and organized farmers when it cancelled their exemption from conscription.

would have its greatest political effect through organization and pressure politics. In a letter published in late 1918 in several farm periodicals, ex-UFA vice-president S.S. Dunham articulated this view. 'The lesson for us to learn from the history of the prior farmers' organizations on the continent,' he argued, 'is that the influence they exerted in political affairs by themselves going into politics as a party could have been exerted just as well, and probably better, had they ... remained out of politics and ... impressed upon the parties existing the principles for which they stood.'[85]

The political activists quickly replied. Quipping that Dunham was a lawyer who farmed 'mostly over the long distance telephone,' League MLA James Weir asserted that independent politics alone could ensure that farmers were not saddled with the war debt. Rice Sheppard pointed out that farmers had made little progress politically with major issues and maintained that a way could be found for the UFA to enter politics without harming the organization. Another farmer simply asked: 'What good is the ballot if we have no option but to vote for men whose interests are directly in opposition to our own?'[86] The day of Dunham, James Bower, P.P. Woodbridge, and the old Henry Wise Wood, the day of movement building and pressure politics, was about to end.

Shaped by the Great War, the movement was fully built from 1914 to 1918 as it developed its culture, doubled its membership, and formed a women's section. Women worked for the movement to further their class and gender interests and to protect the home. The UFA, recognizing women's work on the farm and in the movement, supported their agenda, including their equal rights demands, although it never granted them equality. Women's promotion of causes reflecting their maternal ideology developed a social ethic – a desire for reform through state action – informed by the social gospel, wartime government intervention, and fear that the war might be in vain. War-related state policies and practices and their contrast to UFA/UFWA democracy strengthened members' opposition to the party system. This anti-partyism together with farmers' social ethic, commitment to citizenship, and sense of possibility – tinged with wartime idealism – prompted them to build the movement to create a just and democratic society, first through pressure politics and possibly through direct action.

Chapter Six

Co-operation in the Movement

The co-operative spirit is growing in our vicinity.[1]

Lawrence Goodwyn argues that because of co-operative experience American farmers acquired a movement culture of self-respect and democratic possibility, adopted a radical critique of the financial system, and supported the Populist party in the 1890s. Critics have noted weaknesses in Goodwyn's argument about the strength of the co-operative movement in Populist areas and its contribution to Populist support.[2] Other scholars affirm the reality of a Populist culture, but focus on its non-co-operative origins. Only David Laycock and Ian MacPherson assess the relationship between co-ops and the Canadian farm movement. Laycock argues that co-operative experience gave farmers confidence and developed their ideas about democracy and politics. MacPherson establishes a link between the agrarian movement and a larger co-operative movement, one seeking a social consensus that was neither socialistic nor capitalistic.[3]

Co-operation was not as crucial in developing protest as Goodwyn might argue, but as MacPherson and Laycock suggest, it was significant. Co-operative activity and ideology helped to form, build, and politicize the Alberta farm movement.

In taking co-operative action, Alberta farmers' main aim was to save money at the expense of middlemen and corporations. Their co-operative practice and ideas were based on European, particularly British, co-operative experience and on North American agrarianism. The Grange, the Farmers' Alliance, the Patrons of Industry, and later farm organizations undertook co-operative buying and selling, retailing, banking, wholesaling, manufacturing, and insurance – almost every conceivable kind of co-operative activity.

Unlike most North American producers, Alberta radical farmers lost much of their enthusiasm for co-operation, at least for large-scale projects, because of the failure of their early co-operative endeavours, especially the Society of Equity Co-op. Consequently, few radicals became 'utopian co-operators,' co-operators who closely associated co-operative activity with socialist politics. Many more Alberta farmers were 'liberal co-operators'; they saw co-operation as a way to restore fair capitalism in a monopoly-controlled market place. After the war, as Henry Wise Wood's notion of political action by economic groups became popular, most liberal agrarian co-operators, and some utopians, became 'occupational co-operators,' viewing co-ops 'as essentially assistants to the farmers who owned them and not as elements of a wider movement.'[4]

Because some radicals lost faith in co-operative action after the Equity debacle, they left the initiative to the liberals, so that co-operation had a generally conservative effect on the Alberta movement. With radicals such as W.R. Ball largely abandoning co-operative activity, liberal co-operators were able to convince farmers, with little opposition, that its purpose was simply to correct the market. They also influenced farmers to prefer co-operative over state solutions, while radicals, politicized by the failure of their co-ops, prodded the United Farmers and Farm Women of Alberta (UFA/UFWA) to enter politics earlier than it otherwise would have.

The most important and immediate effect of the co-op disaster was irreparable damage to the credibility of the Society of Equity, which hastened its merger with the Alberta Farmers' Association (AFA), thus helping to form the movement. The Equity co-op failure also revealed the folly of trying to build large co-ops with little co-operative expertise, a lesson that was not lost on several AFA directors, who balked at a proposal that the Association establish packing houses and grain elevators. George MacDonald 'thought the enterprises suggested ... were rather large undertakings for farmers who had no previous experience in managing them.'[5] The AFA's co-operative involvement was limited to buying and selling a few goods locally and helping to organize government co-operative creameries. The Society's co-operative efforts, apart from the Equity co-op, were confined mainly to purchasing binder twine. Further co-operative practice would be needed before farmers would again attempt an ambitious co-operative project.

That experience was rapidly gained through a torrent of early UFA local endeavour. Of the 229 unions returning their annual reports to the UFA office for 1914, 168 reported having done co-operative business. Of these, 137 stated the amount they had turned over, the aggregate total being $287,000.[6] Most UFA locals ordered carloads of goods such as binder twine, wire, coal, lubricants, oil, cement, lumber, building supplies, fence posts, hardware, machinery, chemicals, livestock supplies, clothing, and groceries. The savings over retail prices could be hundreds or thousands of dollars per year. Sometimes unions in a district combined to order larger quantities to save even more. Many unions made bulk purchases through local dealers rather than buy direct from manufacturers or wholesalers. Other locals arranged to have merchants sell to members at a fixed profit, as the Patrons of Industry had done.

There were numerous forms of co-operation. Members of many locals collectively shipped grain or livestock. To facilitate this activity, several unions operated co-operative weigh scales. A number made bulk seed purchases or planted co-operative seed plots to produce grain of a uniform quality so that members could combine their surpluses to fill a railway car. A few set up co-operative credit schemes or made arrangements with banks to get cash for members for co-op buying. In such ways, co-operation was 'the poor man's friend.'[7] To provide a continuous supply of meat for members, many unions organized beef rings. Several bought machinery for co-operative use.

More formal and expensive ventures were undertaken. Many locals built warehouses for co-operative purchases. Some established co-operative mills, creameries, or stores. One early store, run by the Eckville and Gilby Co-operative Company, joined the Co-operative Union of Canada (CUC), the main national co-operative association. Created under the auspices of two UFA unions, the Eckville Society followed true co-operative principles and did $48,000 of business in 1917.[8]

Co-operative education informed and inspired such activity. Starting in 1910, the UFA office answered frequent requests for advice on organizing co-operative societies, stores, mills, and grain elevators and for information on co-operation in other countries, forwarding some queries to the CUC. Following the suggestion of UFA general secretary P.P. Woodbridge, a number of farmers subscribed to the *Canadian Co-operator*, the official CUC organ. A local source of ideas was the Red Deer UFA Co-op, which did $40,000 of business in its first year, selling livestock, hay, and grain. The 1910 UFA convention heard a speech about this co-op, and it sent 200 copies of its constitution to enquiring parties.[9] Farmers also learned about co-operation from articles and secretaries' reports in the *Guide*. Moreover, at conventions of the UFA secretaries there were lengthy discussions about local co-operative activity.

Such discussion revealed farmers' ideologies. Radicals, the carriers of the anti-monopoly tradition, described co-operation as a means of fighting the 'eastern capitalists' and busting the trusts. As well, they saw it as secondary to political action. 'Buy and sell co-operatively whenever you can,' John Glambeck counselled, 'but ... the farmer must be satisfied with nothing less than control of the government.' Glambeck considered co-operation to be a collectivist strategy, though like most UFA/UFWA radicals, he favoured state action when it was feasible. 'Farmers should co-operate,' he declared, 'in all matters where government ownership or operation is impracticable.' Farmers of the liberal wing, seeing co-operation as a form of self-help, generally preferred it to state ownership. They also felt that it should 'intelligently attack monopoly' rather than 'blindly attack capital.' At bottom, they wanted co-operation to make the market efficient, to ensure that farmers received the highest price 'the market could afford.'[10]

Along with other agrarian and co-operative organizations, liberal and radical UFA farmers demanded co-operative legislation. At Ottawa in 1910 UFA general secretary E.J. Fream called for a law to govern the operation of co-operative societies across the country. A convention resolution passed in that year revealed the UFA's 'wish to be part of a national movement based on such a law.' It argued that 'while societies are independent of each other, they are most successful when they act together and develop in unison and sympathy ... a result impossible if each society is dependent upon provincial statutes inconsistent with each other.' Subsequently, many UFA locals signed a *Guide* petition for federal co-operative legislation. In addition, the 1912 convention asked the Canadian Council of Agriculture, the national farm lobby organization, to draft a co-operative bill 'to suit the country and city people and to submit same to the federal government.'[11] No national law was forthcoming, however, and Alberta farmers had to settle for the provincial Co-operative Trading Act, passed in 1913.

As farmers grasped the possibilities of co-operation, they suggested that the UFA become involved in larger projects. The 1911 convention proposed that the organization confer with the Grain Growers' Grain Company about starting 'a farmers' commission house in connection with co-operative stores.' About a dozen resolutions on co-operation were submitted to the 1913 convention. Though many were unrealistic, they exuded collective confidence, based on successful co-operative experience. One resolution declared that 'we, the members of the U.F.A., know that by co-operating we can carry to a successful issue anything we take in hand,' and it 'resolved that we ... build and operate at once a large terminal elevator.' Another argued that merchants' profits were 'enormous' and that 'the only remedy lies in co-operation.' It proposed 'that we ... bind ourselves in such a co-operative union wherein we may ... purchase our goods and thus get them at cost ... In time we could have a store in every railroad town.'[12]

This feeling of co-operative expectancy led to the birth of the Alberta Farmers' Co-operative Elevator Company in 1913. Before 1911 the UFA had called for government owned and operated elevators, but the UFA elevator committee found the Manitoba public elevator plan unsuitable for Alberta conditions and in 1911 asked Premier Sifton to establish a co-operative system similar to that operating in Saskatchewan. Sifton demurred, and the committee presented a modified proposal to the 1913 UFA convention that was based on the Saskatchewan act, while providing for more farmer control and for the company to handle all kinds of farm products. 'By a very large majority,' the delegates endorsed this proposition.[13] The failure of the grain acts to fully regulate the industry, the province's early refusal to create a government elevator system, the financial collapse of the Manitoba public elevators in 1912, the positive example of the Saskatchewan co-op system, and the successes of UFA co-operation hinted at the possibilities of an Alberta co-operative elevator line.

The government dutifully drafted a bill with UFA input to incorporate the Alberta Farmers' Co-operative Elevator Company (AFCEC) Limited. The bill was modelled on the Saskatchewan act, but gave members more control. The province would loan up to 85 per cent of the cost of the elevators; farmers would raise the other 15 per cent from stock purchases. Ultimately, the Grain Growers' Grain Company (GGGC), through which the AFCEC marketed its grain, helped financially. The AFCEC's provisional directors were the UFA elevator committee, less George Bevington. Its first elected directors were also UFA men, including W.J. Tregillus, who became company president. By the fall of 1913 forty-two elevators were under construction and seven had been acquired.[14]

While helping with the AFCEC, the UFA association provided other co-operative opportunities. In 1913 it organized egg circles and egg marketing through the Department of Agriculture, arranged for the GGGC to sell members' produce on commission at the Calgary public market, secured quotations on binder twine for locals, and struck a deal with a B.C. firm to sell fruit to unions at wholesale prices. By 1914 the UFA office had become a clearing house for co-operative buying. Locals received price lists of a wide range of goods they could purchase through the office. Two years later, the UFA made an agreement with a cold storage company for special rates for members and contracted with the Hudson's Bay Company for locals and co-ops to buy provisions at discount prices.[15]

The advent of district associations – groups of affiliated unions – marked the maturation of the UFA/UFWA co-operative movement. These associations, which were formed by the grassroots mainly in the mid to late 1910s, helped locals to co-ordinate their organizing and community work, linked the central office with member unions, and held district conventions that sometimes forwarded resolutions to the annual convention. Their main purpose, however, was to facilitate large-scale co-operative activity. By the fall of 1916 eighteen UFA district associations and a few large unions had incorporated under the Co-operative Societies Act. By the following spring, there were some forty incorporated UFA societies, most of which had an office and warehouse. A half-dozen operated co-op stores. By 1919 there were about sixty-five incorporated societies in Alberta.[16]

These societies did a considerable business. The Ponoka District UFA Association sold $168,000 worth of hogs and bought twenty-eight railway carloads of goods in the first half of 1917. Associations at Manville and Cardston had, in 1918 and 1919, respectively, about $200,000 of revenue. The Blackie Co-op shipped about $1,000 worth of eggs during one month, through an egg circle that the UFWA had organized. In 1916 the Leduc Co-operative marketed 154 railroad cars of potatoes in the United States at a profit of up to $135 a car.[17]

Most co-op associations marketed a variety of products and bought consumer and farm supplies for members. Some also ran co-operative lumber yards and a few sold insurance, but the raison d'être for many associations and some UFA locals was to sell livestock. Members' co-operative loyalty was sometimes tested, since private parties occasionally bought at a loss in order to draw farmers away from their co-ops. The aggressors often lost out, because farmers usually 'stuck' to their co-operative, believing they would be up to 20 per cent ahead in the long run.[18]

Each society had its own by-laws, not all of which conformed to accepted co-operative ideas. All or nearly all societies followed the co-operative rule of 'one man, one vote.' Some paid dividends mainly on the basis of use; others did so more on the amount invested, a policy not endorsed by the international co-operative movement. Some limited the stock that a member could hold; others did not, which again was a variation from normal co-operative practice. Thus, some co-ops were more co-operative, and others were more capitalistic. Almost all paid profits only to shareholders, though many did business with non-shareholders. A few distributed profits by selling at cost. Most built up reserve funds and followed the co-operative custom of selling for cash only. Nearly all followed co-operative principles closely enough to be considered part of the larger co-operative movement.[19]

Secretaries of successful unions argued correctly that co-operation was the key to their locals' growth.[20] The opportunity for saving and making money through co-operative buying and selling attracted new members and kept existing ones in the organization. In this way, co-operation built the movement.

On the other hand, it occasionally hurt or killed unions, because farmers got so involved in their co-ops or co-operative elevator companies that they lost touch with their UFA locals. To address this problem, the UFA association suggested that co-operative societies require shareholders to be UFA members.[21] Following this logic, many co-ops did business only with UFA members, and a number paid farmers' UFA membership fees out of their patronage dividends. Other co-op admitted non-UFA members and often drifted away from the UFA organization, weakening it and dividing the agrarian co-operative movement into UFA and non-UFA camps.

Societies opening their doors to non-UFA members did so because they needed more shareholders or because their leaders, having been trained in the consumer co-operative movement, opposed the idea of a co-op's being for only one occupational group. George Keen, secretary of the CUC and editor of the *Canadian Co-operator*, shared this consumer philosophy[22] and influenced a few UFA societies to admit non-UFA members. UFA co-ops that excluded non-UFA members were not allowed in the CUC and missed benefiting from Keen's advice on co-op management, while the CUC lost the chance to increase its membership and revenues.

Farmers also lost co-operative opportunities with the farmer elevator supply departments. The AFCEC began selling to UFA locals and societies in 1914, and by the year ending August 1917 it had handled almost

2,700 carloads of goods, including flour, fruit, feed, hay, salt, coal, fence posts, lumber, building materials, binder twine, and wire – worth over $1.5 million. In the nine months ending May 1918 the United Grain Growers (UGG), the AFCEC's successor, shipped almost 3,700 carloads to Alberta points, the turnover being nearly $2.5 million.[23]

Despite this business, a minority of farmers criticized the companies' capitalistic features, especially their refusal to pay patronage dividends, prompting the 1915 UFA convention to call for a 'purely co-operative wholesale society' for locals. The directors concluded that this proposal was not feasible and arranged for the AFCEC to act as a selling and purchasing agent for the UFA on specific terms. Because of grassroots protest, however, the UFA did not give the AFCEC a monopoly, but allowed locals and co-ops to continue to deal with other buyers and sellers.[24]

Further criticism of elevator wholesaling surfaced at the 1917 and 1918 UFA secretaries' meetings. Some UFA co-op representatives complained that the companies' prices were high and that co-ops did not get a lower wholesale price than individuals and locals, making it hard for them, with their overhead costs, to operate. Several co-ops therefore bought from other suppliers, although many tried to deal with the elevator companies. It was suggested that the companies act as true co-operative wholesalers to the co-ops by paying them a dividend on their buying volume. The 1918 meetings called for a democratically controlled wholesale department – run by the co-ops, the UGG, and the western farm associations – that would offer low prices.[25]

Discontent with the UGG led to a meeting of eight co-op societies in February 1919. Most, if not all, of them were or had been UFA co-ops, and most, if not all, of the delegates were UFA men. They agreed to use the UGG as a wholesaler when possible, but felt that it had not yet proved itself 'the ultimate buying agency for the retail co-operatives of this province.' They then formed the Alberta Co-operative Union to further their interests. At a later Union meeting, greater antipathy to the UGG emerged. Critical of the company's unwillingness to declare patronage dividends, and angry over its alleged 'fierce' competition with the co-ops through its mail order business and other tactics, the delegates denied membership to the elevator company.[26]

Not all or even a majority of UFA members opposed the UGG or supported the Union. President Wood felt that the Union was 'outside the scope' of the UFA and believed that locals should be 'careful about contributing funds' to it. He did not see how it could 'overcome the difficulties which the U.G.G. had already been trying to overcome.'[27]

This division in the agrarian co-operative movement between anti- and pro-UGG forces spilled into the political field. The Alberta Co-operative Union was a consumer movement whose leaders opposed 'class co-operation,' believing that their co-ops should be open to all, not only UFA members. Guy Johnson, O.L. McPherson, and S. Stevenson, all officers of the Union, took a similar stance in the post-war political dispute, arguing that the UFA political movement should be open to all classes, not only farmers. Wood, on the other hand, an 'occupational co-operator,' was not keen about the consumer movement; he was 'single-mindedly interested in building a multipurpose rural co-operative system' under UFA direction.[28] This agricultural 'class' focus became part of his political doctrine in the spring of 1919. He asserted that farmers must take political action as a class and organization and close the door to other groups. Wood's occupational emphasis, then, like his Union opponents' broader interclass strategy, applied to both the economic and the political fields. Both factions' ideas about co-operation and politics were inseparably linked.

The UGG reacted to the Co-operative Union by trying to improve its service. In 1919 it proposed to open stores where demand warranted, financing them primarily through the local sale of stock. The stores would give patronage refunds and have some local control, although final authority would rest with the company. The latter provision led UFA/UFWA consumer co-operators to reject the plan, because it smacked of the same centralized control that had made them suspicious of the UGG all along.[29]

The 1920 UFA convention was not interested in the UGG plan either. The delegates simply told the officers to encourage the organization of co-op societies and to ask the UGG to open a co-operative wholesale department. But the societies no longer wanted a UGG wholesaler. Instead, fifteen of them formed a 'Central Co-operative Buying Association' in 1921 to supply co-ops in the province with a variety of merchandise at low prices. The idea of a co-op wholesaler, however, was premature. The secretary of the Buying Association found many wholesalers and manufacturers 'ready to give very substantial discounts if they are guaranteed the total business' of the Association's membership. He therefore recommended that 'no attempt be made to establish a wholesale centre or to do any extensive co-operative buying.'[30]

The campaign for a new wholesaler, the meetings of the Co-operative Union, and the criticisms of the UGG revealed tensions in the agrarian co-operative movement and missed chances for united action. Another missed opportunity was a failed attempt to merge several local farmer mutual fire insurance companies into a large UFA business. The 1917 convention approved the amalgamation, but the companies refused to surrender control.[31]

Farmers' lack of support for a proposed pork plant and their manner of selling livestock were among their most serious co-operative failures. The UFA continued the campaign of the Alberta Farmers' Association for a government meat plant and influenced the provincial government to present a proposal to the 1910 convention that a majority of delegates endorsed. It stipulated that the government would build and operate a pork-packing plant if farmers guaranteed to provide 50,000 hogs a year. Individual producers would sign a five-year contract to indicate how many they would supply and commit themselves to sell exclusively to the plant or pay a fine.[32]

The UFA executive urged farmers to sign up quickly, but many soon objected to the contract's terms. They protested that the payment upon delivery was too low and that it was unfair that they should have to sell all their marketable pigs to the plant, beyond the minimum number they would agree to supply. The plant proponents responded that the initial payment could be changed and that producers had to sell all their hogs to the plant to ensure its viability. They also tried to persuade farmers to support the proposal by appealing to their co-operative ethos, calling the plan 'co-operative' and arguing that it would usher in the 'co-operative commonwealth.'[33]

Despite such rhetoric, by the end of 1910 farmers had promised only a quarter of the hogs needed to construct the plant. Undaunted, the UFA pork committee convinced the 1911 convention to approve a new canvass, but only 4,280 hogs were pledged on a pre-canvass guarantee form circulated to the unions. The directors refused to give up, and they sent the 1908 Pork Commission Report to the locals in 1913 with a 'statement showing that the whole proposal is a co-operative one.'[34] Notwithstanding, significant support for a plant could not be raised.

The government pork-plant campaign was effectively over. The terms of the contract, the availability of local markets for hogs, and farmers' growing focus on wheat production contributed to its failure. In addition, some farmers hesitated to commit themselves to a contract, since they had seen pork prices so low that 'they did not pay for the wear and tear on the bale of the swill pail.' On the other hand, high prices during the campaign made farmers 'indifferent'; they could not 'see the need of the proposed co-operative plant.' Individualism – a weak commitment to the co-operative principle – further worked against the campaign. One 'lump of cussed selfishness' would not sign a contract because he reasoned that 'once the plant is erected, I can easily dispose of as many hogs as I desire to the government plant.'[35]

Following a suggestion by the UFA pork committee, farmers began selling large numbers of livestock by the carload, often through the AFCEC. The AFCEC livestock department handled 56,000 hogs and over 1,100 head of cattle in the 1914–15 fiscal year and 36,000 hogs and over 3,500 head of cattle in the following year. In 1915–16 the company handled 628 railroad cars of livestock; in the next year, it handled almost twice as many.[36]

Like the government pork-plant campaign, however, all was not well, co-operatively speaking. Edward Carswell, the manager of the AFCEC livestock department, told the 1915 UFA convention that when commission profits were prorated to shippers in 1914 in the form of stock for a proposed co-operative pork plant, 'we found public sentiment decidedly against the co-operative plan. It was competition our farmers were looking for, and we were received, not as a company of their own creation to be supported and built up by their patronage, but as another buyer for their hogs, competing with the local buyer.' Carswell discovered that many farmers,

> particularly those belonging to the Association, considered that we were simply robbing the farmers who sold us hogs of the five percent retained in this case, and asked us to quote them a net price the same as the other buyers were doing without taking into consideration a future refund, either in stock in the company or otherwise. This appeared to be the feeling in practically every point where we were doing business, and about the middle of May it was necessary, if we were to accomplish anything, to discontinue doing business on the five percent basis and offer a net price we could pay.

Once the company had abandoned the co-operative plan, its business took off. In late 1914, however, lack of capital and inexpert buying forced it to do some commission business.[37]

By the following year, the UFA livestock committee, after investigating co-operative pork packing in the United States, concluded – to the frustration of some UFA members – that a co-operative plant should not be considered until farmers had proved themselves willing to work collectively by shipping large numbers of hogs on consignment through livestock-shipping associations.[38] Farmers did organize more associations, but the required numbers of consigned livestock were apparently not forthcoming. Consequently, the whole co-op pork-plant idea slipped into oblivion. Cautious – perhaps overcautious – leadership, the promise of better prices from several buyers, and a still weak commitment to co-operation among the rank and file spelled its demise.

As P.P. Woodbridge pointed out, that immature co-operative spirit also led to missed opportunities with the AFCEC supply department. An English-trained co-operator, Woodbridge settled at Okotoks near Calgary and joined the UFA in 1910. He was appointed to central office in the following year and was general secretary from 1913 to 1918, when he retired because of poor health and what he believed were undemocratic tendencies in the UFA and lack of concern by UFA and UGG officials for co-op societies. Always frank, Woodbridge laid out in 1916 what the unions had failed to do with the AFCEC. Noting that the handling of supplies by the elevators had killed or weakened several UFA locals, Woodbridge argued – now assuming a scolding tone – that farmers had foolishly abandoned their locals to deal individually with the company. They should have strengthened their unions and co-ops to make them the main, if not the exclusive, buyers from the elevator supply department. They then could have forced, and still could force, the department to pay patronage dividends[39] and thus operate as a truly co-operative wholesaler.

Although farmers missed opportunities with the AFCEC, pork packing, and mutual fire insurance, their support for co-operative hail insurance, dairying, and credit, for the merger of the farmer elevator companies, and for a wheat pool revealed their growing belief in co-operation. Before 1912 the provincial government alone provided hail insurance to those wanting it. In that year the UFA convention, hoping to spread insurance costs around, instructed the executive to lobby for a compulsory hail tax and, if unsuccessful, to propose that each municipality formed under the new act impose a hail tax if it was approved by a majority of its ratepayers.[40]

Having decided to get out of the hail insurance business, the province refused to implement a province-wide tax, but agreed to insert clauses in the Municipalities Act along the lines of the convention's proposal, so that districts could levy a compulsory hail insurance tax upon ratepayer approval. Twenty-six municipalities eventually voted to receive coverage, and a similar system was implemented in Saskatchewan. Before 1917 the insurance in Alberta was funded by a flat tax on all assessable land; in that year an additional charge was levied on crop land. Owing to this new tax and because claimants were not paid on time, farmers became disgruntled about the whole insurance program.[41]

The UFA executive and the provincial Hail Insurance Board devised a new plan that provided for hail insurance in all organized districts, funded by crop land only; the tax on all assessable land would be removed. The compulsory nature of the old scheme was entirely eliminated, since any farmer could withdraw from the program and its tax obligations. Moreover, the tax would be imposed after the hail season, so that a sufficient levy could be made to pay all losses every year, and money could be borrowed to pay claims promptly.[42]

Because it was based on the actual cost of insurance and was voluntary, this was the most co-operative hail plan ever offered to Alberta farmers. The 1918 UFA convention recognized this fact, and one delegate used co-operative discourse to gain support for it. 'If we are a co-operative body, we must all join together,' he declared. 'If there are troubles in one locality and not in another, we must all bear those troubles in order that we may get the full benefit of this co-operation ... [On] my farm ... there ... [has] not been a hail storm ... At the same time, I am willing to pay my proportion of the insurance in order that those who are hailed out can get the benefit.' By endorsing this co-operative proposal and supporting the co-operative program implemented by the government,[43] farmers revealed their growing belief in co-operation.

The UFA appealed to that co-operative ethos to convince members to buy hail insurance through the organization. In 1917 the association was an agent for a company under a quasi-co-operative plan, selling insurance to farmers and earning $4,000. 'A policy written through the U.F.A.,' an advertisement read, 'is a step in co-operation and a blow at private control and monopoly of your business.'[44]

As they did with hail insurance, farmers sought to apply the co-operative principle to dairying. Beginning in the 1890s, a number of government co-operative creameries were established in Alberta, but they had fallen on hard times by the war years – in fact, many had expired – as farmers increasingly patronized large private concerns that paid higher prices. However, following the lead of Saskatchewan farmers, who operated some twenty co-operative creameries in 1917, Alberta producers took over the remaining government-owned creameries, and by 1919 there were apparently fifty-five co-operative, community-owned creameries in Alberta. The UFA also promoted the work of milk producer co-ops in the Calgary, Lethbridge, Medicine Hat, Didsbury, and Edmonton areas.[45]

The first UFA officers (1909). George Long, former president of the Edmonton Agricultural Society and a Society of Equity organizer, is third from the left. James Bower, the first UFA president, is third from the right. On the far right is Strathcona pioneer Rice Sheppard. Seated is secretary-treasurer E.J. Fream. (Glenbow Archives NA-4338-25)

UFA picnic at the '25' ranch near Nanton, 1915. Note the baseball game in progress. (Glenbow Archives NA-3535-142)

The 1916 UFA convention, First Baptist Church, Calgary. (Glenbow Archives NA-4360-6)

The 1918 UFA board of directors. Seated, starting second from the left, are Percival Baker, first UFA vice-president; Irene Parlby, UFWA president; Henry Wise Wood, UFA president; Winnifred Ross, UFWA vice-president; Leona Barritt, UFWA secretary; W.D. Trego, second UFA vice-president. Third from the right in the second row is ex-Kansas Populist governor and third UFA vice-president J.W. Leedy. Third from the left in the back row is UFA general secretary P.P. Woodbridge. Second from the right is Henry E. Spencer, a future UFA member of Parliament. (Glenbow Archives NA-447-1)

Young Farm People's Conference, 1919. The Leavitt Junior UFA band is in the centre. (Glenbow Archives NA-4338-4)

The McCafferty UFA band, Edgerton area. The band was formed in 1920 or 1921 and played at social functions and picnics. (Glenbow Archives NA-4165-2)

The 1921 UFWA board of directors. In the front row, starting from the left, are Jean Field; Susan Gunn, first vice-president; Marion Sears, president; Mrs. O.S. Welsh, second vice-president; Mrs. J.B. Kidd, secretary; Etta Wood (wife of H.W. Wood). (Glenbow Archives NA-3972-1)

UFWA local from Heart Lake, 1921. (Glenbow Archives NA-2691-35)

Farmers' growing support for co-operative dairying and hail insurance paralleled their growing interest in co-operative credit. The increase of agrarian co-operative endeavour across the country, the reluctance of governments to become directly involved in the economy, and farmers' co-operative education and experience cultivated this emerging feeling of co-operative possibility. Western farmers' main complaints about the existing credit system were that producers could not obtain enough credit; interest rates were too high; loan terms were too short; and collection and foreclosure proceedings were unfair.[46]

Responding to these problems, the 1912 UFA convention called for government loans, and at the delegates' request, the central secretary, E.J. Fream, mailed a circular to the unions providing general information about state credit in New Zealand and Australia. In a later circular, he criticized government loan programs, arguing that they might be affected by patronage or plutocratic control. He contrasted them unfavourably with co-operative credit, which, he asserted, substituted 'self-reliance and self-help for state aid.' This analysis, the province's refusal to provide direct loans to producers, and farmers' co-operative successes and learning had their effect. Despite resolutions submitted to the 1913 convention calling for state loans and Tregillus's call for a provincial bank, the delegates did not rule out any credit plan but appeared to favour legislation for co-operative credit societies. Alberta farmers were grasping the possibilities of co-operation, as were producers in Saskatchewan, who also requested co-operative farm credit in 1913.[47]

That trend continued, especially after the 1914 financial crisis and the war made it hard to get loans or renewals, leading the 1915 UFA convention to demand a semi-moratorium on mortgages, land sale agreements, and machinery notes. The convention also approved of co-operative credit, but turned the whole credit question over to the directors for study. The board appointed the president, James Speakman, to examine and report on the subject in the *Guide*, so that members could come to an informed consensus at the 1916 convention.[48]

Born in England, Speakman had homesteaded near Penhold, Alberta, in 1891. He supported the Patrons of Industry, subsequently joined the Alberta Farmers' Association, and played a role in the formation of the UFA, of which he was a director in 1910–11, second vice-president in 1914, and president in 1915 until his death late in that year. A fluent speaker and writer, Speakman was a committed Methodist and an ardent supporter of prohibition, women's suffrage, direct legislation, and free trade.

Speakman studied loan schemes from around the world, but as a liberal, he favoured market-based strategies. He believed that farmers wanted not artificially low interest rates, but the lowest rates good security could obtain in the world's markets. He therefore advocated co-operative mortgage associations that would raise capital by selling debentures on the collective security of members' land. For short-term loans, he proposed co-operative credit societies. He had little use for the New Zealand loan plan favoured by W.R. Ball and the Manitoba Grain Growers' Association. Sounding like E.J. Fream before him, he argued that state loans were open to political influence and patronage and did not provide better terms and interest rates than co-operative mortgage associations. Government loans, he asserted, did not foster 'co-operation' and 'self-reliance'; they made people 'dependent' on the state.[49]

The UFA board endorsed Speakman's co-op proposals, but at the 1916 convention W.R. Ball called for state loans, another delegate wanted a government bank, while former Populist governor John Leedy advocated small private banks. The delegates, however, endorsed the idea of co-operative mortgage societies.[50] The influence of Speakman and the directors and, above all, farmers' sense of co-operative possibility were behind this decision.

At the 1917 UFA convention, the government presented a draft mortgage act, by which the province would lend money to individual farmers at cost. This draft was similar to bills passed by the Saskatchewan and Manitoba governments, which, responding to Grain Grower demands for a mortgage act, had conferred with the Alberta government in drawing up legislation to meet producers' long-term credit needs. Although the UFA had recently declared itself in favour of co-operative mortgage associations rather than government mortgages, the UFA convention, aware of farmers' great need of credit, endorsed the proposal. The bill was enacted but never implemented, initially because of the difficulty of selling bonds during the war to finance the loans. Later in 1917 the Alberta government passed a co-operative credit act to facilitate the formation of co-op societies for short-term credit. It proved almost as useless as the mortgage act because, in contrast to Manitoba's co-operative credit legislation, it did not originally provide for a fixed low rate of interest for borrowers; consequently, few societies were initially organized in Alberta. The only real help Alberta farmers got was a 'Cow Bill' that allowed groups of producers to obtain loans for livestock on the province's credit.[51] This semi-co-operative scheme reinforced farmers' belief that co-op credit could work.

Like their thinking about credit, dairying, and hail insurance, farmers' support for the merger of the farmer elevator companies revealed their growing commitment to co-operation. The AFCEC, the Grain Growers' Grain Company (GGGC), and the Saskatchewan Co-operative Elevator Company discussed amalgamation at their meetings in 1914 and 1915. The powerful Saskatchewan company remained aloof, but the AFCEC, reliant on the GGGC's finances, was interested. In 1917 the possibilities of united effort prompted the GGGC and the AFCEC, with the UFA convention's blessing, to combine to form the United Grain Growers (UGG). With Lakehead terminals, 300 elevators, commission and export businesses, and wholesale warehouses, the UGG became a major force in the western economy.[52]

Farmers' belief in co-operation developed further through their experience with the Board of Grain Supervisors and the Wheat Board, and it culminated in the wheat pool campaign. Farmers had always suspected that the Winnipeg Grain Exchange, which operated until just before the Board of Grain Supervisors was created in 1917, allowed speculators to manipulate prices to the detriment of producers. As a result, farmers generally endorsed price fixing by the Board in 1917–18. Fearing a post-war price drop, some farmers also supported a 1919 UFA convention resolution asking for a fixed wheat price in that year – the Saskatchewan Grain Growers, in fact, endorsed price fixing – but president Wood, an economic liberal, convinced the delegates that fixing prices in peacetime would suggest that farmers were profiteering. The convention therefore simply requested legislation to control grain speculation and asked 'that steps be taken to provide the necessary credit' for producers to hold their wheat until they wished to sell. Although some UFA farmers continued to demand a fixed price, Wood remained adamant that a price guarantee would be a special privilege.[53]

In spite of protests from prairie farmers, the government allowed the Grain Exchange to reopen on 15 July 1919. Wheat prices, which were expected to fall, rose, prompting Ottawa to establish the Wheat Board on 31 July. The Board, which had grain trade, milling, and farmer representatives, including Wood, created a co-operative pool that paid producers a set amount when the grain was delivered and distributed all profits at the end of the season's operations. Many farmers were disappointed when the Board set the initial price at $2.15 per bushel; some did not understand that this was an advance rather than a final price. Wood convinced the 1920 convention that the Board was getting the highest possible price at low cost,[54] and he was vindicated when the

'A Mean Meighen Trick,' by Arch Dale. *Grain Growers' Guide*, 24 Nov. 1920, 6. The Meighen government's decision to dismantle the Wheat Board enraged farmers, which is apparent here, and set in motion the wheat pool campaign.

Board declared an interim payment in May. Farmers were angry, therefore, when the government announced the Board's termination in August. They demanded its reinstatement, especially when prices fell that autumn, a decline they blamed on the return to the open market.

Scholars have suggested that farmers considered forming a wheat pool only after the government had cancelled the Wheat Board; that pooling was their second choice. This belief is generally true, although even before the termination of the Board was announced, some farmers had questions about its composition and wanted an investigation of the possibilities of pooling. The Battle River UFA/UFWA constituency convention was concerned that there were only three farmers on the Board and asked central office to determine how many members would guarantee their wheat to 'a farmers' co-operative selling agency, similar to the one now being organized in Washington.'[55]

The *Guide* had familiarized farmers with the wheat pools in Washington, Idaho, and Oregon and with the fruit pools in California. These pools bound members for five years to deliver all their produce to an agency that sold it and returned all profits to them. The possibilities suggested by this method, the success of the Wheat Board 'pool,' and the achievements of UFA/UFWA marketing convinced the UFA board, with the encouragement of the Bow River UFA/UFWA convention, to ask the UGG and the Saskatchewan Co-operative Elevator Company to consider organizing a pool to deliver western wheat directly to European markets.[56]

The Canadian Council of Agriculture (CCA) still hoped that the Wheat Board might be re-established for the short term, though it had favoured a voluntary pool as a permanent policy even before the dissolution of the Board was announced. Consistent with this position, the CCA appointed a committee, which included Wood, to 'enquire into the feasibility of further development of the farmers' co-operative agencies' for marketing wheat. The committee reported to the December CCA meeting that a pool was feasible if at least 60 per cent of the western wheat acreage could be brought into a five-year contract. The CCA organized another committee from the farmer elevator companies and provincial farm associations to work out the arrangements.[57]

Meanwhile, grassroots support for a pool swept across Alberta. During a UFA/UFWA membership campaign that began in November, canvassers reported 'keen interest in a wheat pool.' One declared that the prospect of a pool made 'the strongest appeal in every instance.' Another stated that 'those of us who worked in the drive would like' to solicit farmers to sign up 'for the wheat pool and are sure the results would be favourable.' Echoing this enthusiasm, the UFA central secretary wrote: 'The sentiment for co-operative marketing has increased a thousand fold in the last few weeks. All but a small remnant of farmers have been driven to realize the hopelessness of the old political parties to help them in their economic struggle ... The farmers are massing in their might to batter down the ramparts of special privilege and usher in a new and better era – a co-operative commonwealth.'[58] Women as well as men were caught up in the pool movement; four resolutions on the subject were submitted to the 1921 UFWA convention. At district conventions and the UFA convention, both sexes endorsed the CCA's proposed pool, although a minority of farmers, mostly radicals, still called for a wheat board.[59]

Outside Alberta, a smaller proportion of farmers shared this sense of co-operative possibility. The influential officers of the powerful Saskatchewan Elevator Company preferred a wheat board, since it would mean guaranteed storage and elevator fees for their company.

'Clearing the Right of Way,' by Arch Dale. *Grain Growers' Guide,* 12 Jan. 1921, 6.
The prospect of creating a wheat pool spawned mass excitement in the Alberta
farm movement. The emphasis in this cartoon is on how pooling would allow
producers to bypass 'speculators, profiteers, gamblers, and middlemen,' giving
them the full benefit of world market prices.

Other Saskatchewan farm leaders feared that they could not sign up
enough farmers to make a pool viable. Moreover, a commission
appointed by the Saskatchewan government was cool to the idea of a
contract pool.[60]

In contrast, most Alberta farmers, because of the success of UFA/
UFWA co-operation, quickly embraced the pooling concept. The many
ex-Americans in the movement were especially interested in pooling,
since it was popular in the United States. Ideological liberals approved
the method as self-help and a way to make 'supply and demand rightly
affect the price of grain.'[61] Co-operative purists were happy that a pool,
unlike the UGG, would return profits according to use, not investment.
Alberta agrarian culture also favoured pooling. The Alberta Farmers'
Association had popularized planned marketing – feeding the market
only when there was demand for grain in order to keep prices up. A
pool could do this. Also, many believed, it could 'control' prices – the

Society of Equity strategy. A contract pool could hold grain off the market to force prices up. This prospect led Charles Harris, a UFA director and an advocate of controlled marketing, to endorse the pool plan.

Alberta farmers did not give up on a pool in 1921, despite the expressed opposition of Saskatchewan farm leaders. The Victoria district convention called on the UFA to organize a pool, although Wood maintained that no pool could be successful without Saskatchewan. The final nail in the campaign's coffin was driven in December, when the CCA committee recommended shelving the pool plan, arguing that it would be impossible to get 60 per cent of the crop under contract or to enforce any contracts signed.[62] The committee knew that most Saskatchewan farmers, who produced a majority of the West's wheat, wanted the Wheat Board reinstated.

The wheat pool was stillborn, but the possibility of creating it contributed to the UFA's political success in 1921. The UFA's political platform and the Farmers' Platform promised to encourage co-operative marketing, which implicitly included pooling. The pool crusade also generated mass excitement that rubbed off on the political campaign.

Farmers' faith in pooling did not die. In 1922 a UFA/UFWA district association proposed to handle all produce 'under the pool system,' with members signing a five-year contract. Similarly, the Calgary Milk Producers' Association, which had been established under UFA auspices, sought to create a milk pool. After the second Wheat Board campaign failed, Alberta farmers, primed with a sense of co-operative possibility, in 1923 created the first provincial wheat pool. The two other prairie provinces followed suit in the next year, and by 1927 the western pools became, with 15 million acres under contract, the 'greatest agrarian co-operative in the world.'[63]

The Alberta pool agitation of 1920–3 was a high point of the UFA/UFWA co-operative movement. Farmers' belief in co-operation – evident in their support for co-operative hail insurance, dairying, credit, and a single farmer elevator company – culminated in the pool movement. Government reluctance to provide state insurance, loans, grain elevators, and a permanent wheat board; co-operative education; and the success of UFA/UFWA co-operative trading: all this fostered farmers' commitment to co-operation.

Co-operative enterprise greatly shaped the UFA/UFWA movement culture. It helped to create a co-operative ethos, a deep-seated commitment to mutuality and group self-help. This ethos was also informed by farmers' economic ties with each other; their community work and social

'The Jonah Man of the Farmers' Organization,' by Arch Dale. *Grain Growers'*
Guide, 12 Apr. 1916, 6. A depiction of the growing co-operative ethos of farmers.

interaction; their practice of mutual aid; their work with the UFA/UFWA
association; their collaboration with other groups; their class battles; and
their radical, co-operative, and social gospel ideologies. Its foundation,
however, was co-operative trading in hundreds of locals and co-ops and
the elevator companies. This activity developed farmers' sense of collectivity, their ability to work together, and their loyalty to the organization.
It instilled self-confidence and suggested, in its successes, that a more co-
operative and less competitive society could truly be realized.

Farmers first articulated their co-operative ethos through helping
each other. 'As to the aims of this local,' wrote one secretary, 'the first
object ... is the working up of a spirit of co-operation and fraternity
among members.' Farmers practised this ethic through activities such as
'co-operative gopher poisoning' or helping to load each others' railway
cars to avoid demurrage fines. Supplying fellow members with seed
before selling elsewhere or collectively pressuring the government was
also called co-operation.[64] Even the building of a UFA hall could be
hailed as 'a triumph of our united effort.' One UFA association in the

southern part of the province sent crews north to obtain hay for the district. This action, too, evinced a 'spirit of co-operation.'[65]

Farmers also applied co-operative discourse to gender relations. Rice Sheppard argued that UFA support for female suffrage revealed 'co-operation.' Once in the movement, farm women aimed to 'co-operate' with the UFA and other reform and women's organizations. At a tea hosted by the Calgary UFWA local and attended by members of the Women's Labour League, the Local Council of Women, the IODE, and the Women's Institute, 'the key note of the remarks was co-operation.' Mrs Sears of the UFWA 'particularly brought out the fact that although we differ on many points, yet we have much in common, and if we learn to work together with a common purpose and for a common cause, we must learn to emphasize our points in common.'[66]

Because of women's concern with children and education, many UFWA locals sought to 'co-operate' with school teachers. Describing one union's efforts to do so, a *Guide* editor commented that 'co-operation between parents and teachers is greatly to be desired and is all too often lacking. Co-operation in this, as in everything else, secures the best results.'[67]

Women also tried to instil a group ethos in youth through junior club work. 'Those who have grown ... in the fixed habits of a narrow individualism,' Irene Parlby explained, 'cannot be expected to throw themselves with any ardor into a movement which is the very antithesis of individualism. That is one reason why we urge the formation of junior branches, that the boys and girls may ... learn to ... co-operate.' Margaret Gunn, a prominent UFWA leader, believed that the junior UFA trained youth for 'future service in the new co-operative community.' In addition, farm women sought 'closer co-operation' with state agencies, including the Departments of Education and Extension. They even felt that 'co-operation' with 'non-English-speaking people' was a 'realizable ideal.'[68]

Many farmers were convinced that co-operation could be the animating principle of all relations – between ethnic and other groups, classes, races, churches, regions, nations, and the sexes. In the 1970s Gunn reminisced that she and other UFA/UFWA farmers had 'visualized society in all its ramifications across national boundaries, creeds, and tongues being transformed through the substitution of co-operative endeavor instead of competition as the dominating factor in society.' Moulded by Christian beliefs, 'co-operation' for many farmers was a fundamentally moral principle; its defining essence was 'unselfishness,' which, according to Irene Parlby, was the only hope for world peace. In 1918 she wrote:

Today the world is bleeding to death in its efforts to conquer a false ideal of nationalism, but the only true nationalism, the only true internationalism, is a spirit of mutual sympathy and understanding among all the people; in other words, the spirit of unselfishness which is the essence of the thing we call co-operation. Until we can bring about the birth of that new spirit among the nations, until we can grow it in our homes, our own communities, our own Dominion, [we might] as well cry out to the tides to cease their flowing ... as bid wars to cease![69]

UFA president Wood argued that the groups and nations of the world, once fully organized, would be forced to co-operate, the only alternative being mutual destruction.

Farmers never clearly described what a co-operative society would be like, and they differed in how they thought it would be created. Many liberals believed it would emerge from a truly competitive capitalism in which the market determined wages and prices without monopolistic interference. Most radicals felt it would require the nationalization of all utilities, banks, and major companies, while co-operative enthusiasts thought it would come through an economy dominated by co-ops.

Despite these differences, the prospect of inaugurating a more co-operative and less competitive society captivated farmers' imaginations. It gave them a sense of purpose and helped them to believe that their agenda would benefit all. This belief generated great energy and commitment, mobilizing farmers to work for the movement – and ultimately to take political action.

Co-operation shaped the Alberta farm movement. The Equity co-op failure encouraged the formation of the UFA; thereafter, co-operation built and later politicized the organization. Although farmers missed co-operative opportunities, co-operation appealed to their pocketbooks and bestowed confidence in the movement, an ethos of collectivity, a vision of a co-operative society, and a sense of excitement. These features attracted farmers to the movement, motivated them to work for it, and contributed to the agrarian revolt. Co-operation thus was integral to the development of the movement.

Chapter Seven

Education in the Movement

A thinking man cannot be kept in slavery.[1]

W.J. Tregillus

Education, and farmers' belief that through it they could solve their collective problems and reform society, helped to form, build, and politicize the movement. Farmers used various types of formal and informal education, including that supported by corporations and the state, for these purposes.

Farmers' commitment to self-education reflected a European and North American popular tradition. Since the early nineteenth century, non-elites had studied their economic and political difficulties and sought solutions in farm, co-operative, socialist, labour, and church organizations. This practice and the rise of mass education fostered a widely held belief in learning for self-improvement. The Grange, the taproot from which many North American farm associations developed, was very committed to education 'for ourselves and for our children.'[2]

Education helped to form the pre–United Farmers of Alberta (UFA) farm movement. The *Edmonton Bulletin* became the first major agrarian educational agency in Alberta. It described the evils of the CPR, the grain trade, and other monopolies; followed the early western farm movement; and admonished farmers to establish co-operatives. Moreover, it supported the Edmonton Agricultural Society, from which many farm leaders emerged, and the Patrons of Industry. It also provided coverage of later Alberta farm organizations and a forum in which farmers could air their views. In these ways, the *Bulletin* contributed to the development of the early movement.

The pre-UFA farm associations had educational objectives, albeit limited ones. The Edmonton Agricultural Society was devoted to farm instruction. The Patrons of Industry introduced farmers to independent political action. The Alberta Farmers' Association taught them about pressure politics and how to improve their production and marketing. The Society of Equity indoctrinated farmers about organization, controlled marketing, government ownership, and a farmer-labour alliance. Through such education, these early organizations brought farmers into the movement and helped in its formation.

Education subsequently built the UFA and the United Farm Women of Alberta (UFWA). The organization's wide-ranging educational goals, stemming from its predecessors' varying agendas, attracted many farmers, stimulating the growth of the UFA/UFWA. At the same time, members were motivated to build the movement as they developed their critical faculties and belief in education. Expressing this belief, W.J. Tregillus declared that 'knowledge is power, gives light, independence, and freedom, while lack of knowledge – ignorance – is weakness, darkness, dependence, and bondage.'[3] Farmers like Tregillus felt that through education they could solve their community, economic, and political problems.

The unions were the foundation of UFA/UFWA education; some locals did little besides educate members. Unions were 'schools of progress' – 'the greatest little thinkeries you ever saw.' At meetings, usually held once or twice a month, farmers 'secured education and information which would otherwise be out of their reach'[4] on subjects such as farm husbandry, community questions, laws, co-operation, economics, the farm movement, and civics. Women's locals studied these and other matters, including health, schools, child rearing, and household efficiency. In the Grange tradition, the only forbidden topics before 1912 were religion and 'party politics.' Yet who could say where party politics began and legitimate education about the 'evil effects of legislation'[5] ended?

Locals used many means to educate. Most often, farmers simply discussed issues, listened to presentations, or held debates. Some locals developed unique educational strategies. Two UFA unions exchanged speakers, and one UFWA local gathered articles from newspapers and magazines for discussion. Another UFWA union used its roll-call as an educational device. Its secretary reported that 'in May each member answered her name by telling briefly of some labor saving idea which she had tried and found helpful. In June we each answered with a current event, and it is surprising how interesting and helpful this can be made and how much general knowledge can be gathered in a few minutes.'[6]

Unions also studied books and material that central office provided, including brochures on specific subjects and routine circulars. The latter contained news of general interest, resolutions other locals had passed, and articles such as those written by the UFA legal department to inform farmers about 'matters of law pertaining to everyday business.'[7] Questions and the department's answers also appeared in the circulars.

The partially realized aim of UFA/UFWA education was to enlighten farmers and teach them to think and express themselves clearly. Although limits remained to farmers' understanding of issues, local secretaries often noted that previously quiet members, having gained knowledge and self-assurance, contributed credibly to discussions. To help women, who were especially unaccustomed to public speaking, some UFWA unions used methods like those of the Blackie local, which got women to talk 'by such devices as putting under a sandwich a little slip of paper on which was written a subject such as "Gardening," "The best food for chicks" ... and it was explained that each lady was expected to say a few words on the subject of her paper. This ... [made] members more confident of their speaking ability.'[8]

UFA/UFWA picnics could also educate. Many featured prominent UFA/UFWA leaders, who spoke on the movement's work. In addition, farmers shared ideas at picnics. Sometimes they 'talked crops and politics until the speaking began from the platform.'[9]

Co-operation was a further source of education. Literature and UFA/UFWA co-operative enthusiasts taught farmers about co-op principles. Farmers also learned from co-operative experience. Dealing with wholesalers, manufacturers, and bankers brought them into 'contact with many of the causes' of their 'oppression.' Moreover, co-operation 'educated' them about 'better business methods.' One co-op had members accompany livestock shipments so that they could understand co-operative marketing.[10]

Farmers frequently 'emphasized the educational benefits' of conventions.[11] At the annual UFA/UFWA conventions and those of the secretaries and district and constituency associations, delegates took information from the addresses and discussion back to their locals. Owing to their importance, the minutes and reports of the general conventions were widely distributed.

Farmers got 'lots of good education' from the *Grain Growers' Guide*, the official organ of the three main western farm organizations. The *Guide* had articles on every topic concerning farmers, from co-operation to reform nostrums to national affairs, as well as letters to the editor. Additionally, each prairie association had a section in which it published notices, articles, circulars sent to the unions, and local secretaries' reports. During the war, other sections appeared that contained reports from locals of the three prairie women's associations and articles and letters by western women dealing with issues of particular interest to them. By 1920 the *Guide*'s Alberta circulation was 22,000, despite occasional complaints about insufficient space for Alberta news and lack of democratic control of editorial policy.[12]

Paul Sharp and W.L. Morton argue that the *Guide* and the farm movement indoctrinated farmers. Strictly speaking, indoctrination means convincing persons to espouse beliefs unquestioningly by discouraging them from thinking critically or considering opposite views. In this sense, farmers were indeed indoctrinated to believe, despite contrary evidence available at the time, that grain prices fell sharply after harvest and that speculators used futures trading to filch producers' profits.[13] The movement taught farmers these 'truths,' without presenting all the facts, to highlight the evils of the grain trade and farmers' heroic efforts, through organization, to protect themselves. It could be said that E.J. Fream and James Speakman indoctrinated farmers to endorse co-operative credit rather than state loans, although their arguments were not exactly indoctrination, since both men tried to present the case for government loans, while proponents of such loans were free to argue their position in the *Guide* and conventions.

Naturally, farmers opposed indoctrination by corporate interests. The 1913 UFA convention believed that those interests were promoting militarism and high tariffs through misleading information in the press and that they were causing schools and colleges to hire protectionist instructors who taught 'false' economics. The convention committed members to inform the executive of any such indoctrination they discovered.[14]

Farmers tried, with some success, to avoid indoctrination within the movement by encouraging the expression of different opinions. *Guide* editor George Chipman published material that challenged his position, including letters by land speculators and tariff protectionists, and he gave the Canadian Manufacturers' Association space to air its views. Chipman did not indoctrinate farmers by allowing only one perspective. Nor did the UFA editor of the *Guide*'s Alberta page; commenting on a letter on that page, he argued that 'the more criticism ... we receive the better it will be for the association.' Such criticism of UFA/UFWA leaders' and others' ideas appeared in every edition of the *Guide*. The locals and conventions also invited dissent, believing that 'dissatisfaction is the law of progress' and that 'only by contradiction can we see all sides of a question in full and decide with full knowledge.'[15]

The locals, conventions, and the *Guide*, then, provided a 'free social space'[16] in which farmers openly discussed issues and came to a consensus, which prompted them to build the movement. By learning about and agreeing on key questions, they were motivated to recruit new members and support the UFA/UFWA to bring about the changes they desired. That they were sometimes wrong did not hurt the movement; what mattered was that they felt they were right and knew that fellow producers, in Alberta and across the West, stood with them.

Farmers used all kinds of education, including that supported by outside agencies, to build the movement. Jeffrey Taylor argues that state education weakened agrarian radicalism in Manitoba.[17] This debatable thesis has little application to Alberta, where farmers showed considerable agency in educational matters. Business- and state-supported education may, in a few respects, have dulled Alberta farmers' radical edge, but they employed these and other forms of education primarily for their own purposes, including for protest.

Alberta farmers had come to believe, partly from reading immigration and railway propaganda, that the West was a region of agricultural prosperity. They used this image for their own purposes, initially to attract prospective settlers and UFA/UFWA members to their districts. Then, as they suffered economically, they blamed governments and corporations for preventing them from profiting from their rich crops and other products. Moreover, as some realized that they had been induced by 'highly rose-colored literature' to settle in Alberta, they demanded state aid.[18]

Farmers also reacted strongly to state and business propaganda that articulated the agrarian myth. They were neither flattered nor pacified; they responded by demanding change. 'If the farmers are the backbone of the country ... as the politicians tell us,' John Glambeck snapped, 'why then are not conditions made more bearable for the farmers?'[19]

As they did with state and corporate propaganda, farmers used Chautauquas for their own purposes. Originating in the United States, Chautauquas were travelling tent meetings supported by 'personally interested business and professional men' that offered high-quality oratory, music, drama, and other entertainment. The programs were designed to educate audiences about science, literature, art, history, sociology, and government. There were forty meetings in the Canadian West in 1917 and about twenty in Alberta in the following year. Whatever the interests of the organizers and businessmen involved, Chautauquas became, to an extent, UFA/UFWA events. They required much local work and sponsorship, which UFA/UFWA members provided,[20] and UFA president Wood was a keynote speaker at some fifty western Chautauquas in 1918. He preached his unorthodox social theory, declaring that the 'false laws of ... competition and autocracy ... have been the ... base of civilization ... and until they are wiped out, there can be no perfect society.' His addresses were a 'stimulant to our organization,' especially since UFA unions were allowed to use Chautauqua tents after to recruit new members. In 1921 UFA unions around Medicine Hat organized an independent Chautauqua, which had music, recitations, dialogues, and lectures, but the 'most successful feature' was debates between locals.[21]

A.E. Ottewell, director of the University of Alberta Department of Extension, spoke at the Medicine Hat Chautauqua. This department had the greatest educational influence of any government agency on the UFA/UFWA. It did not, however, have the conservative effect that Taylor argues the state had on Manitoba agrarianism. Rather, farmers used the department's resources for their own purposes.

University of Alberta Extension work began in 1912 amid controversy about the need for the university and its location and during an attempt to establish a rival institution in Calgary. The Department of Extension was formed to gain support for the university by showing its benefit for all Albertans – thus ensuring its survival. Since the department needed public approval, its material had to be popular; it had no interest in trying to impose a non-radical agrarian ideology on farmers. In fact, the Faculty of Agriculture was not created until 1915, and its role in Extension work was minor until well after the war. The Extension Department therefore, unlike its counterparts in other provinces, gave farmers the broad education they wanted on a variety of topics.[22]

The department had a major educational impact in Alberta. During its 1914–15 session, it reached an estimated 50,000 people through its various activities; by 1920 it was reaching almost 140,000 people. Some 260 lectures were given to 28,000 people in 1914–15 alone. Although department members gave most of the talks, which covered social, historical, literary, scientific, and other topics, the speakers included

J.S. Woodsworth, the future leader of the Co-operative Commonwealth Federation. The department also produced a weekly bulletin of news and information and issued booklets, including 2,000 copies in 1916–17 of 'The Legal Status of Women' by Henrietta Edwards of the National Council of Women.[23] A number of UFWA locals used this pamphlet to learn about and protest the status of their members.

In addition, the department loaned travelling libraries of thirty to forty books, including history, science, and travel books, biographies, works of literature, and texts on geography and rural life. In the year ending 30 June 1921 sixty UFA and twenty-six UFWA locals borrowed such libraries. UFA/UFWA unions were 'the principal agency for serving their communities with library facilities.' Starting in 1914, an open-shelf service provided pamphlets on current events and books on science, social science, education, rural life, and farming. By 1916 the open shelf also issued study guides on topics such as children, home economics, rural problems, and immigration. It was so popular that the women of the Saskatchewan Grain Growers' Association asked their government to establish a similar program.[24]

The Saskatchewan women also asked their university to lend material for debates, as the University of Alberta Department of Extension was doing. This service, which was the most important of the department's services for the UFA/UFWA, was unique in Canadian higher education, and it made the Alberta 'state's' influence on the farm movement unique. None of the debate packages has survived, but they apparently 'attempted a balanced argument' on a wide range of social, economic, and political issues. UFA/UFWA locals held thousands of debates based on department material. In the three sessions starting in 1914, 638, 898, and 955 packages were sent out, many to UFA/UFWA unions. The fourteen most-requested packages in order of preference in the 1915–16 session were on women suffrage, the war, rural life, the tariff, compulsory military training, consolidated rural schools, home economics, science, literature, capital punishment, magazines, education, debating, and co-operation.[25]

Some Extension packages may have worked against UFA/UFWA radicalism, principally those dealing with rural sociology and agricultural and home economics. These topics promoted a liberal-conservative agrarianism, but they were not frequently requested and thus cannot have had much influence.[26] On the other hand, the absence of material on some radical proposals may have made alternatives appear more attractive. Without a package on government loan programs, for example, the one on co-operative credit may have convinced some farmers to prefer this solution over the New Zealand state loan plan, which W.R. Ball advocated.

Other packages may have influenced some farmers to support reforms such as consolidated schools, although the main effect of department material was to arm farmers with arguments in favour of their existing beliefs. Packages like those on women's suffrage and tariffs served this purpose. Others, such as the ones on co-operative trading, provided practical tips. Farmers used still other packages to strengthen their commitment to measures opposed by the the 'state,' such as prohibition and direct legislation. Such packages and others, including those on government railways and the limitation of inheritance, helped farmers to study their political program – the Farmers' Platform. The UFWA executive informed members that information on some of its 'planks can be obtained through the Department of Extension.' Overall, department debating material was less a means by which the state indoctrinated farmers and more a resource they used for their own ends. It is significant that while studying packages pertaining to their Platform and debating political issues with packages such as 'parliamentary vs. presidential government,'[27] farmers rejected the party system and called for a new polity.

Farmers also learned to farm more effectively. This was agrarian tradition; the Grange had made 'instruction in the art and science of husbandry' a major aim. With the same end in view, the Alberta Farmers' Association was involved in seed fairs and farm animal shows, and its constitution, like that of the UFA, required members to discuss 'the production ... of grain and livestock.' UFA officer Daniel Warner invoked this clause when speaking to locals on moisture conservation.[28] Other UFA leaders sometimes wrote articles for the *Guide* or other periodicals about farm production and suggested related topics for discussion. Central office occasionally included notes on the subject in its circulars.

It was not a case of leaders trying to convince a slovenly rank and file to adopt modern farming methods; farmers were keen to learn new techniques, and by helping them to do so, the UFA/UFWA attracted new members. In 1910 general secretary E.J. Fream responded to many enquiries for 'information relating to agriculture, from the growing and harvesting of flax ... to securing rules for the holding of plowing matches.' Unions heard papers and lectures and held debates and discussions on every agricultural topic. They also formed livestock and agricultural societies and held fairs. One local wanted to see 'articles ...

appear in THE GUIDE on such problems as ploughing vs. discing for a second crop on breaking.'[29]

Ideology determined the importance producers ascribed to farm improvement. Believing strongly in self-help, liberals viewed agricultural efficiency as an individual, if not a moral, responsibility and a key determinant of farm income. In contrast, radicals, such as W.J. Tregillus, generally felt that even if farmers adopted the latest methods they would not benefit much because of corporate economic and political control. Still, Tregillus did not consider agricultural education unimportant.[30]

Many farmers looked to and used the state to help them to improve production. UFA locals lobbied for experimental and demonstration farms and for schools of agriculture, and they obtained literature from these institutions and from the Department of Extension. They also held government-sponsored seed fairs and institute meetings. Along with UFWA locals, they secured government agricultural experts as speakers and visited demonstration trains. The 1918 UFA convention called for county agent farm instructors.[31]

Farmers' autonomous use of state and corporate expertise was particularly evident in their reaction to the mixed-farming gospel preached by the press, railways, departments of agriculture, and politicians. Parts of Alberta were well suited to mixed agriculture, but many farmers, especially those on the plains, found it uneconomical to diversify as much as the experts suggested. Therefore, they did so only to the extent it was useful.[32]

The experts initially had more luck convincing farmers to adopt the methods of the Dry Farming Congress. Organized in the United States in 1906, the Congress, which was supported by boards of trade and railways, met annually in western cities to discuss dry-farming techniques and to hold grain fairs. Those attending included politicians and representatives of farm and state agricultural bodies. The UFA was favourable towards the Congress, especially when Alberta won prizes in 1911 and Lethbridge hosted the 1912 Congress. Farmers applied the dry-farming methods of the Congress and various state agencies; the methodology was familiar and seemed to work in most years.[33] But as drought became entrenched in parts of southern Alberta after 1916, many farmers lost faith in dry farming and called for irrigation. Once again, they used an educational resource for their own ends: when its ideas held promise, they implemented them; when those ideas began to fail, they looked for alternatives.

Educational agencies, then, including those supported by the state

'Swat the Flies First,' by Arch Dale. *Grain Growers' Guide*, 24 Nov. 1915, 6. This cartoon suggests that farmers were not brainwashed by corporations or government agencies to believe that better farm production and the adoption of certain methodologies would solve all their economic problems. ·

and business, did not unduly influence farmers to adopt new techniques. Like other business people, most farmers believed that increased efficiency boosted profits, and, like many businessmen, they used government services to improve their operations. In particular, they sought practices that could help them to avoid losses. And while they knew that technique would help only so much, nothing could be gained from poor farming. It was also evident that bad farmers were worse off than good ones.

Farmers were further advised about farm practice by the University of Alberta Faculty of Agriculture, which was established in 1915; by the six provincial schools of agriculture, three of which opened in 1913; and by the Calgary-based *Farm and Ranch Review*. As many North American agricultural colleges did, these agencies admonished farm men and women to adopt industrial methods of production, management, and marketing in their respectives spheres.

This emphasis on business efficiency, rather than government intervention or independent politics, as the solution for farmers' problems challenged agrarian radicalism; however, its effect on the UFA/UFWA was not great. Many farmers read the *Review*, but it was not the movement's official organ; and while many farmers sought information from the schools of agriculture and the Faculty of Agriculture, only a few hundred students each year attended them before the 1920s,[34] and few were UFA/UFWA members. Fewer still became movement leaders. The state did not control or tone down the UFA/UFWA through agricultural education in the period under study.

At the same time, farmers learned some concepts taught in agricultural colleges by studying the country life movement in books and the UFA/UFWA. But as they did with other educational sources, farmers used country life ideas for their own purposes.

The country life movement of the early twentieth century began in the United States and soon crossed the border. Its advocates included agricultural instructors, journalists, teachers, businessmen, clergymen, and farmers. Believing the agrarian myth that farmers were the moral and economic basis of a nation, country lifers feared the consequences of rural depopulation. They argued that rural decline stemmed from poor farm husbandry and management, overwork and isolation, exploitation by middlemen and monopolies, bad legislation, and a lack of credit, amenities, and entertainment. Moreover, parents were not meeting the needs of youth, churches were paying insufficient attention to the social needs of rural communities, and, above all, schools were educating children away from the farm.[35]

Country life solutions included surveys to assess problems and formulate plans; agricultural education and efficiency; co-operative trading and credit; improved rural roads, facilities, and services; agrarian organization; and labour-saving devices. Parents were to provide social occasions for youth and give them a stake in the farm. Churches were to federate or work together, stress rural reform, and serve as social centres. Schools were to organize gardens and teach nature study to create interest in rural living. They were to be vocationally oriented, teaching home economics and all subjects in relation to agriculture. Consolidated schools would best facilitate these reforms.[36]

Country life ideas became prominent in the UFA/UFWA starting in the war years. The slowing of immigration raised fears about rural stagnation – a key country life concern – especially as the exodus began from the dry belt in the late 1910s and the 1920s. Farmers also were aware of the national trend towards urbanization and believed that it would increase their tax burden and weaken their political power. Country life ideology built the movement by attracting farmers hoping to reverse these patterns.

Many locals studied country life subjects. General secretary P.P. Woodbridge recommended discussion topics based on the principles advocated by Horace Plunkett, the widely respected Irish agrarian reformer: better farming, better business, and better living. The Canadian Council of Agriculture's study guide, used by many UFA locals, suggested similar themes as 'proposed solutions' for the 'country life problem.'[37] Better farming meant employing the latest methodology. Better business meant effective farm management: farm men would allocate resources efficiently and keep accounts; women would keep records of household expenditures and organize their housework along the lines of a well-run factory in order to conserve labour power. Better business also meant improved marketing, applying the laws of rural economics, and trading co-operatively. Better living meant enhanced social opportunities and, especially, rural school reform.

Consistent with country life teaching, UFA/UFWA farmers believed that the 'whole of the rural problem' stemmed from inadequate schooling. School conditions in rural Alberta left much to be desired. Most schools were ill equipped; and most teachers were poorly paid, taught several grades in a single room, and received little support from parents and trustees. Many were inadequately trained or left before the end of term. Partly as a result, as late as 1917 only about 10 per cent of rural students attended high school compared with 60 per cent of urban pupils.[38]

In line with the country life movement, a majority of UFA/UFWA farmers, unlike many unorganized farmers in Canada and the United States, believed that consolidated schools would solve such problems. They would be better equipped and could afford good teachers, who would instruct graded classes, including high school classes. A law was passed in 1913, in response to UFA requests, to provide for consolidated schools in districts that voted for them. Following Manitoba, where the consolidation movement was strongest in the Canadian prairies,[39] Alberta had twenty-eight consolidated districts in operation by the end of 1916; by early 1920 it had sixty-four. Starting in 1919, the province also provided loans for teacher training and grants to encourage high school instruction and the construction of teacherages and two-room schools – measures approved of by the UFWA.[40]

The UFA/UFWA also called for greater regulation and centralization of education. The 'state' did not impose these conditions on farmers; they wanted them, partly to ensure that ethnic minorities received adequate English instruction and largely because they believed they would promote better education. Alberta farmers demanded more thorough and frequent inspection of schools and higher teacher qualifications. Like other prairie farmers, they also requested stricter attendance laws,[41] while many sought municipal rather than local school boards. Farm women were glad when the province improved teaching standards and inspection in 1920, but they requested 'more and closer' inspection. The year before, the UFWA proposed the 'standardization or nationalization of education with uniform text books.'[42]

Since many UFA/UFWA school reformers were or had been teachers, they endorsed most of the agenda of the Teachers' Alliance, the provincial association of teachers. Some farmers even supported the idea of higher salaries to attract better teachers to rural schools, though they generally opposed the Alliance request for a minimum salary, preferring that remuneration be based on service and qualifications. To pay for higher costs of education, they proposed a school tax on all land.[43]

Like country lifers everywhere, UFA/UFWA farmers requested curriculum changes. They called for nature study, since 'the love of nature is the first qualification for a happy agriculturalist.' They wanted practical farm instruction, including school demonstration gardens, and teachers who could prepare pupils for rural life and instil in them a sense of 'the dignity of the science by which they live.'[44] UFA/UFWA school reformers also espoused the 'new education,' which sought a 'curricular shift from classical to practical and scientific training.' One farmer argued that a rural high-school program 'must be rooted in the agricultural community.' He suggested that instead of forcing students to learn 'dead languages and "cram" history, classics, and higher mathematics,' schools should 'instruct the boys in animal husbandry, field husbandry, economics, sociology, farm mechanics, and farm management, and instruct the girls in domestic science, home economics, home nursing, and all of the other phases of everyday rural life.'[45]

UFA/UFWA country lifers believed that all subjects in rural schools should relate to farm life. Leona Barritt proposed that rural teachers be given a book applying lessons about length, area, and volume to objects such as silos, grain elevators and bins. Barritt also supported 'child centred' education and John Dewey's idea that children should learn by doing. She endorsed the Ontario system because it taught agriculture

without texts and considered individual development 'of more importance than the giving of information.' She and the UFWA also felt that
students should learn about country life ideals.[46]

Such school reform agitation built the movement by attracting farmers seeking to keep youth – on whom the quality of rural life and the
strength of the UFA/UFWA would depend – from leaving the land.
With the same goal in mind, UFWA country lifers provided recreation
for young people, argued that they should have ownership in the
farm,[47] and organized youth competitions in farm production.

Women also believed, in country life fashion, that education in the
junior UFA/UFWA would give youth 'a correct vision of farm life,' so
they would 'accept farm life as a permanent calling.' The junior section
evolved from rural youth clubs formed during the war as literary or
debating societies. A UFWA officer was appointed to oversee these clubs
in 1916, and a committee on young people's work was created two years
later. Little was done to recognize the clubs officially, however, until
1919, when the UFWA convention and UFA executive adopted a junior-
section constitution. By early 1920 some twenty junior locals, having
officers and holding regular meetings, had reported to central office; a
year later, there were some sixty junior branches, some same sex, some
mixed sex, with a membership of about 1,200, ranging in age from
about ten to twenty-five.[48]

A youth culture emerged among the juniors, based on community
service, the development of citizenship and leadership, and the aims of
the movement. It also included a motto, a watchword, a yell, a slogan, a
pledge, official colours, and songs such as:

> We want boosters for our army;
> There's a work for you to do!
> Help push on this worthy cause;
> Join us now without a pause:
> Come and be a jolly, joyous junior too![49]

Juniors held debates, spelling matches, and skating parties; did charity
and local work; put on socials, concerts, dances, and plays; played sports
and games; acquired sporting and leisure equipment; camped; hiked;
sewed; formed bands; raised gardens; and studied various subjects,
including scientific agriculture and household economics.

The highlight of the year for the junior section was Farm Young People's Week, an annual conference first held in 1919 at the initiative of

the UFWA. Each year 100 to 200 'boys' and 'girls' age sixteen and over attended for recreation, education, and to acquire a 'genuine farm culture.' The 1919 group heard talks on rural life and citizenship, some given by UFA/UFWA leaders, and on literature, spiritual values, and nature study. In addition, the 'boys' were given farm instruction and the 'girls' were offered folk-dancing lessons. Later conferences had a similar program and included junior UFA/UFWA business meetings. The 1920 meeting elected a junior committee to assist an adult committee in directing the junior section. The 1921 meeting created an official junior organization that replaced the junior committee with an elected junior board of an equal number of male and female directors. A president and vice-president, Lawrence Kindt and Donald Cameron, also were elected. They organized several locals later in that year,[50] although UFWA women formed most junior locals.

UFWA women felt that the junior UFA had great educational value. They believed that through meetings juniors learned 'to express themselves clearly, definitely, and concisely' and that by means of papers, talks, and debates they gained 'invaluable training for future leadership.' Moreover, they hoped that the junior section would provide 'a continuous army of men and women trained to take up the responsibilities of leadership in the local communities, at the head of our organization, in the political fields.' Margaret Gunn argued that junior activity inculcated a co-operative ethos. 'All this co-operative study, co-operative work, co-operative play,' she explained, 'is merely building for the future co-operative community. Boys and girls trained in this group activity are learning ... how to work with others to mutual advantage, are practicing the co-operative principle, and are discarding the competitive system.'[51]

To teach business skills to juniors, women organized 'dollar contests,' giving each member of a junior branch a dollar with which to make as much money as possible through farm-related activities. Whoever made the most by a set date won. One such contest apparently taught juniors

that thinking before investing, that making a definite plan before starting brought the best returns. It taught them that only by keeping track of everything can the real results of their labor be ascertained. They learned that by purchasing a small quantity of pure seed the crop turned out better than when a larger quantity of just any old seed had been sown. It taught them that one who grew his potatoes under the proper conditions ... and dug them when new potatoes were a luxury received more for his crop than if he left them ... until everybody was digging them.[52]

All such junior educational activity built the movement. It drew in young people while attracting and inspiring women who, imbued with country life ideology, sought to keep youth on the land. 'If country life makes a powerful appeal to those of teen age,' Gunn promised, 'it is not likely they will be drawn to the city by a "tinsel show and a' that."'[53]

Country life ideology and education also politicized the movement, despite their anti-political thrust. Farmers quickly realized that many country life reforms required political action, even independent action. Government aid was needed to establish the schools and rural facilities the country life movement called for; sweeping tariff reform was required to enable farmers to buy the labour-saving devices, household conveniences, and farm machinery that, according to country lifers, farmers needed in order to be efficient; lower tariffs were necessary if farmers were to have the time and money to provide youth with healthy recreation so they would not drift to the cities.

Country life education also politicized farmers by bolstering their self-confidence. It convinced them they were scientific 'professionals' and encouraged them to demand reforms consistent with this status. Furthermore, to the extent that they met the requirements of country life teaching, they found its promises wanting. They had improved rural schooling and educated youth about the benefits of farm life; they had built a great co-operative movement; they had organized themselves effectively; they had become better farmers and business persons – but they still were not prosperous and contented with country life; young people still left the land. Farmers soon concluded that direct political action was needed to realize their country life ideals.

New educational sources also politicized the movement. In 1919 the *Western Independent* became the voice of the UFA Political Association, a body that oversaw the organization's political activities. Edited by William Irvine, the *Independent* influenced many farmers to favour direct political action. UFA support for the paper ended, however, after the Political Association was dismantled in early 1920. At that time, the central office began preparing bulletins for the directors that raised their political consciousness by criticizing the old parties and highlighting attacks on the farm movement. In the following year, an educational department was created that did research, prepared pamphlets and articles, and became a political arm of the organization. During the Medicine Hat by-election, it took charge of publicity for the local UFA constituency association. During the provincial election, it devoted itself almost entirely to politics, providing information on provincial affairs and electoral conduct. For the federal election of that year, it sent out a description of the Elections Act and handled correspondence about the election, while issuing pro-UFA political literature.[54]

After deciding to enter politics in 1919, the UFA/UFWA emphasized – as did the farm movement across the country – the need for education in citizenship. This meant that farmers should become informed about social, economic, and political matters and their responsibilities as voters. They did so through formal study, political skits, and the use of parliamentary procedure in their locals. They also acquired ideas about citizenship from the teachings of leaders such as Henry Wise Wood and from their experience with delegate democracy. The latter taught them that if they wanted grassroots democratic control, they had to select and instruct their political representatives and pay their campaign expenses, just as they chose and instructed their convention delegates and paid their expenses. UFWA leaders felt that education in citizenship was especially necessary for women, given their lack of electoral and political experience:

> Farm women for centuries had remained out of public life and suddenly found themselves possessed of all citizenship rights and responsibilities ... How were women to be educated to meet these responsibilities intelligently? Only by participation in public life and the forming of groups to discuss and consider matters of vital importance to them ... Here was a great ... training school for citizenship.

Lucy Peterson, district director for Lethbridge, admonished women to educate themselves about 'our public administration and present day problems so that when we vote we can register an opinion instead of just writing an X beside a name.'[55]

The UFA/UFWA also educated farmers for direct political action. Political conventions, described by Henry Wise Wood as political 'schools,' were held first in the federal constituencies in 1919 and later in the provincial ridings. The delegates, from locals within the constituency boundaries, debated how to take political action, when to nominate a candidate, and other political and non-political matters. According to Wood, the conventions were 'designed to educate the people in regard to the political problems and the co-operative methods necessary' to solve them. He promised that if farmers attended every year, they would 'develop an understanding of political affairs and a capacity for dealing with them a hundred times more rapidly' than they ever had done before.[56]

UFA political candidates were educated for their tasks through these conventions and in other ways. Most had experience in local and school politics, and many had been prominent movement leaders. The first UFA premier, Herbert Greenfield, was a founder and president of the Union of Alberta Municipalities, a school trustee, chairman of the local council of his district, vice-president of the Alberta Educational Association, and in 1919 he was elected to the UFA executive. Like many farmers, Greenfield also received leadership training in his local. To some extent, many unions followed the practice of one woman's local in which 'the secretaries hold office for only one year. After they have had that experience, they will always take part in the proceedings. Half of our local is trained as leaders so that the affairs of the local are carried on whether our president or secretary is any good or not.' In the light of such experience and the UFA's decision to take political action, the 1919 secretaries' conventions suggested that central office advise the locals of the advantages of periodically changing their officers.[57]

Locals held mock elections to teach members about the electoral process and proportional representation. Some unions took a direct part in municipal elections. After 1918 most studied the Farmers' Platform and topics such as 'the political situation' or books such as J.D. Hunt's *The Dawn of a New Patriotism*. The results of women's education were evident in the Medicine Hat by-election. According to one observer, 'women took part in the campaign and proved to be successful campaigners. Workers in that campaign stated that each audience addressed was composed of women as well as men, and more than one speaker was questioned by women in an intelligent and frank manner. In many districts, women called special meetings in order to go over voters' lists to see that no names were omitted.'[58] Education had politicized the UFA/UFWA. It gave farmers the political know-how and confidence to take independent action.

Education developed the Alberta farm movement. It attracted farmers to the UFA/UFWA and its predecessors, helping to form and build the movement. It also built the movement by enabling farmers to come to a consensus on key issues, which prompted them to act. They used various educational agencies and ideologies, including those supported by the business community and the state, for their own purposes: to develop their agenda, to improve profits, to keep youth on the land, and to build the organization. Education ultimately politicized farmers, spurring them to take independent political action while training them for it.

Chapter Eight

The Politicizing of the Movement, 1919–1921

Ye farmers of this mighty land,
  Organize, oh, organize;
Its bulwark ever more to stand,
  Organize, oh, organize.
For with the flag of right unfurled,
In spite of darts against you hurled;
You still must feed this hungry world;
  Organize, oh, organize.[1]

Official UFA/UFWA campaign song

During the war, the Alberta farm movement was fully built. It gained a large membership and a women's section and developed its movement culture, which moved it towards direct politics. From 1919 to 1921 the United Farmers and Farm Women of Alberta (UFA/UFWA) was politicized. Farmers committed the organization to independent political action, were prodded to take such action by their culture and understanding of events, gained women's political support, created political structures, and launched the agrarian revolt – the movement's culmination.

It can be argued that a movement is pushed to attain a higher level of development when its members have 'rising expectations' that they can collectively overcome their problems and improve their lives and have made progress towards those ends until a setback reverses that trend, which makes them more determined to achieve their goals.[2] So it was with the UFA/UFWA by 1919. Its members had come to Alberta expecting a better life, and although they had encountered obstacles, they had gained unshakable confidence in both the Alberta and the larger farm movements and were convinced that the war had paved the way for a new society, a true democracy that they must inaugurate. Yet having accomplished so much before 1914, they had often been stymied during the war by governments and political parties that seemed either preoccupied with the war effort or hopelessly corrupt. Farmers responded with even greater resolve to see their aims realized, and in so doing, they brought on a new phase of movement development: its politicization.

The 1919 UFA convention made the fateful decision to allow direct UFA/UFWA political action. The resulting political excitement contributed greatly to the movement's incredible growth from some 18,000 UFA, UFWA, and junior members in early 1919 to about 37,500 by the end of 1921. In 1919 alone, UFA membership swelled from around 16,500 to over 25,000, while UFWA membership more than doubled from over 1,400 to 3,000. As of 31 December 1921, there were some 31,500 UFA, 4,500 UFWA, and 1,450 junior members.[3]

Believing that 'every additional member linked up with our great organization is another step toward success at the polls,' the movement made unprecedented recruiting efforts after the war. Progress was hampered in parts of southern Alberta, however, because crop failure and low product prices prevented many from paying membership dues and forced others to leave the area for good or to search for temporary wage work. Notwithstanding, UFA/UFWA support remained strong in southern constituencies, since hard times seemed to 'bring in more members and arouse keener interest.'[4] Southern Alberta farmers hoped that the UFA could organize a wheat pool and force governments to lower producers' costs and assist with irrigation. And were not diversion and a sense of community helpful in difficult times? The UFA/UFWA met these needs too. In the far north of the province, the movement benefited from new settlement, including that by veterans, although poor railway service ultimately hindered population and UFA/UFWA growth in the region.

While locals continued to do most of the recruiting, the central association played an increasingly important role. The directors formed many new unions after the war in concert with paid organizers and constituency association officers. The central also organized membership drives. During the 'fall drive' of 1920, which was held by all three prairie farm associations, a mass of unpaid canvassers in Alberta collected $6.00

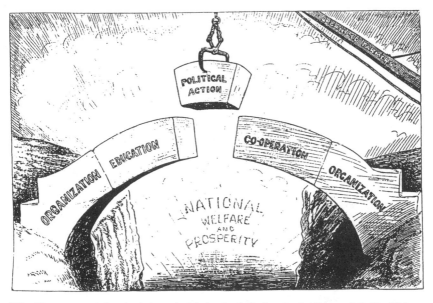

'The Keystone of the Arch,' probably by Arch Dale. *Grain Growers' Guide*, 28 Jan. 1920, 6. As this illustration implies, the politicizing of the movement, which began with the decision to take direct political action, was the final phase of development, and it rested on a foundation of movement building.

from individual farmers for a *Guide* subscription and membership in the UFA/UFWA and its political associations. 'I am going to make another call on some of the farmers,' one canvasser pledged, 'and am going to try again and again until I get them into the U.F.A.' While fully achieving its goal in only one Alberta constituency, the drive raised over $100,000 for the UFA/UFWA and secured many new members.[5]

Growth threatened democracy in the organization, but rank-and-file supremacy was maintained. That democratic control was temporarily weakened when UFA president Henry Wise Wood, not wanting radicals on the executive, convinced the 1919 convention to end the election of officers by proportional representation. The 1920 convention, however, reasserted its democratic prerogative by reintroducing the election of the executive on the proportional system. One delegate argued that it would have been 'impossible' for the leadership to manipulate the convention in that year, because 'it would be most difficult to find a set of men with more determination and intelligence.' The delegates, he boasted, 'as a rule had a good grasp of the question before the house and voted to the best of their judgement.'[6]

Further weakening post-war UFA democracy was the fact that many local resolutions were 'crowded out' of the convention or were 'handled too hurriedly.' A related problem was the 'growing tendency towards substitution of executive resolutions for ... several locals' resolutions.' Beginning in 1920, these difficulties were largely solved when the constituency conventions, at the UFA board's suggestion, screened and consolidated their locals' resolutions before submitting only relevant ones to the annual meeting.[7] Now, district conventions of local delegates, rather than the executive alone, determined which resolutions the general meeting would consider and in what form. Grassroots control over the annual convention had been maintained.

While preserving democracy in the UFA convention, farmers ensured that their political platforms were democratic. In 1919 William Irvine of the agrarian Non-Partisan League accused the Canadian Council of Agriculture of unilaterally drafting the Farmers' Platform and imposing it on farmers. Henry Wise Wood, who was president of the Council, immediately corrected 'Mr. Irvine, who had put us in the position of handing down a platform developed from above.' Wood pointed out that the Platform 'began to develop right in our own locals, and the best of the many ideas sent in were taken and were afterwards discussed and ratified at our convention.' The Council drafted planks consistent with resolutions passed by the four great farm associations of the West and Ontario and submitted the Platform and proposed amendments to the conventions, which made changes and additions. The UFA/UFWA provincial political platform was created by a similar process. Following a 1921 convention directive, a committee of delegates from the federal political associations – not the central executive – drafted a platform for members to discuss. The provincial constituency conventions later adopted the platform, in a few cases with slight amendments.[8] Farmers did not simply endorse their platforms; they constructed them democratically.

Farmers also took democratic political action, thanks to their post-war notion of citizenship. Before the war, most had felt that they could improve society and their own lot through the old parties. When this strategy proved ineffective, their belief in citizenship told them that to succeed politically they must get involved in every facet of the political process, which meant independent political action. They began by holding political conventions, first in federal and then in provincial constituencies, where at least 10 per cent of the locals requested them.[9] The delegates, representing individual unions, elected a chairperson and appointed committees, set and voted on an agenda, and formed a constituency association and elected its officers. Later conventions nominated political candidates and adopted a political program. Each association ran its candidate's campaign and financed its activities by assessing the locals in its constituency. Associations also appointed scrutineers and made sure that UFA voters got to the polls.

All this was done by the grassroots, not the leadership – farmers' notion of citizenship responsibility demanded nothing less. Wood spoke to the 1921 Medicine Hat federal constituency convention only after the delegates had chosen their candidate. He later described the impossibility of the central's controlling the 1921 UFA provincial election campaign and the role of democratic citizenship in what transpired:

> This provincial election was sprung in order to take us by surprise. We had no political organization in the ordinary sense of the word. But we had something better ... an intelligent citizenship ... The result was that when the election was announced, the people organized themselves. Within ten days, every constituency in the province had formed its own organization. I had nothing to do with this organization work, and the central had nothing to do with it. We could not have made a beginning on such an enormous task in such a short time. To say that the thing was handled from above is nonsense. Every local, every constituency, exercised a free and unhampered choice under the most democratic conditions. The central had no hand in the selection of candidates, and to say that I 'hand-picked' them is absurd. Why, half of them were men I had never heard of before the election.[10]

Farmers' commitment to citizenship and their experience with UFA/ UFWA democracy contributed to their belief that just as locals instructed delegates about how to vote at conventions, constituents should be able to 'dictate' to their elected members. And if constituents were to control representatives, members had to be free to vote against a bill without fear of defeating the government. This idea, popularized by the Non-Partisan League, became a plank in the UFA platform that made a 'powerful appeal to the electorate.'[11] It promised to break cabinet control and party discipline and render the 'elected representative answerable directly to the district organization that elected him.' Farmers also felt that UFA members should report to constituents after each legislative or parliamentary session, just as convention delegates reported to their locals. To provide further accountability, many UFA candidates, like UFA officers, signed recalls.[12]

While politicizing themselves by devising a new political model based on citizenship and UFA/UFWA experience, farmers demanded political reform consistent with their democratic beliefs. Radicals, in particular, supported civil rights and called for the repeal of the Wartime Elections Act, opposed the deportation of persons without trial, and condemned restrictions on freedom of the press. In concert with farmers across the country, the UFA/UFWA also requested Senate reform and the publication of campaign contributions. 'Tell me from what sources the secret campaign funds of the political parties in power come,' declared one future UFA MLA, 'and I will tell you what invisible forces control the government.'[13]

Reflecting this disdain for the old parties and their methods, the UFA/UFWA attracted many voters by eschewing mudslinging and trying to use reasoned arguments to focus on its program. Farmers were sick of 'partyism' and the tactics of professional politicians, and the UFA seemed to offer a refreshing new approach to politics. The conduct of Wood and UFWA president Irene Parlby during the 1919 Cochrane by-election, as described by Wood, appealed to many farmers:

> Now they [the *Calgary Herald*] suggest that Mrs. Parlby and myself at Cross-field gave a 'clean bill of health' to this government. Bless your heart, we are not veterinarians, and we did not examine it ... We went up there on another mission. We did say that the Honorable Chas. Stewart [the Liberal premier] was an honorable, upright citizen, doing the best he could under difficult circumstances, and I reiterate that. If I have got to tear down the character of an honorable man to build up something that I want, I am not going to build it up. If we have not got better material than personal slander, we had better, as a representative of the government at Edmonton told the U.F.A. convention in 1912, 'Go home and slop your pigs.'

In similar vein, a UFA director argued that Robert Gardiner won the Medicine Hat by-election partly because he 'discussed the issues involved and left out personality and recrimination.'[14]

Such political victories were dependent on the electoral support of women, which the UFA encouraged by working more actively to bring them into the organization, by giving them a measure of equality in the political movement, and by backing their post-war agenda. UFA men believed that the UFA/UFWA would train farm women to vote for their class and that their spiritual qualities would uphold the movement's ideals, keeping it from becoming materialistic.[15]

Therefore, while some men remained indifferent to recruiting women or 'did not know how,' UFA officers and unions organized unprecedented numbers of UFWA locals and persuaded many women to join the UFA. Some UFA unions also helped UFWA locals with financial and other aid. 'We owe our heartiest thanks to the men of the community,' wrote one UFWA secretary, 'who have always been ready with both the encouraging word and the open pocketbook.'[16]

In spite of these efforts, women's home duties, their inability to pay membership fees and limited access to transportation, the competition of other women's organizations, and sometimes the opposition of husbands kept UFWA membership well behind that of the UFA. Some women did not join the UFWA because there were too few of them to form a local or because they preferred to stay in UFA locals.[17] Many in the latter formed 'women's committees,' which received UFWA literature and did much the same work as UFWA locals.

There were unexpected benefits for the UFA in having women in the movement. Sometimes UFWA locals revived UFA unions by holding joint socials, which drew back old members and attracted new ones, and a few UFWA women organized UFA locals. Both sexes spoke of the organization as an integrated whole, not as two separate gender-based sections. Practically, this meant that women, being members of the one organization, whether the UFA or UFWA, could vote in UFA annual conventions, but men could not vote in UFWA conventions or join UFWA unions, even though 'one or two women's locals had been desirous of taking in men members.'[18]

Despite this different treatment of the sexes, the UFA, wanting women's support for UFA politics, granted them a measure of equality in the political movement. UFWA locals were given the same right as UFA locals enjoyed to elect delegates for the constituency political association conventions. Partly because of this provision, the proportion of prairie women attending such conventions was highest in Alberta, although UFWA locals were generally underrepresented compared with UFA locals, since many wives felt it 'next to impossible ... to leave their homes for the necessary length of time.' Nevertheless, women were elected to the position of vice-president in nine of the twelve political associations in 1919, and Emma Root was named to the UFA Provincial Political Association executive. Furthermore, starting in 1920, several associations appointed women to committees and elected an equal number of male and female directors.[19] All in all, given their comparatively small numbers in the organization, women were fairly well represented in the policial movement leadership, but they were not given top positions – if, in fact, they wanted them.

They were not, however, always happy with their status. Though not endorsed, a resolution presented to the 1920 UFWA convention called for the removal of the constitutional clause prohibiting the UFWA from petitioning governments 'independent of the central.' Moreover, women sometimes resented the fact that the UFA made decisions without their input. The 1920 Battle River UFA/UFWA constituency convention protested that the UFWA had not been consulted about the dissolution of the Provincial Political Association.[20]

Notwithstanding such complaints, women were generally satisfied with the UFA because, needing their political support, it lobbied for their agenda. The UFA endorsed women's requests for equal homestead, inheritance, divorce, and guardianship rights and for restrictions on a husband's right to dispose of property without his wife's consent. Additionally, the 1921 UFA convention approved a UFWA demand that men be held financially responsible for their illegitimate children. The very few UFWA resolutions not supported by the UFA after the war included a request for drought insurance and other requests dealing with relatively unimportant, non-gender issues. The UFWA accepted such screening and invited constructive criticism of its resolutions. Irene Parlby told the UFA board that women wanted their resolutions 'considered carefully by the men's convention'; they did not want the UFA to endorse them 'merely because the women had passed them.'[21]

UFWA respect and support for the UFA and the political movement were reinforced by conflicts with other women's groups. In 1919 the Graduate Nurses Association strongly opposed a UFWA proposal that nurses be trained and licensed as midwives for districts without doctors. The UFA, however, endorsed the UFWA proposal, strengthening farm women's belief that the organization would implement their agenda if elected. Their commitment to the UFA grew as the state-assisted Women's Institutes competed with the UFWA for members. Parlby maintained that opposition to the UFWA 'had been a determined and growing' Liberal policy that was 'dividing the women of the country into two hostile camps.'[22] The solution seemed to lie in backing UFA politics and turning out the government.

Farmers used gender discourse to encourage each other to do this.

Rice Sheppard argued that manliness required 'men' to take direct political action for their family and nation. 'God expects us to be men,' he asserted, 'and ... we are commanded to feed and care for our families ... Let us ... change conditions ... Let us be free from all party ties and prepare to stand as men to work for ... all the people ... Only by independent action can the peoples of our Dominion rise to the higher plane of justice.' UFWA leaders told women that they could 'house-clean' politics – a 'mess' men had created – and fulfil their prime duty of protecting the family by supporting the UFA political movement. Their lack of political entanglement would ensure success.[23]

Assumptions about gender shaped the movement's social ethic – its belief that the state must reform society – which politicized farmers as they concluded that their proposals required direct political action. Believing it was their social maternal duty, UFWA women helped the Red Cross to distribute clothes and raise money for southern Alberta drought victims. Such work – along with low product prices, short crops, and a sense that plutocrats had grown fat on the war – convinced farmers that governments should promote greater equality of condition. 'We are trying to build,' wrote one UFA officer, 'a democracy ... which ... will transform the economic status of the farmer, the worker, the tradesman, and will bring a fairer division of the wealth that is created.' To that end, the 1919 UFA convention prompted the Canadian Council of Agriculture to amend the Farmers' Platform to call for a 'sharply' graduated tax of up to 2 per cent on incomes of $2,000 per year, increasing to 50 per cent on incomes over $100,000. The UFA also opposed a proposed tax on small incomes.[24]

Influenced by women's desire to 'mother' society, farmers' social ethic moved them to endorse social welfare measures to protect the family. In 1919 the UFA supported a UFWA demand for mothers' pensions. When the province introduced an act to assist impoverished widows and the needy wives of insane men, the UFA/UFWA boards asked that deserted mothers and mothers with invalid husbands be eligible. The Battle River constituency convention urged governments to improve the condition of pregnant women and women with young children and demanded better screening and supervision of adoptive parents in order to protect adopted children.[25]

The obvious need of veterans for government aid did much to develop farmers' social ethic. The Farmers' Platform called for state insurance for high-risk unpensioned veterans, training for those unfit to return to their former occupations, and assistance for those wishing to farm. The UFA/UFWA generally did not want Ottawa to loan money to veterans to buy farm land, preferring that it commandeer land from speculators to provide homesteads for ex-soldiers and war nurses. In addition, the UFA requested veteran bonuses and monies for dependent parents of deceased soldiers, while the UFWA proposed generous pensions for disabled soldiers and their families.[26]

The UFA/UFWA became politicized as farmers felt that their proposals for veterans, taxation, and social welfare required independent politics, a conclusion reinforced by social gospel convictions. Farmers believed that political action would inaugurate the kingdom of God by ensuring that the state brought in reform. In a debate in the columns of the *Western Independent,* the organ of the UFA/UFWA political movement, most farmers agreed that Christianity could have a beneficial effect on the UFA/UFWA and society. One contributor argued emphatically that the UFA should 'enter religion the same as politics.' He declared that this policy would be 'all the better for religion, and if at the same time a larger element of religion enters the U.F.A., the benefit will be mutual.' He concluded that greater Christian influence in the movement would have a real impact on 'the legislation of the future.'[27]

Evangelicalism also politicized farmers, even though it suggested, in the words of Irene Parlby, that 'social evils were traceable to bad home conditions' and that moral teaching and healthy family living, more than legislation, would regenerate society.[28] What was wrong with politics, in Parlby's mind, was that there were not enough men 'of strong moral and independent characters in the legislatures at any one time.' The old parties hated persons of integrity, preferring 'the machine type of man or woman who will meekly keep to heel.' Only UFA political action would allow farmers to choose candidates for their 'moral worth, strength of character, and ability.'[29]

Evangelicals and, especially, social gospellers acquired what Franklin Foster calls a 'millennial-like vision of a possible future society.' Farmers' religious ideals, liberal ideas about social perfection, social-Darwinian notions about societal progress, faith in self-education, the reform ethos of the age, the UFA/UFWA's successes and growing power, and a desire to ensure that wartime successes were not in vain spawned this feeling that an ideal society was about to emerge from the old corrupt order. 'I believe we are entering the dawn of a new era,' declared W.T. Lucas, a future UFA MP, 'and that it is the desire of the United Farmers ... to act in sympathy with all other democratic forces in the spirit of true co-operation and go into the new day together.' Agrarian political successes heightened farmers' sense of expectancy. Referring to the United Farmers of Ontario victory in 1919, one local UFA secretary wrote that 'this should be an opportune time for holding "revival meetings." Interest in the organization is being much stimulated.'[30]

Foster contends that UFA/UFWA millennialism was mainly 'civil millennialism': man would build 'the new world; he would be following God's laws, but there would be no direct Divine intervention needed.' This was certainly the millennialism of Henry Wise Wood and William Irvine, who believed that God was synonymous with the natural laws driving social progress. Most farmers, however, felt that a personal God would help to usher in the new day. Still, Wood's use of biblical metaphors, his depiction of 'us' versus 'them' and of the conflict between good and evil, and his apocalyptic imagery reflected a general millennialist outlook that rang true to many farmers. Describing the impending struggle between the people and plutocracy, Wood declared:

> The conflict is just beginning, and the people will utterly fail unless they mobilize their forces and stand as a solid wall of citizenship in defence of their rights ... It will be the epic of ages. God will marshall and direct the forces of the people; Mammon, the forces of the beasts. Either Mammon will be overthrown and the beasts destroyed, or the people and the beasts both go down together and God stand alone on the wastes of social isolation.

This outlook and farmers' social gospel and evangelical beliefs contributed to the agrarian revolt. A quantitative study found that areas with 'high proportions of Protestants tended to give disproportionately strong support' to Progressive candidates, including UFA candidates.[31]

The revised Farmers' Platform also politicized the movement. Issued in late 1918 and called the 'New National Policy,' it was more than a farmer's wish list; it was a symbol of the movement, a rejection of things as they were, and a vision of what Canada could be. Organized farmers from Alberta to New Brunswick believed that the old National Policy benefited industrialists at the expense of the many, but that the New National Policy, with its low tariff, progressive taxation, and welfare planks, would help the masses; it was the country's first truly democratic program. Although the Canadian Council of Agriculture announced the Platform with 'no expectation that on the strength of it a demand for direct political action would be made,' its impact on the 1919 western farmers' annual conventions was striking, as noted in the *Guide* with some exaggeration:

> When the series of recommendations which constitute the Farmers' Plat-
> form ... were placed before the farmers' conventions of last winter, they
> were seized upon with avidity and made the basis for a new party move-
> ment. The delegates at those conventions, with united voice, declared that
> they had waited long enough upon the two old parties. If the measures
> advocated in the Farmers' Platform were to be realized at all, it was felt that
> steps must be taken to launch a new party which would be free from old
> centralized autocratic influences and whose elected representatives in par-
> liament would stand uncompromisingly by the New National Policy.

A UFA poem is suggestive of the Platform's politicizing effect on the movement:

> The platform that we now endorse
> Must rule the vast domain;
> Stand firm and fast, ye leaders all,
> For good and not for gain.
> Let party politicians be
> Submerged in farmers' laws;
> Democracy shall reign supreme
> For every noble cause.[32]

The policies of 'party politicians' further politicized farmers. During the war, the movement's lack of legislative success pushed farmers towards independent politics. After the UFA approved such action in 1919, the provincial Liberals, hoping to head off the new political movement, met many UFA/UFWA demands. But because of their culture and determination to justify UFA politics, farmers saw such responsiveness as expediency or evidence of agrarian political power, views that strengthened their political resolve. On the other hand, they condemned the government when it did not meet their requests. It was a no-win situation for the Liberals.

Largely at the UFA/UFWA's behest, the province improved rural schooling and spent millions on railways and telephones after the war. In 1921 a UFA demand that an oil pipeline bill include a common carrier clause prompted the bill's withdrawal. Responding to the UFA/ UFWA in the previous year, the government had granted equal intestate

inheritance rights for women and equal parental rights in the guardianship and estate of infants. These successes bolstered farmers' political
confidence, while the province's unwillingness to make wives' signatures
necessary for land transfers and its refusal to form a committee to oversee road contracts[33] sharpened the movement's political edge.

The government's handling of prohibition greatly raised farmers'
political consciousness. The UFA/UFWA demanded stricter enforcement of the law and control of abuses such as doctors' overprescribing
alcohol as medicine. Encouraged by the 1919 Volstead prohibition Act in
the United States, the 1920 UFA convention called for a plebiscite, as provided for by a federal statute, on the importation of liquor into the province. A plebiscite was held in that year in all three prairie provinces, and
the prohibitionists won – thanks to the support of the farm organizations
– but the majorities were much slimmer than they had been during the
war. The public was obviously growing weary of prohibition, and the
Alberta government was unwilling to fully impose the measure, suggesting to farmers that the Liberals 'should be thrown out, neck and crop.'[34]

The government's health policies brought farmers to the same conclusion. The influenza epidemic of 1918–19 had revealed 'the total
inadequacy of medical and nursing aid in the rural districts.' The UFWA
therefore asked the province to provide a short course in nursing and
yearly medical inspection of schools. Irene Parlby suggested that municipalities be permitted to hire doctors and nurses.[35] The UFA called for
the enforcement of quarantines, higher hospital grants, a cap on medical fees, and state-funded doctors for outlying areas. The government
responded by sending out more public nurses to look after maternity
cases, inspect schools, and do general health work. It also increased the
hospital grant in 1921 and allowed districts to engage a doctor. Many
farmers, however, were not satisfied; they believed that such legislation
showed that 'the state under our present political system will only creep
along as public opinion and political expediency permit.'[36]

Government debt further undermined the Liberals' credibility. Farmers concluded that the old parties, being reliant on patronage, would
never impose the 'rigid economy' demanded by producers. 'The debt of
the province ... is $34,635,200,' the *Independent* noted. 'Is it not time for
a business administration?'[37]

The government's response to farmers' debt and credit problems also
tarnished its image. Frontier and wartime conditions contributed to
high debt loads and interest rates for Alberta producers; declining product prices, drought, and tight money after the war drove many to the

wall. Farmers were angry that until 1920 the province did not follow Manitoba's lead and set the interest rate at which banks must lend to co-operative credit associations. Many of the delegates at the 1921 UFA convention were also piqued by the provincial treasurer's unwillingness to create a government savings bank like that in Manitoba, which accepted deposits from the public to provide co-op credit societies with cheap money. Only in later 1921, on the eve of the election, did the Alberta government take effective action to help the co-op credit societies by fully guaranteeing bank loans made to them.[38]

Farmers were also unhappy with the province's response to the farm mortgage crisis. Foreclosures and threats of seizure were endemic in some districts. Thousands of producers lost their farms. Some farmers called for a moratorium, but most simply wanted the government to implement the 1917 Farm Loan Act whereby it would finance mortgages by selling bonds. The Liberals hemmed and hawed and did little, which was especially frustrating given that Manitoba and Saskatchewan had established state mortgage programs for their farmers.[39]

The Alberta government's lack of credit assistance politicized even liberal farmers and made them receptive to American soft-money doctrines and the social credit ideas of C.H. Douglas and Arthur Kitson, which were introduced to the movement in 1921. Farmers came to believe that financiers, through their control of money and credit, had brought on the post-war price decline. Disillusioned with the province's unhelpfulness and influenced by ex-American UFA radical credit experts, such as W.R. Ball and George Bevington, farmers demanded state banks. The 1919 UFA convention called for provincial government banks, and in 1921, with product prices plummeting and the dry belt shrivelling, most farmers wanted nothing less than the 'nationalization of our banking and credit system.' The desperation behind these demands fuelled the agrarian revolt as farmers sought credit relief through political means.[40]

Dry-belt farmers also were dissatisfied with the province's irrigation policies. By 1919 certain areas had experienced three consecutive years of drought. Lethbridge farmers responded in 1920 by forming the Northern Irrigation District, but the province would guarantee only two years' interest on the bonds issued by the district to finance its proposed irrigation projects. Consequently, the bonds did not sell. The UFA insisted on a full loan guarantee, and although the government finally consented in 1921,[41] some farmers resented that it had taken the Liberals so long to act.

In the far north of the province, railways were the key political issue. Railway rates were high, and service, particularly on the badly maintained Edmonton, Dunvegan, and B.C. line, was poor. Moreover, many farmers were far from any railway. Northern locals and conventions, with the support of the larger UFA/UFWA, demanded lower rates, better service, more extensions, and a west-coast link. There was some improvement after 1920, when the CPR assumed operation of the E.D. and B.C. line and the province took over the Alberta and Great Waterways Railway, but northern farmers were exasperated, having waited years for help and having been promised lines that never appeared. So angry were they that when the 1921 election was called, they resolved, 'Let's make a clean sweep; things couldn't be worse.'[42]

Across the province, farmers suspected that the Liberals favoured urban over rural areas in their education, road construction, and taxation policies. They were keenly upset that the government imposed the supplementary revenue tax at a higher rate on rural land than it did on urban land. They were also displeased that the premier had failed to keep his promise to introduce proportional representation.[43]

As their political strength grew, farmers became truculent. UFA officer W.D. Trego was indignant that the minister of municipal affairs refused to amend the Hail Insurance Act, as the 1920 UFA convention had demanded. 'This raises the question,' he asked ominously, 'who is this minister – a servant of the people or a dictator of the people?' Trego snorted, 'If this is the kind of service we are to get from the present incumbents in office,' there was no reason for delaying UFA political action 'beyond the next provincial election.' As time went on, the government found it nearly impossible to neutralize UFA/UFWA criticism. The *Independent* cynically commented that the UFA's growing political influence did not mean that the Liberals had undergone a 'sound conversion'; they were merely playing 'another phase of the old political game.'[44]

The UFA/UFWA was in revolt against 'partyism' as well as Liberal policies. The pre-1905 tradition of non-party government in the Northwest, a railway scandal involving the provincial Liberals in 1910, rumours of corruption in the government during the war, the Non-Partisan League's agitation for a non-partisan 'business administration,' and the collapse of the Alberta Conservatives, many of whom switched their allegiance to the UFA political movement,[45] proved fatal to the government and the party system.

If the provincial Liberals were doomed in many farmers' eyes, much more so was the dominion government. At least the Liberals had passed a fair amount of pro-agrarian legislation after the war; the same cannot be said of the governing Union/Liberal-Conservative party in Ottawa. Articulating the frustration of many farmers, John Slattery, a UFA/ UFWA political association secretary, noted that producers had been 'begging for economic justice for years,' and he concluded that direct political action was needed. The cancellation of the Wheat Board in 1920 drove many western farmers to the same conclusion. It indicated, one future UFA MP predicted, that the government's political campaign against them would be 'merciless.'[46]

Post-war protectionism suggested to farmers throughout the country that they could expect little from the government. Having endured increased duties during the war, they believed that they were now entitled to lower tariffs, especially since protected manufacturers demanded that their inputs be put on the free list. Farmers were incensed when, despite their arguments before the Tariff Commission, Ottawa raised tariffs in the 1921 budget. The previous budget had already politicized them by throwing 'down the gauntlet to the ... supporters of the New National Policy.' Arguing that the government was 'determined to maintain protection ... to secure the war profiteers in ... their ill-gotten gains, and to compel the workers of Canada to carry the burden of the war debt,' the *Guide* prophesied that 'the challenge' would be 'taken up at the earliest opportunity.'[47]

The defeat of a motion in Parliament in 1921 to ratify the Reciprocity Agreement further incited farmers' ire. What was particularly galling to them was that sixteen western members representing pro-reciprocity constituencies had voted against the pact; had they voted for it, the resolution would have carried. Constituents' wishes clearly had been sacrificed to party discipline. The *Guide* warned that during the next election farmers would remember 'the action these "representatives" took when they had an opportunity to secure wider markets for the produce of Canadian farms.' When the American Congress imposed heavy duties on Canadian wheat and livestock later in the year, farmers' cup of wrath ran over.[48]

They did not turn to the federal Liberals for relief. Had not the party's protectionist wing worked against reciprocity in 1911? Moreover, the *Guide* noted that Liberals had made pro-tariff remarks in Quebec in 1921, and UFA propaganda denounced Lomer Gouin, a prominent high-tariff Liberal politician, as the 'Czar' of that province.[49] Most farmers were convinced that corporate interests directed the tariff policies of both parties.

Broader foreign policy also politicized the movement. Farmers from coast to coast were against any move to strengthen the imperial link without public approval. Influenced by Queen's University political economist O.D. Skelton, they sought national self-determination. In their Platform they argued that 'further development of the British Empire should be sought along the lines of partnership between nations free and equal.' They asserted that farmers were 'strongly opposed to any attempt to centralize imperial control,' maintaining that 'any attempt to set up an independent power to bind the Dominions, whether this authority be termed parliament, council, or cabinet, would hamper the growth of responsible and informed democracy in the Dominions.' The *Guide* repudiated what it believed was the government's policy of weakening Canada's status won at the Peace Conference, stating that this was one of the 'real issues' of the 1921 election.[50]

Retreating to their pre-war stance, prairie farmers were strongly critical of militarism and navalism. 'Do we want to build expensive war ships ... with the financial position that this country is in?' T.A. Crerar asked the UFA convention. Western and Ontario farmers were resoundingly opposed to compulsory military training, believing that it cultivated a taste for war. The *Independent* argued that the government's defence policies would be 'one of the main reasons for turning it out.'[51]

Poor railway service hurt the political fortunes of the federal and Alberta governments. The UFA/UFWA clamoured for more branch lines and the completion of all lines started before the war. After the bankruptcy of the Canadian Northern and the Grand Trunk Pacific and the onset of depression in 1920, however, little railway extension was undertaken. The construction of the Hudson Bay Railway also was frustratingly slow.

Farmers felt that greater state involvement in major industries would solve such infrastructure problems. The Farmers' Platform called for public ownership and control of railways, utilities, and the coal industry. Consistent with this proposal, the 1920 UFA convention opposed the alienation from the Crown of resources such as timber, gas, and oil and asked the government to develop them 'in the interests of the people.' Farmers believed that state ownership and operation of resources and key industries would lower consumer costs and create more revenue for the government, so that the tariff could be lowered. The issue took on a sectional flavour as farmers called on Ottawa to hand over control of resources to the prairie provinces.[52]

The call for government control of major industries was an expression of farmers' demand for a more activist state, a demand stemming from wartime experience with state intervention, from radical ideology and the 'new' liberalism, and from expediency. Although some Alberta farmers were uncomfortable with this trend, most supported state-assisted wheat and livestock marketing, government control over land speculation, and even a cap on milling company profits.[53] While the old parties met such requests to a degree, many farmers concluded that independent action was needed to create the interventionist state they wanted.

Western farmers were further politicized by their changing perception of the state. Before and during the war, they generally saw government boards and commissions as expert, non-partisan, and impartial arbiters between groups. The early work of the Grain and Railway boards seemed to validate this view. But farmers increasingly believed that such agencies worked in the interests of politicians or plutocrats. The Railway Board's approval of a freight rate hike of 35 per cent in 1920 and its refusal to hear a UFA presentation on the effect of high railway rates on agriculture 'dissipated' farmers' faith in that body. By 1921 farmers also felt that the Grain Board should be investigated. Given their cynicism about such boards, farmers naturally opposed the idea of a permanent commission to help the government to determine tariff policy.[54]

The problem with commissions and boards, UFA/UFWA farmers concluded, was the party system; the old parties corrupted them through patronage. If honest and competent persons were put in these agencies, they would be effective. But only a non-party government would appoint such commissioners without trying to influence them in their work.

Disappointed with government policies, commissions, and boards, farmers were annoyed by the parties' political tactics. At two UFA/UFWA political constituency conventions in 1919, the provincial Liberals suggested that they and the UFA nominate joint candidates. The delegates perceived this offer as a ploy to co-opt UFA political action, and they turned down the proposals 'amid hilarious applause.' Farmers were also offended by the amount of money spent by the parties in their campaigns and their use of practices such as padding voters lists.[55]

Clause 10 of the 1920 Franchise Act, an apparent federal attack on

'A Rotten Foundation Eventually Spells Disaster' and 'Up She Goes Again!' by Arch Dale. *Grain Growers' Guide*, 15 Mar. 1916, 6; and 15 Sept. 1920, 6. A comparison of these two cartoons reveals farmers' loss of faith in commissions. In the 1916 cartoon (top), commissioners are presented as workmanlike representatives of the people. In the 1920 cartoon (bottom), the Railway Board is depicted as a bloated plutocrat; farmers now suspected that corporations influenced commissions by controlling the political parties.

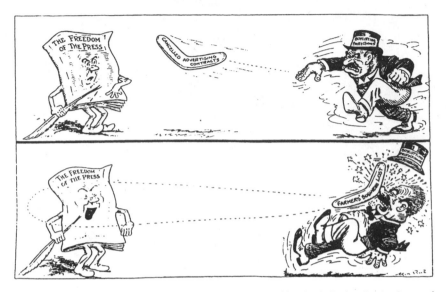

'The Farmers Can Make the Boycott a Boomerang,' by Arch Dale. *Grain Growers'*
Guide, 3 Mar. 1920, 6. The decision of certain manufacturers to cancel their
advertising in the *Guide* because of its low-tariff position politicized farmers, and
they responded, as this cartoon shows, by refusing to buy those industrialists'
products.

non-party political organizations, raised farmers' anger another notch.
The clause stipulated that only associations incorporated solely for
political purposes could provide money for political use. Farmers 'bitterly' condemned this restriction as a pernicious attempt to bar them
from taking independent action. Although the UFA took steps to protect itself from a legal challenge under the act,[56] the clause suggested
that the government would do anything to hamper farmers' political
efforts.

   Farmers faced another politicizing challenge in 1920, when a number
of companies, at the behest of a former manager of the Canadian Manufacturers' Association, cancelled their advertising in the *Guide* because
of its tariff stance. UFA/UFWA locals saw this move as a barefaced
'attack on the freedom of the press' and on the agrarian political movement, and along with other prairie farmers, they resolved not to buy
from manufacturers who boycotted the paper.[57]

   A poem by Herne Liddell captured the politicizing effect of clause 10
and the *Guide* boycott on the UFA/UFWA:

But when we form a party
At politics to play,
They up and do their darndest
To block the right-of-way.
They class it class distinction,
And other nasty things;
And bring up bills in Parliament
To clip the farmers' wings.

And when a farmers' organ,
That's called the G.G. Guide,
Begins to quote opinions
Of farmers far and wide,
They start a little boycott,
That boodle-bird's brigade,
And ask their friends to please refuse
Their advertising trade ...

The moral of this ditty
Is mighty plain to read,
They deal us lots of taffy,
But that ain't what we need.
So think it over farmers,
Too long we've been the goat;
And when the next election comes
Let's take and use our vote.[58]

The 1921 Grain Inquiry, which focused on alleged illegalities involving the United Grain Growers, further politicized farmers. They quickly concluded that it was a thinly veiled attempt to discredit the company, its president, T.A. Crerar, and the national political farm movement he headed. Crerar debunked the Inquiry's accusations to farmers' satisfaction, leading them to believe that the Meighen government was unfit to govern – if it had to resort to such tactics to stay in power. Meighen sank still lower in farmers' estimation when he allegedly called Crerar and Henry Wise Wood 'Bolsheviks' and 'enemies of the state.'[59]

Economic adversity hardened farmers' political resolve. Higher prices for what they bought and the post-war drop in the prices of grain and livestock created severe hardship. Citing statistics showing these trends and arguing that farmers were operating at a loss, Donald Cameron, a

'The "Safe and Sound" Party Conducting an Election,' by Arch Dale. *Grain Growers' Guide*, 23 Nov. 1921, 4. The Grain Inquiry, portrayed here as the product of a 'scandal mill,' raised farmers' ire against the Meighen government and the party system.

UFA man, blamed the party system. 'In the face of such evidence,' he reflected, 'and much more like it, so apparent to the average thinker, our politicians and the subsidized press do not seem to understand the fundamental principles underlying the new movement for political emancipation that is now rocking their old worn-out structure of party politics to its foundations.' 'We must destroy this party system,' Cameron resolved, 'not only in the federal field, but in the provincial field as well.' Many farmers believed that speculators and corporations had brought on the price squeeze, which was all the more reason to take direct political action. Red Lodge UFA local wondered

> why the price of grain went down so quickly and freight rates went up, and why it still takes $7.50 to $8.00 to buy a sack of flour and $1.50 to $1.75 for a 20 pound sack of rolled oats, although we are being paid 35 cents to 40 cents at the local elevator. And why it takes the price of two cow hides to buy a pair of shoes, and many other things need explanation ... If ever, now is the time for the farmers to unite and organize and see if they can have a hand in legislation.[60]

'The Mud Slinger,' by Arch Dale. *Grain Growers' Guide*, 6 Oct. 1920, 6. The national agrarian political movement, in its literature and in this cartoon, accused Prime Minister Meighen of calling organized farmers 'Bolsheviks.' Whether or not the allegation was true, it hardened farmers' political determination.

In some districts, climatic disaster inclined farmers to support UFA politics. Describing the 'starved cattle and farmers without feed' he witnessed in 1920, John Glambeck admonished producers to 'organize, both economically and politically, in order to retain more of their products in good years so that they may have something to fall back on in lean years.'[61]

Movement confidence emboldened farmers to take political action. This self-assurance developed from study of 'the political situation and the Farmers' Platform'; from agrarian political victories; from legislative and co-operative successes, which suggested that farmers had only 'begun to act in a "collective capacity"'; and from rousing speakers: 'Boy howdy, didn't he shoot the ginger into us!' Above all, the rapid expansion of the movement imparted a sense of power. 'A feeling grew out of the strength of the organization,' one prominent UFA member recalled years later. Farmers felt that 'they could do greater things if

'Is There Any Connection?' by Arch Dale. *Grain Growers' Guide*, 9 Mar. 1921, 6. As shown here, farmers suspected that financiers controlled price trends through their control of credit. This perception inclined farmers, especially those facing severe economic difficulty, to support the independent political movement, which they hoped would end such price manipulation.

they were in charge themselves.'[62] So armed, they launched the agrarian revolt.

The 1919 convention permitted UFA political action and instructed the central to call political conventions in federal ridings upon request of 10 per cent of the locals in the constituency. Soon after, the Non-Partisan League approached the UFA executive about a possible merger. A joint committee was appointed, which endorsed, with a few amendments, an agreement drafted by the League as a basis for amalgamation.[63] The agreement was later considered by the UFA/UFWA constituency conventions, which, as stipulated by the annual convention, determined how, or whether, they wished to take political action.

The agreement proposed to create a non-party 'business administration' in which all schools of political thought would be represented. It favoured provincial as well as federal action and insisted that farmers meet all costs of their political activities. It suggested that a separate UFA political office be opened and that the UFA/UFWA constituency

'What Happened in the Dark?' probably by Arch Dale. *Grain Growers' Guide*, 8 June 1921, 6. This cartoon depicts farmers' bewilderment over post-war price spreads – the widening gap between what they received for their products and what they had to pay for finished goods. Their anxiety about this issue had a politicizing effect on the movement.

associations adopt their political platforms clause by clause.[64] The League promised to cast its lot with the UFA if its constituency conventions accepted these principles.

Conventions were held in all federal constituencies by mid-1919. Most approved the joint committee agreement in its essentials. A number endorsed the Farmers' Platform; others committed their members to study the Platform with a view to adopting a program later. In two conventions, Non-Partisan League supporters tried to get 'League' included in the names of the constituency associations, but only the Macleod convention agreed to this suggestion.[65]

The main point at issue in the conventions was whether the political movement would be restricted to UFA/UFWA members or open to anyone who believed in the movement's cause. League supporters, who were mostly radicals, and a few others called for the 'open door,' arguing that a strictly UFA political movement could not attract enough voters. Henry Wise Wood disagreed and insisted that broadening out would weaken the movement by diluting its central focus – class interest – and by permitting the infiltration of political manipulators. This view prevailed at the conventions, owing to Wood's influence and farmers' class consciousness.

Nevertheless, the movement never ruled out involvement in UFA politics for non-farmer UFA/UFWA members[66] such as teachers and clergymen. The Calgary East and West convention even allowed persons of other classes to become 'associate members' of its political movement, though with fewer rights than regular members enjoyed. Some conventions permitted their constituencies to nominate non-farmer UFA political candidates, but others required their candidates to be 'bona fide farmers,' so that no professional politicians could be nominated.[67]

The conventions were major events in the politicization of the movement, as was the UFA/UFWA's absorption of the League in mid-1919. Although the UFA/UFWA would not endorse a wide-open multiclass strategy, the League was satisfied that the conventions had adopted most of the joint committee proposals. With the merger of the rival organizations, the political movement could grow and develop undivided. Had the two remained apart, fighting one another, agrarian politics in Alberta would have been seriously weakened, as the farm movement would have been if the Alberta Farmers' Association and the Society of Equity had failed to unite to form the UFA.

Once the conventions were over, the constituency associations created the UFA Provincial Political Association (UFAPPA) to co-ordinate their political work. Because many former League members were elected to the Association board, it advocated the open-door political strategy, despite the UFA constituency associations' approval of Wood's closed-door policy.

The result was another run-in with Wood during the October provincial by-election campaign in Cochrane. In this, the movement's first political test, the UFA candidate, Alex Moore, challenged the Liberal standard-bearer, E.V. Thompson. On the hustings, Wood first enunciated his group-government theory, arguing that occupational groups should replace parties in Parliament and the legislatures. This was a logical extension of his desire to keep the UFA/UFWA political movement for members only. Other 'class' organizations would do likewise and elect their own representatives. League MLA James Weir and a few UFAPPA members, including Guy Johnson, publicly repudiated Wood's ideas.[68] Despite this tactic and the support of prominent Liberals for Thompson, Moore won.

It was a landmark victory for the UFA; had Moore lost, the political movement would have stalled. Soon after, another important politicizing step was taken when William Irvine, editor of the *Independent* and the main spokesperson for the open-door plan, joined the Wood camp and convinced many radicals to support Wood's doctrines. Radicals and liberals now had a common political ideology on which to unite.

Some opposition to Wood's position continued, however, although the issue was resolved at the 1920 annual convention, where Wood accused the UFAPPA of telling him during the Cochrane campaign that he 'could not talk about the great principle of group government and group organization.' UFAPPA president O.L. McPherson countered that he had not objected to Wood's expressing his views, but he was upset that Wood reportedly had stated them as the UFA's official position before the annual convention had declared on the question. The election of the UFA president settled the matter. The contestants were Wood and Archie Muir, vice-president of the UFAPPA and an open-door advocate. Wood won by a five-to-one margin, and the convention endorsed his notion of economic group organization for politics. It also passed a resolution that weakened the UFAPPA by subordinating it to the UFA board. The UFAPPA, as a result, decided to disband, handing responsibility for co-ordinating the constituency associations' political work to the central.[69] All in all, it was a decisive victory for Wood, class politics, and group government.

In 1921 the politicization of the movement reached fruition. The annual convention recommended provincial political action in every constituency and endorsed the choice of T.A. Crerar as leader of the Progressives, the national agrarian political party formed in 1920 from a group of eleven cross-benchers. Then, in late June, the UFA candidate, Robert Gardiner, polled over 9,700 more votes than his only opponent in the Medicine Hat federal by-election, giving Alberta farmers unshakable political confidence just as the provincial Liberals called an election for 18 July. The UFA/UFWA quickly organized itself in some thirty new ridings and placed forty-four candidates in the field[70] and won thirty-eight of sixty-one seats. This victory – the UFA would form a majority government – spawned a new wave of excitement that carried into the December federal election in which all ten UFA candidates and the two labour and independent candidates endorsed by the UFA were elected. In several urban-rural ridings during the election campaigns and the Medicine Hat by-election, the UFA and labour agreed to run and support only one class of candidate. In only two constituencies did the UFA and the Labour party pit candidates against each other – to the detriment of the Labour candidates.

The agrarian political fire, most intense in Alberta, was aflame across the prairies and had spread into Ontario, the Maritimes, and even British Columbia. Having been sparked by a few agrarian by-election victories in 1918–19 in Ontario, Saskatchewan, New Brunswick, and Alberta, it had been set ablaze by the astonishing victory of the United Farmers of Ontario, which formed the provincial government in 1919. It was stoked the following year by the equally surprising election of seven provincial farmer candidates in Nova Scotia and ten in New Brunswick, the latter holding a balance of power in the legislature. At this time, the farmer political movement was starting to burn brightly across the prairies: twelve Progressives gained seats in the 1920 Saskatchewan provincial election, and the same number carried the day in Manitoba in that year, depriving the Norris government of a majority.[71] This fiery political fervour swept into Alberta and contributed to the great UFA triumphs of 1921: the defeat of the old parties both provincially and federally. The federal UFA candidates were part of the national Progressive party, which won sixty-five seats in the election, mainly in the West and, to a lesser extent, in Ontario. It was enough to qualify the Progressives as the official opposition.

Responsible for this great national achievement were the provincial farm organizations and their constituency associations, which essentially had conducted their campaigns independently. Some members of the Canadian Council of Agriculture (CCA) had tried to link the provincial political movements, and a loose co-ordinating committee was formed.[72] But Wood, who was CCA as well as UFA president, successfully blocked all attempts, including those by Progressive leader T.A. Crerar, an open-door proponent, to create a centrally organized national party. Wood and other organized farmers, especially in Alberta and Ontario, were determined to have direct democratic control over their political movements. They believed that candidates must belong to their constituents; they must be nominated, financed, instructed, and elected locally. Anything else would be partyism – exactly what farmers were in revolt against, especially in Alberta.

From 1919 to 1921 the UFA/UFWA was politicized. It committed itself to independent politics, gained women's political support, and created political structures. The organization's growth, its democratic ethos, its sense of citizenship responsibility, its social ethic and Platform, and its religious ideals motivated farmers to pursue this political path, as did state actions, economic adversity, political victories, and eventual consensus on strategy. Under these influences, farmers launched what would be the most resilient agrarian political crusade in North American history.

Chapter Nine

The Philosophy of the Post-War UFA/UFWA

Democracy may be simply defined as the people in action.[1]

Henry Wise Wood

Many scholars portray the UFA/UFWA's post-war social and political philosophy as a concoction of Henry Wise Wood, based on his class experience, reading, and American background.[2] A few see it primarily as William Irvine's creation, grounded in British socialism. These interpretations present UFA/UFWA doctrine as a foreign construct that charismatic leaders imposed on the rank and file, or as a reflection of farmers' 'small commodity producer' outlook. But the UFA/UFWA philosophy stemmed from more than a 'great man's' social position, education, or history; as David Laycock suggests, it expressed a movement culture,[3] which is why it inspired farmers politically. Wood, the main voice of UFA/UFWA theory, and Irvine, who helped to popularize and develop it, were as much synthesizers of movement ideas as they were prophets.

Henry Wise Wood was born on a farm in Missouri in 1860 and settled near Carstairs, Alberta, north of Calgary, in 1905. He was a member of the Society of Equity, a UFA director in 1914, a vice-president in 1915, and president from 1916 until he retired in 1931. He also was on the Board of Grain Supervisors and the Wheat Board from 1917 to 1920, was president of the Canadian Council of Agriculture from 1917 to 1923, and was president of the Alberta Wheat Pool from 1923 to 1937. Wood possessed a homely charisma, an earnest sincerity, and an earthy humour that few who knew him ever forgot. Attired in academic robes to receive an honorary degree of doctor of law from the University of Alberta in 1929, he dryly remarked, 'This is like putting a show harness on an old Missouri mule.'[4]

Although he attended a private school and Christian University in his home state, Wood was largely self-educated. He had a voluminous library in his Carstairs home where, into the wee hours of the night, he read political economy, sociology, philosophy, natural history, and literature.[5] He was also a keen observer of American farm organizations – and a one-time member of the Farmers' and Laborers' Union of Missouri – whose political forays convinced him of the dangers of third-party politics.

The burden of Wood's social philosophy, which he began preaching right after the war, was that history flowed from a dialectic between the two 'social laws' of competition and co-operation. Competition 'acted' to force a 'reaction' – the formation of larger co-operative units. These units competed at higher levels, prompting the creation of still greater co-operative units for competitive use. In this way, competition for survival and trade drove the earliest peoples to form family groups, family groups to form tribes, tribes to form nations, and nations to form allied units. According to Wood,

> Germany and her allies represented the greatest co-operative national unit of strength that the world had ever seen. This strength was all built by co-operation, but built for competitive purposes. Germany threw this strength competitively against certain other nations and would have destroyed them if her opponents had not succeeded in building a greater co-operative unit of strength than Germany had built. This they finally succeeded in doing, and this greater strength reacted in the overthrow of the German strength. Thus, competition, begun by individual savages, had driven co-operation up through the various increasing units until practically all of the nations of the world were embraced in two great co-operative units. Speaking from a national and a military standpoint, competition can drive co-operation but one degree higher, when all of the nations will be embraced in one co-operative unit and military competition will have been destroyed.[6]

International competition, in short, had become so dangerous that higher levels of military efficiency could destroy the world and were therefore unthinkable. Competition was forcing nations to pursue co-operation. But peace would be impossible until the cause of war – international trade competition – was eliminated. War in modern times was a means by which commercial aggregates, known as countries, and allied units sought economic domination:

> War is not an end within itself. Germany did not wage war primarily for military supremacy. Her real object was commercial supremacy ...
>
> True, the brute call to man and to nations has often been strong enough to cause them to fight for glory and power. But through the ages greed like a great octopus has been sending its tentacles out through the fabric of the social system, sapping the strength and the life blood of the people through the pores of trade and commerce till it has acquired the power ... of a god and is enthroned as Mammon, directing the competitive activities of the nations and the peoples of the earth. Mammon, by holding dominion over commerce, holds it also over war ... Under his edicts the nations have broken themselves against each other ... Unless his reign over the realms of trade and commerce can be broken, he will continue to lead the forces of military conflict until the war drums beat the funeral dirge of civilization.[7]

Specifically, the economic and political control that plutocracy – powerful industrial and financial interests – had over the nations was responsible for recent wars. If the plutocrats' grip on commerce and politics were broken, however, and fair prices, wages, and free trade were established between classes and countries, international commercial competition would be ended and world peace would ensue. 'Commerce systematically used in accordance with the true social laws of life,' Wood promised, 'would be the greatest binding tie in the social system. It would draw the nations of the earth together in one great indissoluble union.'[8]

Wood explained how plutocracy had come to dominate, and how it might be destroyed, by examining the dialectic of competition and co-operation in the commercial field. There, the process had been slower than it had been in the national and military arena because before the industrial revolution there was insufficient trade competition to force commercial co-operation. Manufacturing was done by artisans who supplied local markets with little selling competition between themselves; this system made co-operation unnecessary.

During the industrial age, however, improved production and transportation brought industries into competition. The rivalry 'acted' to drive weak firms out of business and pushed others to 'react' by creating co-operative units in the form of combines. Competition between those conglomerates became so fierce that the manufacturers, realizing that their whole industry might be wiped out, turned to the only solution possible – co-operation – and the national manufacturers' associations were born.

These associations, by eradicating competition between manufacturers of the same country, enhanced the industrialists' competitive strength towards their counterparts in other countries – leading to trade war and military conflict – while increasing their economic and political power over domestic groups like farmers. And because the level of organization and co-operation of such groups was so low by comparison, they could not defend themselves against the manufacturers and their plutocratic allies, especially bankers, who controlled the parties and press 'through the systematic use of money.' The industrialists exercised their control by having tariffs imposed, while financiers brought on deflation in the early 1920s to profit on money, with disastrous consequences for agriculture.[9]

The weaker groups were 'reacting' to this plutocratic power by co-operating. Reinforcing that external pressure to combine – perhaps even stimulated by it – was 'a germ developing in the human race.' This 'germ' was an innate voice of nature that had prompted individual regeneration, or the development of a co-operative spirit, and was now prodding people to undertake social regeneration, or the creation of a co-operative order, by defeating plutocracy. Having effectively organized as an occupational group, the manufacturers had unwittingly shown the other groups what to do. Economic interest was the only feasible basis for organizing; it was the only 'viewpoint' that could bind a group together. As rivers flow to the sea via the easiest course, 'class' organization was 'the way of least resistance.'[10]

Wood warned that social, economic, and military advancement had recently been so rapid that if the people did not promptly organize to oppose plutocracy, civilization would veer off the path of progress into a morass of autocratic rule and warfare. Yet he never doubted that the people would succeed. They would respond to the competitive force of plutocracy and to the germ within them: nature's call to group organization. Social and natural law could not be ignored. Once the people had developed their group 'intelligence' and 'citizenship strength' to the highest degree through education and organization, they would 'federate' their economic groups into a great co-operative and democratic force and meet plutocracy in an apocalyptic 'showdown.' 'When these forces are finally thus marshalled,' Wood prophesied, 'the irrepressible conflict will be on. The conflict between democracy and plutocracy, between civilization and barbarism, between man and money, between co-operation and competition, between God and Mammon.'[11]

The victory of the people would be the culmination of the struggle for democracy that began when absolute monarchy was challenged. The war over, the democratic classes would meet on an even level with the former plutocrats – now stripped of their autocratic powers – in the commercial and political arenas in order to adjust, in a way agreeable to all, trade relationships, wages, and prices. The nations, no longer controlled by plutocracy, would similarly settle trade disputes. The result would be peace and a just and democratic order – the 'kingdom of heaven.'[12]

Despite the graphic drama, the apocalyptic confrontation was not a military engagement or a rebellion. It was an economic and political fight the people would win over time by co-operatively opposing plutocracy through commercial and, to a lesser extent, political action – first, within the party system, then, as Wood changed his thinking, through group government. Wood was a gradualist, not a revolutionary. Seeing society as an organism, he believed that 'incessant and minute change is one of the conditions of life, but great and sudden change is disease.'[13]

Consistent with this organic view of society, Wood felt that social progress was inevitable because it was driven by 'immutable' natural and social laws:

> To say that democracy will fail will be to say that the design of nature in creating a social being and bringing him into obedience to social laws has failed ...
>
>   It will not fail ... because the Supreme Power that flung the numberless hosts of worlds out into infinite space, set them whirling in their fixed courses, lit them with effulgent splendor and revealed them to the eye of man, has this work in hand and will not let it fail.

Still, there was a role for human agency; Wood argued that progress would be accelerated or hindered depending on the degree to which the people co-operated with nature's laws.[14]

As scholars have argued, many aspects of Wood's philosophy can be traced to his American background and reading of European and American works, although exact books cannot always be pinpointed. Sometimes one can only draw parallels or suggest possible influences. Wood's belief in social laws was consistent with positivism and a tendency in late nineteenth-century thought to replace theology with social science. His exposure to evolutionary and social-Darwinian theory clearly informed his gradualism and determinism. These sources, perhaps with his reading of Walt Whitman's poetry, helped him to see society as an evolving democratic organism. His vision of social progress and ultimate perfectionism revealed his liberalism and understanding of writers such as Herbert Spencer and Tennyson. The latter he considered the 'greatest prophet of modern times.'[15]

Wood apparently learned that co-operation was the true social law and competition the false law at university in Missouri.[16] His belief in social co-operation reflected the American radical tradition. Thinkers such as Edward Bellamy and social gospellers such as Washington Gladden considered competition 'selfishness' and longed for a co-operative society. Social gospel ideas certainly developed Wood's thinking about competition and co-operation and his vision of the 'kingdom of heaven.'

Wood loathed the individualistic struggle-for-existence ethic. He criticized Darwin, Huxley, and Haeckel for failing to discern that humanity must 'throw off this animal spirit' and develop a co-operative spirit. 'Science tells us that the law of the survival of the fittest is the true primary animal law,' Wood conceded, 'but only the fool will tell us that it is the true ultimate social law.' Here Wood echoed evolutionists such as Henry Drummond and Kropotkin, who, like him, saw group co-operation – between families, tribes, nations, and classes – as integral to survival and progress.[17]

Wood's love for democracy was Jacksonian, a product of the Democratic South and a Missouri where the democratic ideals of 'Old Hickory' reigned supreme. His idea about an innate democratic 'germ' was an adaptation of the theory that the ancient Teutons possessed racially inherited 'seeds' of liberty – an inherent democratic impulse – which their descendants carried to Britain and America.[18] His charge that financiers had brought on deflation is reminiscent of the 'Crime of "73"' controversy in the United States, when financial interests influenced the government to stop minting silver coins, causing prices to stagnate or drop.

Wood's Campbellite background also affected his thinking, although by the time he developed his philosophy he no longer believed in a Christian God; his god was little more than natural and social law.[19] Nevertheless, he retained his love for the Bible and believed that it confirmed his theory; he convinced himself that Jesus had preached co-operation as the 'primary rule' of life[20] and that the Gospels and book of Revelation were prophecies about the evolution and ultimate triumph of democracy. Biblical influence is unmistakable in Wood's rhetoric and moral tone and in the apocalyptic climax to which his history unfolds.

Wood's conviction that right trading relationships fostered social health was rooted in his reading of Adam Smith and J.S. Mill. His idea of a dialectic between competition and co-operation was largely his own, but the notion of a dialectical process he took from Marx, Emerson, or M.P. Follett, whose Hegelian treatise, *The New State*, Wood knew well. His call for 'class' organization based on economic interest may also have been Marxist in origin, while his analogy of this strategy being 'the way of least resistance,' akin to water flowing to the sea by the easiest course, is what one might expect from a man who studied Alberta's geological history in his spare time.[21]

Moulded by these intellectual sources, Wood's social philosophy revealed his concern for the post-war world. The war had made a deep impression on him; he feared that another might destroy civilization. He felt that if co-operation did not replace competition in social and international relations, the world might cease to be. He sought to show people how to bring about peace through democratic class organization.

But Wood's philosophy was more than a product of the war and his reading and American background; it embodied the movement culture he had absorbed as a UFA member. Many of his doctrines reflected movement assumptions; his theory was not purely his own. He was as much a preacher of existing UFA ideas as a prophet of new ones.

A key movement culture notion expressed by his social philosophy was a sense of class-conscious opposition to corporate power. While his hostility to plutocracy was born in the Jeffersonian milieu of Missouri and was nurtured by his reading of authors such as Frank Norris, his philosophy articulated Alberta farmers' tradition – one he had come to share – of antipathy to metropolitan economic and political control. And while his belief in agrarian organization also began in Missouri,[22] his theory enunciated a long-standing UFA/UFWA argument, which he had heard many times in Alberta, that farmers must organize to protect their interests. Well before Wood became a UFA leader, yet sounding like him, W.J. Tregillus described the evolution of social organization, with a lesson for farmers: 'In olden times, men fought single-handed; that would be useless now. Later in clans and tribes; that would also be useless in our day. Now every civilized nation has a perfectly organized and trained army that works with the ... precision ... of a watch, and that is the kind of organization we want if we are to get what belongs to us.' The purpose of organization in Wood's philosophy was to mobilize class strength to establish equitable trade relationships. UFA general secretary P.P. Woodbridge had similarly argued, before Wood outlined his theory, that farmers must organize their 'full strength' to force an adjustment in 'their relationship with other classes' and with governments.[23]

Wood's belief that class competition would ultimately lead to social co-operation, though partly a result of his study, was a further expression of UFA/UFWA culture. Long before Wood had influence in the UFA, the movement had built a co-operative ethos, a belief that co-operation should infuse all human relations. This notion was evident in a motion debated by Mayerthorpe local in 1913: 'That co-operation is more beneficial to the human family than competition.' Two years later, Edwell union heard an address on the 'history and ethics of co-operation.' The listeners learned of the 'value of co-operation and the virtue of unselfishness.' Wood's argument – and even the rhetoric he used – about social co-operation was not new to Alberta farmers. Nor was his contention that to fight plutocracy democratic groups must develop their highest 'intelligence' through education. The UFA had always taught farmers that 'knowledge is power.'[24]

Wood's social philosophy, then, contained several key UFA/UFWA ideas and sentiments. It represented a conjunction of his personal experience and the movement culture that had shaped his thinking since he arrived in Alberta in 1905.

Wood's group-government theory, which he first broached during the Cochrane by-election campaign in October 1919, was a modification of the political component of his social philosophy. To create a group government, the democratic groups, while continuing to battle plutocracy in the commercial realm, would cease fighting them through the party system; instead, they would elect non-party occupational representatives according to each group's numerical strength through a proportional representation system. Small groups, to have a political voice, would support the candidate of a larger group that came closest to representing their class interest. Electoral co-operation between larger groups was possible on a restricted basis. One group could support another's candidate rather than split the progressive vote, but it could not endorse that candidate's platform; to do so would be to jeopardize its class principles.

Nor could the two groups draft a joint platform. Any such compromise program would be based on superficial and ultimately divisive issues.[25]

Moreover, there must be no merger of the groups; that would be creating a political party. Lacking a unified class interest, parties were easily manipulated by plutocracy and were therefore corrupt and unstable. They also appealed to voters' prejudices, obstructing the development of democratic thought and dividing voters of the same class into opposing partisan camps, which prevented the people from working together to fight plutocracy. The only proper basis for political organization was the occupational group; only 'class' education and political experience could create the 'intelligence' needed to transform the weak 'citizenship strength' of individual voters into a collective voting power able to resist the wiles of partyism.

Group government would be introduced gradually. The example of early group-elected members would encourage other groups to organize and elect 'class' representatives. Then, by co-operating with each other without amalgamating or without joining or forming a party, the elected members of the groups would weaken the existing parties – the bastions of plutocracy – and eventually drive them out of Parliament and the legislatures. This was how the democratic forces would politically defeat the plutocrats in Wood's post-1918 apocalyptic vision.[26]

With the parties gone, the group-government members, as delegates of their 'class' who embodied their groups' 'intelligence,' would debate issues freely to 'settle class differences.' If any group tried to secure unfair legislation, the others would block that attempt.[27] All statutes would represent an agreement of the groups; each group in competing for itself would be forced to co-operate with the others. Political co-operation would produce laws that fostered equitable trade, which, with industrial action, would promote the social and world harmony that Wood forcast in his social philosophy.

Wood never indicated how a group government would conduct its business without a party responsible for introducing and processing legislation. Nor did he say how a 'class' member could speak for an occupationally heterogeneous constituency. He did not, at least for the immediate future, favour replacing geographical constituencies with economic ones.[28] He also failed to explain how or when the democratic groups would 'federate' to defeat plutocracy. He emphasized only that groups must initially keep their organizations separate from one another. He was especially suspicious of farmer-labour parties, owing to their past political failures. Nonetheless, he encouraged democratic groups to co-operate immediately, where possible, and once they had built their 'citizenship strength' to the limit, they would form a closer commercial and political association, the nature of which Wood never described. If, however, any alliance were consummated before the groups had realized their full strength, their organizations would disintegrate, succumbing to the confusion, bickering, and plutocratic manipulation Wood believed would follow any attempt to harmonize immature class viewpoints. How the groups would know when they had achieved their highest 'intelligence' and 'citizenship strength,' Wood did not say.

Wood was also unclear about how decisions would be made in a group government. While he did not rule out the possibility of a majority vote, he likely favoured W.F. Cooling's argument that group decisions should involve a consensus of representatives. He apparently borrowed Follett's notion that a group decision should be a synthesis resulting from a dialectic of members' opposing ideas – witness his comment about a 'reaction' of divergent views producing a 'common ground of settlement': 'We [farmers] are human, the same as everybody else, and I do not deny that if we were the only class organized we would make unjust demands; but other classes will organize and resist unjust demands, and out of this reaction they will find a common ground of settlement.'[29]

All 'legitimate interests' would participate in this decision-making process. Only the plutocrats would be excluded. However, once plutocracy was overthrown – once manufacturers and financiers were divested of their excessive power – the former plutocrats would be encouraged to elect group members. The task of the democratic forces was to destroy plutocracy, not their industries, which Wood believed Canada needed. Group government would force all 'classes,' out of self-interest, to co-operate and find solutions that were fair to all.

Like his larger social philosophy of which it was a component, Wood's group-government theory was partly a product of his reading and the historical context. Most generally, it reflected the search of the age for a more democratic polity, a quest that led political pluralists such as Harold Laski and M.P. Follett to argue, respectively, that governments should have occupational and consumer Houses and that neighbourhoods rather than parties should be the basic political unit. The most important book for Wood's political thinking, it seems, was Walter Cooling's *Public Policy*. Like Wood, Cooling advocated industrial and proportional representation, although unlike Wood, he foresaw group representatives working within existing parties or organizing new ones. Probably also from Cooling came Wood's idea that group members should embody their groups' 'intelligence' and that class selfishness in a group government would impel intergroup co-operation to ensure the passage of just laws.[30]

Moulded by these sources, Wood's group-government theory was, above all, a pragmatic response to political developments he could not control. Before 1919 he opposed independent politics, fearing that it might destroy the UFA as it had other farm bodies. He urged farmers to nominate good candidates in the old parties and to collectively lobby for legislation rather than create a new party.[31] Why did Wood eventually reject this advice to preach class politics and, soon after, group government – a doctrine requiring the overthrow of the party system he had earlier supported?

Wood had felt the tremors of the agrarian revolt that was rumbling across the country. In January 1919 the annual UFA convention endorsed direct political action. Subsequently, independent farmer candidates won by-elections in Ontario, New Brunswick, and Saskatchewan; the United Farmers formed the government in Ontario; and Alex Moore ran in the Cochrane by-election as the UFA candidate. Meanwhile, Non-Partisan League members were trying to open the UFA political movement to 'progressive' members of all classes.

Wood knew that this political uprising could not be stayed, and, as a democrat, he bowed to the people's will. Yet there remained that nagging lesson of history: third-party action could kill a farm organization. Wood concluded, therefore, that the UFA must not join or create a new party, neither a low-tariff party advocated by other farm leaders nor a Non-Partisan League political movement, which he felt would also become a party by virtue of its class heterogeneity. Instead, farmers must enter politics as a 'class' organization, which, united by economic interest, would avoid the pattern of third-party disunity and destruction. By the fall of 1919 Wood had crystallized these ideas into his group-government theory. 'When I could not keep the organization out of politics,' he reminisced years later, 'I conceived the idea of going in as an organization instead of as a party. I conceived that group government might succeed.'[32] Group government thus was a pragmatic response to the agrarian revolt, a theory that Wood developed to save the UFA/UFWA from third-party annihilation. If members had not insisted on taking direct political action, he would never have devised his group plan.

Wood also believed that class action and group government would save the UFA/UFWA from economic radicalism. He feared that if the League's socialist leaders succeeded in making the UFA/UFWA political movement a multiclass party, radical labour leaders and intellectuals would join and would shift it to the left. But if farmers entered politics as a class, they would not be tempted by outsiders to support legislative panaceas, and Wood and the UFA/UFWA would be able to guide the movement along a liberal path.

Beyond this, Wood's group-government scheme, like his larger social philosophy, expressed aspects of the UFA/UFWA movement culture. Group government was not an American ideology he imposed on farmers. He was not even the first to advocate group politics in the UFA. At the 1910 convention, Angus Macaulay had proposed a political system that would guarantee farmers a 'fair share of direct representation' in the legislature by allocating, initially, fourteen of the forty-one seats for independent farmer candidates to contest. Eventually, the independent members 'might form a government.' In the meantime, given their number and the likelihood that they would hold a balance of power, they would have more success procuring good legislation than the UFA would if it elected third-party candidates in the field 'anywhere and everywhere.'[33]

This proposal's resemblance to Wood's group-government strategy is striking. Both aimed to reduce the field for party politics and avoid third-party action while facilitating direct action. Under both plans, farmers would immediately form an occupational bloc, influencing and perhaps forcing the government to act. Both envisaged that farmers ultimately would become the dominant group in the legislature, although the immediate goal was to secure fair representation and input into law making.

The convention did not endorse Macaulay's proposal; the UFA was not yet politically radicalized. The plan did reflect, however, a movement culture sense of opposition to partyism that Wood's theory would articulate. Sown in the era of non-party Territorial politics; germinating in an immigrant population lacking commitment to the Canadian parties; nourished by a 1910 provincial Liberal railway controversy; watered by the defeat of reciprocity; fertilized by the 'crooked' Alberta election of 1913, which revealed dirty politics at its worst;[34] cultivated by graft and rumours of corruption at all levels of government during and after the war; brought to maturity by a perception, confirmed by the Riordon affair,[35] that the Union/Liberal-Conservative party was, like its parents, a tool of plutocracy; and ripened by the Non-Partisan League's agitation for a 'business administration': farmers' hostility to partyism – a metaphor for the sordidness and inefficiency of the old parties – was ready for harvest by 1919 and found full expression in a group-government theory that sought the end of the party system.

Class politics and group-government doctrines flowed logically from this anti-partyism, and they may have arisen in some form without Wood's lead. There was support for group political action outside Alberta – among the provincial agrarian independents in Saskatchewan and Manitoba and especially among the United Farmers of Ontario – and it is not certain that all this support came from direct familiarity with Wood's teachings. It is interesting that the farmers' clubs of Manitoulin, Ontario, which helped to elect an independent farmer candidate in 1918, expressed something very like the group-government concept in September 1919, before Wood had articulated his theory in any systematic way. They explained that 'in place of partyism we would substitute a fair and equitable representation of all the interests of the country, meeting in Parliament, not to struggle against each other as though the government of our country were a game, but to unite in promoting the general welfare of the commnity.'[36] It seems, then, that the notion of group-based politics was not an American construct that Wood imposed on farmers; it was, to some extent, a natural outgrowth of an anti-party agrarian culture that, although strongest in Alberta, was shared by many Canadian farmers.

While articulating anti-partyism, Wood's group-government doctrine expressed farmers' movement culture belief in direct democracy and citizenship responsibility. It required them to nominate, elect, and instruct – like convention delegates – their group representatives and possibly recall them, like UFA officers. It also incorporated the idea popularized by the Non-Partisan League that members should be allowed to vote freely, without fear of defeating the government.[37] By its very nature, group government required frank input from all representatives and made no provision for a government's resigning if one of its bills was defeated.

Group government, in short, like the larger social philosophy of which it was a part, reflected Wood's experience, concerns, and study, as well as the UFA/UFWA movement culture. Although one writer argues otherwise, Wood explained his ideas in many local meetings, conventions, and the press,[38] and his notions were widely discussed and well understood by UFA/UFWA leaders, political candidates, and members. One farmer commented about group politics: 'It is doubtful if any public issue in Alberta has ever received greater publicity, more hostile criticism, and more serious consideration. And all the while the idea has steadily gained favor with the people, so that to suggest that the action of the convention [in endorsing group political action] was due to a lack of understanding of the proposition or to the personal influence of Mr. Wood, is as ridiculous as it is insincere.'[39]

Because Wood's doctrines were well known and expressed as well as developed the movement's culture, they were popular and played a role in the 1921 elections. One anti-UFA local newspaper attributed the UFA candidate's victory in the federal election to an 'unshakable confidence in the group idea' among voters.[40] 'Class' politics and the group-government theory captured farmers' imaginations by showing how a true democracy could be realized. It also provided an effective means of electoral co-operation between farmers and labourers.

Group doctrines, while enjoying some support throughout the country, were most popular in Alberta. In the foothills province, frontier conditions, geography, and climate gave rise to high debt loads and transportation costs as well as drought and wide crop yield variability, all of which made farmers receptive to radical political solutions. Besides having generally less extreme economic pressures, other provinces had neither a Wood to preach class politics nor as high a proportion of American settlers. Such settlers, being unattached to the British parliamentary and party system, were more open to unorthodox populist political ideas than British or Canadian farmers. Moreover, they brought with them an uncompromising commitment to grassroots democracy, which the group-government theory embodied. Ex-Americans strongly backed Wood's group-government theory because they had shaped the political culture of rural Alberta, a democratic culture his theory articulated.

William Irvine also influenced Alberta farmers to endorse group politics. Born in the Shetland Islands, where he imbibed labour and socialist literature, Irvine came to Canada in 1907, graduated from Wesley and Manitoba colleges in 1914, and arrived in Calgary in 1916. There, he became a Unitarian clergyman and the editor of the radical *Nutcracker* (1916–17), the *Alberta Non-Partisan* (1917–19), and the *Western Independent* (1919–20), the organ of the UFA Provincial Political Association. In 1920 he published *The Farmers in Politics*, a lucid exposition of Wood's ideas. Like Wood, Irvine had a delightful sense of humour. In a 1918 edition of the *Alberta Non-Partisan*, he printed, with no comment but the heading 'Oh,' a note he had received from a reader: 'Stop my subscription to your anarchist paper at once.'[41]

A few scholars argue or imply that Irvine, more than Wood, developed and popularized the idea of group organization and politics in the UFA/UFWA. 'From such diverse sources as his early found socialism,' writes Anthony Mardiros, 'the politics of the U.S. Non-Partisans, the ideas current among western Canadian farmers, and finally from the ponderings of Henry Wise Wood, he was able to construct a social philosophy which was in large part adopted by the U.F.A.' John Hart suggests that Irvine's group-government theory was not really based on Wood's, averring that it 'resembled Cole's guild socialism much more than it did the ideas of Wood.'[42]

Irvine did help to spread group doctrines, primarily through *The Farmers in Politics*, and he gained support for notions implicit in group government, such as the idea that backbenchers should be able to vote freely without fear of defeating the government. But his apologists overstate the originality of his group theory and his influence in getting farmers to endorse class politics.

The fact is that until the late fall of 1919 Irvine opposed occupationally based political action, and he clashed with Wood at the UFA/UFWA constituency conventions of that year, arguing that the organization must open its political movement to non-farmers. Wood won over the majority of Alberta farmers, however, and Irvine, soon convinced by Wood's arguments, sensed the direction in which the wind was blowing and jumped on the bandwagon, realizing that continued opposition to Wood would only weaken the political movement. The eventual result was *The Farmers in Politics*.

This lively book presents all the essentials of Wood's philosophy; in no real sense is it an original work. Following Wood, Irvine describes the operation of the 'laws' of competition and co-operation in history: how competition prompted the creation of successively larger co-operative units – tribes, nations, allied units – and how those same laws drove manufacturers to form associations and drove other classes, including farmers, to organize for protection. Irvine's critique of the party system is also like Wood's, though it is more complete. In addition, he makes a similar case for industrial organization, arguing that only occupational groups, rooted in class interest, could resist divisive and superficial party appeals and develop democratic thought and in this way mobilize the masses. Furthermore, Irvine presents the same arguments about group government as Wood: occupational representatives would be forced to co-operate out of self-interest, passing laws acceptable to all classes while blocking bills favouring any one group.[43]

In these key respects, Irvine repeats Wood's points, but he often develops them. For example, he extends the logic of Wood's group-government theory to argue that a group cabinet would consist of members in proportion to their numerical strength in the government.[44] Yet despite its greater detail, Irvine's group-government scheme does not, Hart to the contrary, resemble guild socialism 'much more' than it does Wood's plan.

Although mainly an elaboration of Wood's ideas – and an expression of the UFA/UFWA movement culture – *The Farmers in Politics* certainly bears Irvine's imprint. It is set more explicitly in an organic evolutionary framework than Wood's writings are. Perhaps owing to this social science emphasis as well as to his Unitarianism, Irvine omitted Wood's biblical depiction of an apocalyptic battle between democracy and plutocracy. And while Wood's message was mainly for farmers, Irvine appealed also to workers, placing labour into his discussion. Additionally, Irvine's concept of class was somewhat different from Wood's. While calling all occupational groups classes as Wood did, Irvine sometimes adopted a more traditional class analysis, referring to the conflict of the two basic classes of capital and labour. He argued that farmers would bring peace between these groups by showing them how to co-operate.[45]

The major difference between *The Farmers in Politics* and Wood's teachings is that Irvine, while noting that group governments would have business representatives, looked forward to the gradual collapse of capitalism and its replacement by socialism. At the same time, he avoided the latter term for fear of alarming liberal farmers, using instead rhetoric such as 'the commonwealth' and the 'humanizing of the social system.' Wood's philosophy, in contrast, implied that his true democracy would be capitalistic, although he said little about how society would be organized. This lack of specificity, and Wood's use of non-liberal notions of class conflict and class co-operation, enabled Irvine to cast Wood's theory in a radical light.[46]

Because of Wood's ambiguity and Irvine's hints about the eventual triumph of collectivism, most radicals accepted group action and government. They were also pleased that Wood permitted a measure of farmer-labour co-operation. With both radicals and liberals supporting group organization and politics, Wood's philosophy and Irvine's version of it became the UFA/UFWA philosophy. That theory inspired farmers politically by promising to end party rule and corporate exploitation while assuring them that their utopias – whether liberal or radical – would be ushered in.

Henry Wise Wood's social and political philosophy was a product of his class experience, reading, American background, the historical context, and the UFA/UFWA movement culture. Expressing that culture, his theory was readily accepted by farmers. Interpreted in a socialist way by William Irvine, it appealed even to radicals. Supported by both wings, it became the UFA/UFWA philosophy and was an intellectual force in the agrarian revolt. It also entrenched a populist 'bias' for grassroots democracy in Alberta political culture that lingers to the present.

Epilogue

What profit has a man from all his labor in which he toils under the sun?

One generation passes away, and another comes; but the earth abides forever.

The sun also rises, and the sun goes down, and hastens to the place where it arose.

The wind goes toward the south, and turns around to the north; the wind whirls about continually, and comes again on its circuit.

All the rivers run into the sea, yet the sea is not full; to the place where the rivers come, there they return again.

All things are full of labor; man cannot express it. The eye is not satisfied with seeing, nor the ear with hearing.

That which had been is what will be, that which is done is what will be done, and there is nothing new under the sun.

Ecclesiastes 1:3–9[1]

By the end of 1921 one of the greatest mass democratic and agrarian movements in North American history had reached its peak. At that dizzy moment, the UFA/UFWA had some 37,500 paid-up members, including almost 40 per cent of Alberta's male farmers. It had developed an impressive co-operative movement, had gained important legislation for farm women and men, and had defeated the old parties, federally and provincially.

The movement culture that lay behind these achievements would sustain a core of committed UFA/UFWA members through the 1920s and into the 1930s. Yet as the heady excitement of the 1921 elections subsided, the organization began a long period of stagnation; never again would it regain the vibrancy of the immediate post-war years. The movement had been politicized, had thrown itself into the campaigns, had succeeded beyond its wildest expectations, and now its force was waning. For many farmers, there seemed nothing more to do. The UFA was in power; the kingdom would come as a matter of course. The fight was over, plutocracy was defeated, or would be shortly. With many farmers feeling that 'the U.F.A. does not need me now,' UFA/UFWA membership dropped by half in 1922,[2] a fall from which it never really recovered.

Having become politically conscious, many farmers lost sight of the organization's educational and community work. Because of their political victories, they also saw less reason to accommodate ethnic minorities. This attitude and renewed immigration caused nativism to rear its head in the 1920s as it never had when the movement had endeavoured, for political reasons, to recruit all producers. Non-Anglo-Celtic members and potential members became alienated and drifted away from the UFA/UFWA.[3] Women from a variety of backgrounds were repelled by the opposition of UFA men to their agenda in the 1920s; a real contrast, they felt, to the encouragement they had received when the organization had sought their political support to topple the old parties.

But the UFA/UFWA was more than a victim of political success and a resurgence of nativism and sexism. Co-operative activity, which had helped to develop the movement, now helped to spell its demise. Frustration with the grain and meat trades, the termination of the Wheat Board, and a desire to save money through co-operation had drawn thousands to the UFA/UFWA. The long-awaited Alberta Wheat Pool, however, shifted farmers' focus away from the UFA/UFWA as 'pooling became the panacea for growers' problems.'[4] In fact, the farm movement – in Alberta and across the West – did not so much dissipate as it moved partly into a new institution. The UFA/UFWA became, to an extent, the pool movement.

In addition, economics conspired against the UFA/UFWA. The movement – in Alberta and elsewhere – was a child of adversity; hardship had propelled farmers into the agrarian revolt. But with the UFA in power – one main goal achieved – many Alberta farmers experiencing difficulty in the early 1920s were no longer willing to pay membership fees to the organization. Then, as conditions improved later in the decade, there seemed less need for a UFA/UFWA. And when the 'dirty thirties' came around, who could afford to pay dues to the association when the kids needed shoes?

The conduct of the UFA government also hurt the UFA/UFWA organization. Many farmers were happy with the government's conservatism and saw no reason to try to change its policies by joining the UFA/UFWA, which continued its role as a political pressure group. Other farmers became disillusioned with the UFA/UFWA's inability to influence 'their' government: some women were upset with the administration's lack of equal rights legislation, and farmers of both sexes were angered by the government's record in other areas, especially its lack of credit reform. The resulting frustration, which became acute in the 1930s, pushed thousands away from the UFA/UFWA and into the arms of William Aberhart, whose charisma and religious appeal harkened back to Wood and the glory days of the movement.[5]

The decline of UFA/UFWA education further weakened the organization. In 1922 *The U.F.A.* replaced the *Guide* as the UFA/UFWA's official organ. The *Guide* had been an open forum in which prairie farmers debated issues and developed movement policies; *The U.F.A.* was essentially the voice of UFA/UFWA leaders and the UFA government. Some members wanted more space in the paper for their opinions,[6] but this request was not granted. Despondent, they lost interest in the UFA/UFWA.

The leaders' control of *The U.F.A.* was but one indication of the growth of executive power in the UFA/UFWA, which was another blow to the organization. This centralization of power drove a wedge between the rank and file and the leadership, especially as the officers sided with the UFA government when members sought policy changes. UFA/UFWA democracy – that dynamic impulse of the earlier movement – began to suffer, and the zeal of many members faded as they lost their grip on the movement's helm.

The decline of support for reform in general also worked against the UFA/UFWA and the larger farm movement. To some extent, this waning enthusiasm stemmed from success – many reforms had been achieved, including women suffrage – but it also stemmed from the decline of idealism, which had been blighted by the carnage of the war and by the post-war depression. In this climate, and with the secularization of the social gospel,[7] the UFA/UFWA's crusading spirit was blunted.

The gradual absorption in the 1920s of the national Progressive party by the Liberals further damaged the farm movement across the country. By the middle of the decade, it was clear that the dwindling numbers of Progressives would never form the government, and since the UFA members were unable to accomplish much in opposition, increasing numbers of rural Albertans concluded that it was useless to vote UFA, and they returned to their old parties. Although the UFA continued to send sizable numbers of MPs to Ottawa until 1935, the federal UFA vote slipped from 52 per cent in 1921 to 31 per cent in 1925, and the Conservative candidates in Alberta obtained more votes than the UFA candidates in the 1925 and 1930 federal elections.[8] Thus, the failure of the Progressive movement, the ineffectiveness of the UFA MPs – the latter rendered powerless by the two-party British parliamentary system – and the persistence of traditional party loyalties eroded the credibility of the farm movement, including that in Alberta.

This erosion was exacerbated by the cleavage in the national agrarian political movement between the advocates of occupational representation, who were mostly Albertans led by Wood, and the majority of Progressives outside the province, who saw Progressivism as little more than a means of forcing the Liberal party to reform itself and return to its low-tariff roots. The controversy between these two groups, although evident as early as 1920, had been buried during the 1921 elections, but it arose with a vengeance thereafter. It split the Progressive party in 1924, when a faction of uncompromising proponents of constituency autonomy, who were mainly Alberta members, left the party because of its cabinet control and organized their own parliamentary group known as the 'Ginger group.' Although the UFA/UFWA approved this action, and although the UFA remained politically successful provincially and even federally until 1935 – long after independent agrarian politics had withered and died elsewhere in the country – the lack of unity among farmers over political strategy had a corrosive effect on the grassroots farm movement, even in Alberta. The sense of oneness with farmers in other provinces that had built the UFA/UFWA before 1922 was shattered.

In the 1930s the UFA organization suffered from its association with the UFA government, which was overwhelmed with the Great Depression and plagued with sex scandals. Moreover, by this time the UFA/ UFWA had lost prestige because it no longer spoke for rural Alberta; its hearty endorsement of a proposed UFA government education bill in 1929 was repudiated by a majority of farmers.[9] Its affiliation in 1932–3 with the Co-operative Commonwealth Federation (CCF), which certain UFA leaders and MPs had helped to create, was at best a mixed blessing for the farm movement. While radicals and economically pressed farmers were enthusiastic, most liberals were shocked by the CCF platform;

much of its rhetoric was familiar, but its Fabian socialism was foreign to the UFA/UFWA movement culture.

In spite of its decline, the UFA/UFWA etched an indelible mark on Alberta political culture. The movement's emphasis on democracy and its culture of opposition to metropolitan power forged a permanent populist 'bias' in Alberta politics. Woe to the party that fails to appeal and listen to 'the people' and to fight, if necessary, the 'East' on their behalf! Moreover, in spawning a political movement that defeated the Liberals, absorbed many Conservatives, and held power provincially for fourteen years – all the while eschewing partyism – the UFA/UFWA established a pattern in provincial politics of one-party dominance and political eccentricity, or at least a willingness to try new political movements. Never again would Albertans be beholden to the traditional parties. Furthermore, and more immediately, by exposing farmers to radical monetary doctrines, the UFA/UFWA prepared the way for Social Credit, another unorthodox populist movement, which stormed to power when the UFA failed to solve the riddle of the Depression.

By no means are these the only legacies of the UFA/UFWA and the larger farm movement. The organized farmers helped to fight for women's rights and contributed to the development of the national co-operative movement, particularly the producer co-op movement, which has flourished. They were at the forefront of the agitation for direct and graduated taxation, which was implemented during the war and eventually became the cornerstone of the Canadian tax system. Thus, the concept of a modest redistribution of wealth through the state was accepted and made part of Canadian political culture. The farmers also fought, with partial success, for political reform. Although patronage was by no means eliminated – it seems as inevitable as death and taxes – its practice became less blatant and pervasive in response to agrarian pressure, and the principle of merit was factored into the hiring of civil servants.

To the farmers must also go credit for making third parties an enduring feature of the Canadian political landscape. Not only did the Progressives give rise, in a very real way, to the CCF and Social Credit, they were responsible for changing parliamentary rules to accommodate a third party in the House. Moreover, their struggle, carried on primarily by UFA members, for recognition of the principle of constituency autonomy – the accountability of the representative to his or her constituents – was not entirely in vain. It weakened, if only slightly, the power of the caucus and the whip in Canadian political life,[10] and the ideal of grassroots political control remains alive, especially in Alberta. In particular, the appeal of direct democracy – the initiative, the referendum, and the recall – has shown remarkable staying power in the prairies, thanks largely to the democratic culture left by the farm movement, especially the Alberta movement.

It can also be said that the organized farmers helped to foster acceptance – for good or for ill – of the idea of government ownership of key industries, the most notable example being public support for railway nationalization; and they promoted the concept of a limited welfare state, particularly in their demands for measures to assist war veterans and their families. More generally, they popularized the notion that the state should control certain sectors of the economy. In applying this principle, the Progressives' greatest success was the restoration of the Crow's Nest Pass Agreement in 1922. And while their efforts to reinstate the Wheat Board were unsuccessful after the war, such a body was finally created in 1935. The mainstream of the early farm movement, though by no means proto-socialist or even necessarily left of centre, was emphatically not laissez-faire in orientation.

In one key area the UFA/UFWA and the larger farm movement of the day would feel vindicated if they could have looked into the future: free trade has been established with the United States. They had very little success, however, in their own crusade for lower tariffs; while they forced post-war governments to refrain from increasing duties and even forced the King government to lower some tariffs slightly, the National Policy of protectionism remained impregnable. Moreover, farmers did not inaugurate a new heaven and a new earth.

During the four decades up to 1921 the Alberta farm movement and its culture were 'made' in response to frontier and environmental conditions, capitalistic pressures, and government policies. From 1879 to 1908 the movement was formed as farmers began questioning the status quo, articulating a nascent movement culture that led them to create several farm associations and ultimately the UFA. Then, from 1909 to 1918 the movement was built: it gained a substantial membership base, established a women's section, and fully developed its culture, which, under the stress of the Great War, moved the organization towards the brink of direct political action. Finally, from 1919 to 1921 the movement was politicized as farmers dedicated themselves to independent politics, were confirmed in that decision by their perception – shaped by their culture – of their post-war experience, gained women's political support, set up political structures, and entered the 1921 elections.

The movement culture helping to drive farmers through these phases comprised feelings of community; a sense of class opposition; assumptions about gender; commitment to organization, co-operation, democracy, citizenship, and education; a social ethic; religious convictions; agrarian ideals; collective self-respect and self-confidence; and two ideologies, one liberal, one radical. The emergence and development of this culture, in reaction to structural and other forces, help to explain the forming, building, and politicizing of the Alberta farm movement – one of the most fascinating and successful mass movements in North American history.

The wind continues to howl outside the old UFA hall, whistling through the cracks and banging the door, open and closed, open and closed. The sun, no less relentless, beats down on the broken shingles and the dry, splintering wood siding of the building.

In time, the sun begins to set, the wind changes direction, and rain clouds pass quickly overhead, releasing their heavy drops on the roof and surrounding thistle-choked fields. Inside, water starts dripping from the ceiling, forms a puddle on the hardwood floor, and slips slowly between the cracks, finding its way to the earth beneath.

And I set my heart to seek and search out by wisdom concerning all that is done under heaven; this grievous task God has given to the sons of man, by which they may be exercised.

I have seen all the works that are done under the sun; and indeed, all is vanity and grasping for the wind.[11]

Notes

UFAF   United Farmers of Alberta Fonds
UFWA   United Farm Women of Alberta. Minutes of Conventions and Execu-
        tive and Board
WI   *Western Independent*

Note: The archives in which sources were found are cited only the first time those sources appear in the notes of each chapter. Periodicals and pamphlets for which no archives are cited were found at the University of Calgary. All errors in spelling, punctuation, and grammar in the original quotations that appear in this book have been corrected.

Introduction

1 David Embree, 'The Rise of the United Farmers of Alberta' (MA thesis: University of Alberta, 1956), 253; AGI, UFAF, M1749, Box 1, File 8, *The Great West*, 20 Jan. 1909, 3.
2 The UFA had 40 per cent of the province's farm operators on its membership rolls at the height of its success, compared with 35 per cent for the Saskatchewan Grain Growers' Association, 31 per cent for the United Farmers of Manitoba, and 32 per cent for the United Farmers of Ontario. Calculated from AGI, MRAC, 1922, 73; Paul F. Sharp, *The Agrarian Revolt in Western Canada: A Survey Showing American Parallels*, with introductions by William Pratt and Lorne Brown (Regina: Canadian Plains Research Center, 1997; originally published by the University of Minnesota Press, Minneapolis, 1948), 117; *CAR*, 1922, 761; Melville H. Staples, *The Challenge of Agriculture: The Story of the United Farmers of Ontario* (Toronto: George N. Morang, 1921), 66; Census of Canada, 1921, vol. V, 78. The UFA's membership also compared very favourably with that of American farm organizations: in 1921 the UFA's membership was almost 5.5 per cent of Alberta's total population; with the UFWA and the junior UFA included it was almost 6.5 per cent. By comparison, the state Granges at their peak in 1875 had organized, on average, less than 3.5 per cent of their states' total population; the North Carolina Alliance had organized about 6 per cent of its state's population by 1890; the Kansas Northern Alliance, likely the strongest of the northern state Alliances, had organized around 10 or 11 per cent by the late 1880s; and the North Dakota Non-Partisan League had organized, at most, 7 per cent (and probably less) when it reached its high point in the late 1910s. Calculated from MRAC, 1922, 73; Census of Canada, 1921, vol. I, 5; Theodore Saloutos, *The Farmer Movements in the South, 1865–1933* (Lincoln: University of

Nebraska Press, 1964), 33; Carl C. Taylor, *The Farmers' Movement, 1620–1920* (New York: American Book Company, 1953), 213, 217, 437; U.S. Bureau of the Census, *Historical Statistics of the United States, Colonial Times to 1957* (Washington, DC, 1960; 1961 reprint), A 123–80.

3 Louis Aubrey Wood, *A History of Farmers' Movements in Canada: The Origins and Development of Agrarian Protest, 1872–1924*, with an introduction by Foster J.K. Griezic (Toronto: University of Toronto Press, 1975; originally published by Ryerson Press, Toronto, 1924); Sharp, *The Agrarian Revolt*; W.L. Morton, *The Progressive Party in Canada* (Toronto: University of Toronto Press, 1950); Ian MacPherson, *Each for All: A History of the Co-operative Movement in English Canada, 1900–1945* (Toronto: Macmillan, 1979); David Laycock, *Populism and Democratic Thought in the Canadian Prairies, 1910–1945* (Toronto: University of Toronto Press, 1990); William Kirby Rolph, *Henry Wise Wood of Alberta* (Toronto: University of Toronto Press, 1950); Anthony Mardiros, *William Irvine: The Life of a Prairie Radical* (Toronto: James Lorimer, 1979); J.E. Rea, *T.A. Crerar: A Political Life* (Montreal & Kingston: McGill-Queen's University Press, 1997).

4 Richard Hofstadter, *The Age of Reform: From Bryan to F.D.R.* (New York: Alfred A. Knopf, 1955; 1968 reprint); Paul Voisey, *Vulcan: The Making of a Prairie Community* (Toronto: University of Toronto Press, 1988); Robert Irwin, 'Farmers and Managerial Capitalism: The Saskatchewan Co-operative Elevator Company,' *Agricultural History* 70, 4 (Fall 1996), 626–52. The argument here is not that this view is 'wrong'; certainly, there were many entrepreneurial farmers, as Voisey shows, and some 'managerial' farm enterprises, as Irwin reveals. The point is that UFA/UFWA farmers cannot, as a whole, be fitted into this paradigm.

5 James Henretta, 'Families and Farms: Mentalité in Pre-Industrial America,' *William and Mary Quarterly* 35 (1978), 3–32; Lawrence Goodwyn, *The Populist Moment: A Short History of the Agrarian Revolt in America* (New York: Oxford University Press, 1978); Steven Hahn and Jonathan Prude, eds, *The Countryside in the Age of Capitalist Transformation: Essays in the Social History of Rural America* (Chapel Hill: University of North Carolina Press, 1985; 1987 reprint); MacPherson, *Each for All*. MacPherson and John Herd Thompson make the latter argument in 'The Business of Agriculture: Prairie Farmers and the Adoption of "Business Methods," 1880–1950,' in Peter Baskerville, ed., *Canadian Papers in Business History* 1 (Victoria: Public History Group, 1989).

6 The only scholarly book on organized Alberta farm women is Nanci Langford's *Politics, Pitchforks, and Pickle Jars: 75 Years of Organized Farm Women in Alberta* (Calgary: Detselig, 1997). Because she covers such a broad sweep of time, her analysis of the earliest years is sketchy.

7 C.W. King, *Social Movements in the United States* (New York, 1956), 27, cited in
  Walter D. Young, *The Anatomy of a Party: The National CCF, 1932–61* (Toronto:
  University of Toronto Press, 1969), 4.

8 Goodwyn's argument can be found in *The Populist Moment.* Critical articles
  include Stanley B. Parsons et al., 'The Role of Co-operatives in the Development of the Movement Culture of Populism,' *Journal of American History* 69
  (1983), 866–85; Robert Cherny, 'Lawrence Goodwyn and Nebraska Populism: A Review Essay,' *Great Plains Quarterly* 1, 3 (Summer 1981), 181–94.
  Scholarly works that effectively use the concept of a movement culture
  include Steven Hahn, *The Roots of Southern Populism: Yeoman Farmers and the
  Transformation of the Georgia Upcountry, 1850–1890* (New York: Oxford University Press, 1983); Robert C. McMath, Jr, 'Sandy Land and Hogs in the
  Timber: (Agri)cultural Origins of the Farmers' Alliance in Texas,' in
  Hahn and Prude, eds, *The Countryside in the Age of Capitalist Transformation*,
  205–29.

9 What follows is an adaptation of Lawrence Goodwyn's stage theory of movement development as outlined in *The Populist Moment*, xviii.

10 Robert Darnton, *The Great Cat Massacre and Other Episodes in French Cultural
   History* (New York: BasicBooks, 1984), 4.

11 Ibid., 78; *GGG*, 24 Jan. 1912, 12; 12 July 1916, 12.

12 Labour histories written from a cultural perspective include Bryan D.
   Palmer, *A Culture in Conflict: Skilled Workers and Industrial Capitalism in Hamil-
   ton, Ontario, 1860–1914* (Montreal & Kingston: McGill-Queen's University
   Press, 1979); Gregory S. Kealey and Bryan D. Palmer, *Dreaming of What Might
   Be: The Knights of Labour in Ontario, 1880–1900* (Cambridge: Cambridge Uni-
   versity Press, 1982). Among the few rural histories demonstrating the explan-
   atory power of culture are J.I. Little, *Crofters and Habitants: Settler Society,
   Economy, and Culture in a Quebec Township* (Montreal & Kingston: McGill-
   Queen's University Press, 1991); John C. Lehr, '"The Peculiar People":
   Ukrainian Settlement of Marginal Lands in Southeastern Manitoba,' in
   David C. Jones and Ian MacPherson, eds, *Building Beyond the Homestead*
   (Calgary: University of Calgary Press, 1985; 1988 reprint), 29–46.

13 See Clifford Geertz, *The Interpretation of Cultures* (New York: BasicBooks,
   1973), 204–5, 219–20.

14 Barry Ferguson analyses this strain of liberalism in *Remaking Liberalism: The
   Intellectual Legacy of Adam Shortt, O.D. Skelton, W.C. Clark, and W.A. Mackintosh*
   (Montreal & Kingston: McGill-Queen's University Press, 1993).

15 See Joy Parr, *The Gender of Breadwinners: Women, Men, and Change in Two
   Industrial Towns, 1880–1950* (Toronto: University of Toronto Press, 1990),
   6–11.

Chapter One: The Forming of the Movement, 1879–1909

1 AGI, *EB*, 15 Dec. 1883, 2.

2 Producerism was the notion that farmers and workers, as the producers of all wealth, had a common identity and a common enemy: the non-producing capitalist class. Anti-monopolism was an aversion to monopolistic or corporate power. Equal rights was a protest against 'special privileges' for corporations, such as bonuses and tariffs.

3 Carl C. Taylor, *The Farmers' Movement, 1620–1920* (New York: American Book Company, 1953), 495; Louis Aubrey Wood, *A History of Farmers' Movements in Canada: The Origins and Development of Agrarian Protest, 1872–1924*, with an introduction by Foster J.K. Griezic (Toronto: University of Toronto Press, 1975; originally published by Ryerson Press, Toronto, 1924), 13.

4 David Embree, 'The Rise of the United Farmers of Alberta' (MA thesis: University of Alberta, 1956), 1–5. The author is indebted to Embree's thesis for this chapter; readers wanting further information on the pre-UFA Alberta farm movement should consult his excellent study. Hereafter cited simply as 'Embree.'

5 Embree, 8–14.

6 Ibid., 15–16, 20–3.

7 *EB*, 5 Dec. 1891, 2; 16 Apr. 1892, 1; Wood, *A History of Farmers' Movements*, 119–20, 138–9; Brian Robert McCutcheon, 'The Economic and Social Structures of Political Agrarianism in Manitoba, 1870–1900' (PhD thesis: University of British Columbia, 1974), 279, 328–9, 341.

8 Jeffrey M. Taylor, 'The Language of Agrarianism in Manitoba, 1890–1925,' *Labour/Le Travail* 23 (Spring 1989), 96–7; Ramsay Cook, 'Tillers and Toilers: The Rise and Fall of Populism in Canada in the 1890s,' *Historical Papers*, Canadian Historical Association (1984), esp. 14–15.

9 Regarding the populist influence of Scandinavians and Ukrainians on prairie politics, see Robert C. McMath, Jr, 'Populism in Two Countries: Agrarian Protest in the Great Plains and Prairie Provinces,' *Agricultural History* 69, 4 (Fall 1995), 528–9.

10 Embree, 24–8; Wood, *A History of Farmers' Movements*, 144; *EB*, 21 May 1894, 4.

11 *EB*, 1 Nov. 1894, 1, 4; 1 June 1896, 1; 2 June 1896, 2.

12 Embree, 34–7; McCutcheon, 'Economic and Social Structures,' 342–3.

13 The CPR adopted this policy because grain could be loaded into railway cars more quickly from elevators than from flat warehouses. The latter were trackside grain containers owned by independent grain dealers who competed with the elevator companies in buying grain.

14 Many farmers preferred to load their grain directly from their wagons into railway cars and ship it to market themselves, rather than sell it to the grain elevator companies.

15 Charles F. Wilson, *A Century of Canadian Grain: Government Policy to 1951* (Saskatoon: Western Producer Prairie Books, 1978), 25–8; D.J. Hall, 'The Manitoba Grain Act: An "Agrarian Magna Charta"?' *Prairie Forum* 4, 1 (1979), 106–11.

16 *EB*, 29 May 1899, 2; 23 Oct. 1899, 4; Embree, 59–62.

17 Hall, 'Manitoba Grain Act,' 113–15; Embree, 65–6.

18 *EB*, 11 Nov. 1901, 6; 6 Dec. 1901, 2; 9 Dec. 1901, 2; 20 Dec. 1901, 2.

19 Ibid., 27 Dec. 1901, 8; Embree, 73–4.

20 Wilson, *A Century of Canadian Grain*, 32–4; Hall, 'Manitoba Grain Act,' 116.

21 *GGG*, 26 June 1918, 11; Embree, 86.

22 Embree, 86–7, 89.

23 *EB*, 1 Dec. 1902, 7; Embree, 89–92.

24 *EB*, 23 Jan. 1903, 4; 12 Feb. 1903, 3; Embree, 107–8, 92.

25 Embree, 93–5, 97.

26 1906 Census of the North-West Provinces, 91; Embree, 98–9.

27 AGI, Rice Sheppard, M1135, 'Twenty Years in the Great North-West,' unpublished manuscript, 1922, 52.

28 AGI, M1747, Eileen Birch, collector, papers and pamphlets on UFA, 'The Early History of Canadian Society of Equity,' 1; Taylor, *Farmers' Movement*, 365–6; *EB*, 25 Nov. 1904, 3; AGI, Norman F. Priestley Fonds, M1003, File 6, Keen to Priestley, 6 Sept. 1929; *CAR*, 1908, 486; 1919, 357.

29 *EB*, 1 Mar. 1905, 7; 18 Feb. 1905, 6.

30 Embree, 114–16.

31 Ibid., 103.

32 *EB*, 30 Mar. 1905, 6; 6 June 1905, 5.

33 Embree, 119–20; 1906 Census, 91.

34 Embree, 124, 121–5.

35 AGI, *FRR*, May 1906, 19; *EB*, 27 Nov. 1905, 4.

36 AGI, COR, handwritten letter, Keen to Clark, 6 Nov. 1905; typed correspondence, Keen to Clark, 6 Nov. 1905; Embree, 143.

37 Embree, 144–5; AGI, Alberta Farmers' Association, M1745, Minutes of Conventions and Directors' Meetings, 22; *EB*, 13 Dec. 1905, 3.

38 Embree, 148–62; *FRR*, Apr. 1906, 10; May 1906, 19.

39 Robert Joseph Gowen, 'Canada and the Myth of the Japan Market, 1896–1911,' *Pacific Historical Review* 39 (1970), 63–83; AFA Minutes, 5–6, 17; *SN*, 29 Dec. 1906, 11; 26 Jan., 1907, 10.

40 *SN*, 19 Jan. 1907, 11, 13.

41 Embree, 156.

42 *SN*, 3 Nov. 1906, 3; AFA Minutes, 55, 57; Embree, 167.

43 AFA Minutes, 54.

44 Ibid., 55; *FRR*, Jan. 1907, 8.

45 *SN*, 9 Mar. 1907, 10; 13 Apr. 1907, 11.

46 COR, Minute Book of Bon Accord S of E union, 20 Jan. 1906; *SN*, 24 Nov. 1906, 16; 20 Apr. 1907, 10; 26 Jan. 1907, 11; AFA Minutes, 37.

47 *EB*, 10 Feb. 1906, 5; Embree, 189.

48 *MA*, 13 Nov. 1907, 1.

49 *EB*, 7 Apr. 1906, 3.

50 AFA Minutes, 66; *FRR*, June 1908, 13.

51 *SN*, 29 Dec. 1906, 10; Embree, 191–2.

52 Embree, 197.

53 Ibid., 199–200; COR, circular letter from Keen to the unions on behalf of 'Canadian Society of Equity, Limited,' 7 Jan. 1907; Robert H. Bahmer, 'The American Society of Equity,' *Agricultural History* 14 (1940), 53.

54 AGI, UFAF, M1749, Box 1, File 10, S of E constitution, 1; Embree, 201, 200, 198.

55 Embree, 200–2; Bahmer, 'American Society of Equity,' 54–5; *SN*, 15 June 1907, 6, 8; 22 June 1907, 8, 10.

56 Embree, 198; *SN*, 22 June 1907, 8.

57 Embree, 215–19; *MA*, 15 Nov. 1907, 1.

58 *MA*, 16 Nov. 1907, 5; *CH*, 14 Nov. 1907, 2.

59 *MA*, 18 Nov. 1907, 1; 16 Nov. 1907, 1.

60 Ibid., 18 Nov. 1907, 1, 5; *CH*, 18 Nov. 1907, 2.

61 Embree, 230, 228.

62 *SN*, 31 Aug. 1907, 6; 4 May 1907, 11; 11 Jan. 1908, 2; AFA Minutes, 86; *GGG*, June 1908, 8–11.

63 AFA Minutes, 23, 62, 83; *GGG*, 22 June 1910, 16; *SN*, 26 Jan. 1907, 11; 27 July 1907, 10; 11 Jan. 1908, 2; *CAR*, 1907, 481–2; 1909, 545.

64 Embree, 240, 241–4.

65 Ibid., 245–7.

66 Sheppard, 'Twenty Years,' 65; Embree, 245–51.

67 Embree, 253; UFAF, Box 1, File 8, *The Great West*, 20 Jan. 1909, 3.

Chapter Two: The Building of the Movement, 1909–1913

1 *GGG*, 2 Mar. 1910, 22; David Embree, 'The Rise of the United Farmers of Alberta' (MA thesis: University of Alberta, 1956), 248.

2 *GGG*, Feb. 1909, 37. The fee was not increased until 1918, and then to only $2.00. Half of the fee went to the local union, half to the central association.

3 AGI, MRAC, 1910, 27; *MA*, 25 Feb. 1910, 2–3; L.G. Thomas, *The Liberal Party in Alberta: A History of Politics in the Province of Alberta, 1905–1921* (Toronto: University of Toronto Press, 1959), chap. 4. Thomas argues that the scandal 'profoundly' affected Albertans' political behaviour and may have been 'the critical episode in the political history of the province' (58).

4 *GGG*, 2 Mar. 1910, 16.

5 Ibid., 21 Dec. 1910, 39, 4; *CAR*, 1910, 265–330. The Canadian Council of Agriculture, the main national farm lobby group, was formed in 1909 by the UFA, the Saskatchewan Grain Growers' Association, the Manitoba Grain Growers' Association, and the Dominion Grange and Farmers' Association (Ontario's major agrarian organization). Other farm groups later joined the Council.

6 *GGG*, 7 Dec. 1910, 32; 28 Dec. 1910, 8; 21 Dec. 1910, 39–40.

7 Ibid., 1 Mar. 1911, 18; 18 Jan. 1911, 11.

8 Ibid., 2 July 1913, 14; 24 Dec. 1913, 7.

9 Ibid., 4 May 1910, 16; 18 Oct. 1911, 12; 8 June 1910, 16; 29 June 1910, 16; 21 Dec. 1910, 12.

10 Ibid., 21 Dec. 1910, 4.

11 Ibid., 20 Sept. 1911, 12; 1 Mar. 1911, 42; 22 Mar. 1911, 26; *CAR*, 1911, 246.

12 *GGG*, 30 Nov. 1910, 17; 8 Feb. 1911, 15; 22 Mar. 1911, 14; 29 Mar. 1911, 10.

13 MRAC, 1913, 28; *GGG*, 19 July 1911, 7; 22 Mar. 1911, 8.

14 *GGG*, 14 Dec. 1910, 16; 3 May 1911, 12; 10 May 1911, 13; 14 Dec. 1910, 16; 30 Nov. 1910, 17.

15 Ibid., 19 Apr. 1911, 14; 19 Apr. 1916, 6; 9 Aug. 1916, 10; 30 Aug. 1916, 12.

16 W.L. Morton, *The Progressive Party in Canada* (Toronto: University of Toronto Press, 1950), 26.

17 MRAC, 1913, 9; Henry George, *Progress and Poverty: An Inquiry into the Cause of Industrial Depressions and of the Increase of Want with Increase of Wealth; the Remedy*, abridged edition edited by A.W. Madsen, with a foreword by James M. Roberts (New York: Robert Schalkenbach Foundation, 1970), ix, xi.

18 *GGG*, 27 Apr. 1910, 13–14; 9 July 1913, 8; 4 Oct. 1911, 12; MRAC, 1913, 9.

19 MRAC, 1912, 53; *GGG*, 11 Oct. 1911, 22. Calls for similar single-tax measures by organized farmers in Saskatchewan and Manitoba are recorded in *CAR*, 1910, 499; 1911, 562–3; 1913, 609; 1915, 648.

20 *GGG*, 18 Sept. 1912, 10; *CAR*, 1914, 654.

21 *CAR*, 1911, 590; 1912, 584; *GGG*, 18 Sept. 1912, 10.

22 *CAR*, 1913, 642–3; 1914, 662.

23 *GGG*, 18 Sept. 1912, 10.

24 *CAR*, 1912, 573–4; 1913, 591, 601; 1914, 626.
25 Paul F. Sharp, *The Agrarian Revolt in Western Canada: A Survey Showing American Parallels*, with introductions by William Pratt and Lorne Brown (Regina: Canadian Plains Research Center, 1997; originally published by the University of Minnesota Press, Minneapolis, 1948), 51.
26 MRAC, 1913, 19–20; *GGG*, 6 Mar. 1912, 17, 24–6.
27 *GGG*, Feb. 1909, 38; 15 Feb. 1911, 30; 1 Mar. 1911, 9.
28 MRAC, 1910, 29, 35; 1911, 10, 3.
29 Ibid., 1911, 39; 1913, 35; *GGG*, 17 July 1912, 10; 31 Dec. 1913, 15; 16 Nov. 1910, 24; *CAR*, 1913, 609; 1914, 640.
30 Thomas, *Liberal Party in Alberta*, 135–6.
31 *CAR*, 1911, 541; 1912, 551; 1913, 294–5, 299, 267.
32 Ibid., 1913, 232–3.
33 Louis Aubrey Wood, *A History of Farmers' Movements in Canada: The Origins and Development of Agrarian Protest, 1872–1924*, with an introduction by Foster J.K. Griezic (Toronto: University of Toronto Press, 1975; originally published by Ryerson Press, Toronto, 1924), 217–19; Charles F. Wilson, *A Century of Canadian Grain: Government Policy to 1951* (Saskatoon: Western Producer Prairie Books, 1978), 43–5; MRAC, 1913, 10.
34 MRAC, 1910, 7–8; 1912, 13; 1914, 12; *GGG*, Feb. 1909, 37; 16 Mar. 1910, 11.
35 *GGG*, 28 Sept. 1910, 16; 28 Dec. 1910, 12–13; 21 Dec. 1910, 4.
36 Ibid., 18 Dec. 1912, 11; MRAC, 1911, 13–14; 1912, 14, 25–7; 1913, 13; 1914, 13; 1915, 10.
37 *GGG*, 24 Aug. 1910, 10; 21 Sept. 1910, 12; 28 Dec. 1910, 12; MRAC, 1912, 5; 1913, 11; 1914, 13.
38 Ian MacPherson, *Each for All: A History of the Co-operative Movement in English Canada, 1900–1945* (Toronto: Macmillan, 1979), 32–3; MRAC, 1913, 10, 27. Grain mixing was permitted by legislation allowing samples markets.
39 *GGG*, 6 Aug. 1913, 8; 30 Apr. 1913, 7; MRAC, 1914, 11–12; 1913, 16–17; 1911, 3.
40 *GGG*, 3 Aug. 1910, 23; 25 Jan. 1911, 15.
41 Ibid., 28 Feb. 1912, 16; 7 Aug. 1912, 15.
42 Ibid., 9 Nov. 1910, 24; 16 Nov. 1910, 17; 2 Nov. 1910, 16; MRAC, 1911, 16.
43 *GGG*, 17 Apr. 1912, 18; 22 Jan. 1913, 11; MRAC, 1912, 3.
44 MRAC, 1911, 8; *GGG*, 1 Jan. 1913, 9; 17 Apr. 1912, 18.
45 *GGG*, 16 Feb. 1910, 18.
46 Ibid., 28 Sept. 1910, 14.
47 Ibid., 29 June 1910, 17; 22 Mar. 1911, 16.
48 Ibid., 8 May 1912, 20.
49 MRAC, 1918, 55.

50 *GGG*, 13 Apr. 1910, 17; MRAC, 1912, 18, 16; 1911, 25.
51 AGI, UFAF, M1749, Box 1, File 10, UFA constitutions, 1909–10, 1, 3; William McIntosh, 'The United Farmers of Alberta, 1909–1920' (MA thesis: University of Calgary, 1971), 5, 7, 37, 52, 66–7; *GGG*, 13 Nov. 1912, 11.
52 McIntosh, 'United Farmers of Alberta,' 106. Tregillus's statement favouring a new party is recorded in MRAC, 1914, 8. The convention did not endorse UFA political action until 1919 – over four years after Tregillus had died.
53 *GGG*, 13 July 1910, 13; Thomas, *Liberal Party in Alberta*, 93–4. Tregillus was particularly critical of A.C. Rutherford, Alberta's first premier, and Duncan Marshall, the minister of agriculture. *MA*, 25 Feb. 1910, 2–3.
54 *GGG*, 3 July 1912, 8; 11 May 1910, 13; 9 Nov. 1910, 16; 12 July 1911, 10.
55 Thomas, *Liberal Party in Alberta*, 94; *GGG*, 5 Oct. 1910, 32; MRAC, 1911, 34; 1912, 48.
56 *GGG*, 23 Nov. 1910, 24; 16 Aug. 1911, 13; 13 Aug. 1913, 15; 23 July 1913, 8.
57 Ibid., 11 Jan. 1911, 13.
58 Ibid., 21 Sept. 1910, 32; 20 Nov. 1912, 11; MRAC, 1910, 27; 1911, 3, 31, 38; 1913, 27; 1914, 6.
59 *GGG*, 1 Jan. 1913, 7; *CAR*, 1912, 494–6; 1913, 300.
60 MRAC, 1913, 8; *GGG*, 11 Dec. 1912, 9; 20 July 1910, 14; 13 Aug. 1913, 15.
61 MRAC, 1913, 8.
62 Robert Irwin, 'Farmers and Managerial Capitalism: The Saskatchewan Co-operative Elevator Company,' *Agricultural History* 70, 4 (Fall 1996), 626–52; McIntosh, 'United Farmers of Alberta,' iii; *GGG*, Feb. 1909, 37–8; MRAC, 1910, 27.
63 MRAC, 1910, 31. The latter statements are based on a careful count and analysis of resolutions dealing with matters that were not simply internal to the organization.
64 MRAC, 1911, 36–8.
65 Ibid., 1913, 31–2, 29–30; 1910, 27; 1912, 56.
66 *GGG*, 16 Mar. 1910, 18; 14 June 1911, 16.
67 MRAC, 1911, 36; *GGG*, 16 Feb. 1910, 17; 21 Dec. 1910, 24.
68 Starting in 1912, unions were allowed a delegate for every ten, and major portion of ten, members.
69 *GGG*, 4 Nov. 1914, 13; 26 Apr. 1916, 11. At least three-quarters of the women's unions were represented at the 1917 convention: there were fifty women's locals at the time, and delegates representing thirty-six locals answered the convention roll-call, while several came in later. MRAC, 1917, 137, 49.
70 MRAC, 1911, 34.

71 Ibid., 34–5; 1912, 46; UFA constitutions, 1911, 11; 1912, 2–4. Under the old constitution, the executive comprised the president, the secretary-treasurer, and three directors chosen by the ten directors. Under the revised constitution adopted by the 1912 convention, the directors on the executive were replaced by three vice-presidents elected by the convention.

72 *GGG*, 24 May 1911, 13; 1 Nov. 1911, 12.

73 Ibid., 21 Feb. 1912, 12; 17 Aug. 1910, 12.

74 Ibid., 15 May 1912, 13; 26 July 1911, 17; 3 Jan. 1912, 23; 16 Aug. 1911, 20.

75 Ibid., 16 Aug. 1911, 20; 7 Feb. 1912, 23. The winner was F.B. Sulman, a prominent local UFA leader.

76 *GGG*, 3 Jan. 1912, 23; 31 May 1911, 21; Alison Prentice et al., *Canadian Women: A History* (Toronto: Harcourt Brace Jovanovich, 1988), 200.

77 MRAC, 1912, 56.

78 *GGG*, 27 Aug. 1913, 14; 26 Jan. 1910, 5.

79 Wood, *A History of Farmers' Movements*, 27; Leslie Robinson, 'Agrarian Reformers: Women and the Farm Movement in Alberta, 1909–1925' (MA thesis: University of Calgary, 1979), 95–6.

80 *GGG*, 18 June 1913, 14.

81 Ibid., 23 Oct. 1912, 12; 22 Jan. 1913, 11; 6 Aug. 1913, 11; MRAC, 1913, 34.

Chapter Three: The Rural Economy and the Movement

1 AGI, MRAC, 1910, 12.

2 The notion that a wheat staple economy was quickly established in the West can be found in W.A. Mackintosh, *Economic Problems of the Prairie Provinces* (Toronto: Macmillan, 1935); Vernon C. Fowke, *The National Policy and the Wheat Economy* (Toronto: University of Toronto Press, 1957); Howard Palmer with Tamara Palmer, *Alberta: A New History* (Edmonton: Hurtig, 1990), 51. The idea that this wheat economy was a major catalyst of farm protest is expressed in William Kirby Rolph, *Henry Wise Wood of Alberta* (Toronto: University of Toronto Press, 1950); Paul F. Sharp, *The Agrarian Revolt in Western Canada: A Survey Showing American Parallels*, with introductions by William Pratt and Lorne Brown (Regina: Canadian Plains Research Center, 1997; originally published by the University of Minnesota Press, Minneapolis, 1948). In *A History of the Canadian Economy*, 2nd ed. (Toronto: Harcourt Brace, 1996), Kenneth Norrie and Douglas Owram similarly argue that wheat 'was the dominant field crop from the beginning' and that it 'underlay a regional identity and political perspective that has continued to the present' (237, 227).

3 Census of Canada, 1911, vol. IV, xcii–xciii, 411; 1921, vol. V, xxxv. There were

(rounded to the nearest one) 34 head of cattle, 10 horses, 9 sheep, and
5 hogs for every Alberta farm in 1901, and only 20 head of cattle, 6 horses,
5 sheep, and 2 hogs for every Saskatchewan farm.

4 Census, 1921, vol. V, lx, lxxii; 1911, vol. IV, li, liii.

5 Ibid., 1911, vol. IV, xcii–xciii.

6 *CAR*, 1911, 582; 1913, 658; 1914, 671; 1915, 707; 1917, 791; 1918, 717.

7 Taken or calculated from Census, 1921, vol. V, lxi; Prairie Census, 1916, xlvi,
li, lii, lxiii, 300.

8 Mackintosh, *Economic Problems of the Prairie Provinces*, 7; Census, 1921, vol. V,
lxvii, lxxxvi. The average number of livestock per farm in Alberta in 1921 was
10 horses, 17 cattle, 5 sheep, and 5 hogs; the average numbers per
Saskatchewan farm were 9 horses, 11 cattle, 2 sheep, and 4 hogs.

9 These conclusions are based on calculations from the Census, 1921, vol. V,
xli. The values for livestock and their products in 1920 were $395 for
Saskatchewan and $488 for Alberta. The value of wheat was calculated as
65 per cent of the value of all field crops (see lxxiii).

10 Jeffrey M. Taylor, *Fashioning Farmers: Ideology, Agricultural Knowledge, and the
Manitoba Farm Movement, 1890–1925* (Regina: Canadian Plains Research
Center, 1994), 9–10. Prices are for No. 1 Northern, cash basis Lakehead
(122).

11 Paul Voisey, *Vulcan: The Making of a Prairie Community* (Toronto: University of
Toronto Press, 1988), 87–90.

12 Ibid., 86, 90, 92.

13 Census of Population and Agriculture, 1906, xviii.

14 *CAR*, 1911, 582; 1912, 591.

15 Voisey, *Vulcan*, 77–80, 93–7.

16 Mackintosh, *Economic Problems of the Prairie Provinces*, 24.

17 AGI, *EB*, 29 Dec. 1905, 6.

18 AGI, COR, letter from G. Harcourt, Department of Agriculture, to 'Sir,'
12 Dec. 1906.

19 AGI, UFAF, M1749, Box 1, File 10, UFA constitution, 1909, 1.

20 MRAC, 1910, 34; 1916, 25, 27, 54. The table on the latter page shows that
the northern constituencies contained about 44 per cent of the membership.

21 MRAC, 1922, 64.

22 Ibid., 1910, 10–12. The 1910 convention approved Bower's report making
these recommendations (20).

23 MRAC, 1910, 12; *CAR*, 1911, 119.

24 *GGG*, 2 Nov. 1921, 11; 17 Mar. 1915, 13; 8 Mar. 1916, 36; MRAC, 1917, 39;
1916, 17.

25 *GGG*, 14 Dec. 1910, 24; 15 May 1912, 14; 2 Nov. 1910, 17; 20 Apr. 1910, 17; 8 June 1910, 11; 24 May 1911, 15.

26 MRAC, 1914, 14; *GGG*, 3 Sept. 1913, 16; 6 May 1914, 12; 10 June 1914, 12; 29 July 1914, 12; 24 Feb. 1915, 12; 12 Aug. 1914, 14; 25 Nov. 1914, 13.

27 QUA, CP, Coll. 2117, Box 107, File 25, Fream, E.J., UFA circular no. 9, 15 Sept. 1912; *GGG*, 2 Jan. 1918, 12; 19 Feb. 1919, 21; 12 Nov. 1919, 32; 26 Nov. 1919, 49.

28 UFA constitution, 1909, 15; 1917, 22; *GGG*, 9 Nov. 1910, 26; 11 Jan. 1911, 17; 19 Apr. 1911, 23.

29 *GGG*, 16 Nov. 1910, 25; 16 Oct. 1918, 10; CP, Box 108, File 25, Fream, E.J., Aug. 1913 – Aug. 1914, UFA circular no. 14, 7 Dec. 1913.

30 UFA constitution, 1909, 15; 1917, 22; Cecilia Danysk, *Hired Hands: Labour and the Development of Prairie Agriculture, 1880–1930* (Toronto: McClelland & Stewart, 1995), 55; *EB*, 18 Feb. 1905, 7; Douglas McCalla, *Planting the Province: The Economic History of Upper Canada, 1784–1870* (Toronto: University of Toronto Press, 1993); J.I. Little, *Crofters and Habitants: Settler Society, Economy, and Culture in a Quebec Township, 1848–1881* (Montreal & Kingston: McGill-Queen's University Press, 1991); Rusty Bittermann, Robert A. Mackinnon, and Graeme Wynn, 'Of Inequality and Interdependence in the Nova Scotia Countryside, 1850–70,' *Canadian Historical Review* 74, 1 (Mar. 1993), 1–43; David McGinnis, 'Farm Labour in Transition: Occupational Structure and Economic Dependency in Alberta, 1921–1951,' in Howard Palmer, ed., *The Settlement of the West* (Calgary: University of Calgary Comprint, 1977), 174–86.

31 *GGG*, 21 Oct. 1914, 13; 28 Oct. 1914, 13; 28 June 1916, 10; 30 Aug. 1916, 12.

32 AGI, MREB, 1916, 88; *GGG*, 12 Nov. 1913, 13; 16 Mar. 1921, 22; 6 Apr. 1921, 20; Danysk, *Hired Hands*, 137.

33 Palmer, *Alberta*, 157–8; *GGG*, 30 Nov. 1910, 27; AGI, United Farmers of Alberta, Beaverlodge Local Fonds, BE Peace River, microfilm, Minute Book, 4, 6, 10, 12, 15, 17.

34 *GGG*, 20 Aug. 1919, 15; PAA, Premiers' Papers, Acc. 69.289, File 7, letter to R.B. Banber, 28 Dec. 1921.

35 The information on Sutton in this and the following paragraphs is taken or calculated from the entries and tables in his diary, which is in PAA, Acc. 66.119, Box 1, Files 1 and 2. A small amount for lost time was deducted from the wages indicated.

36 The 21 June 1913 entry says that he was poisoning gophers on the homestead and '20.'

37 Nancy Grey Osterud, 'Gender and the Transition to Capitalism in Rural America,' *Agricultural History* 67, 2 (Spring 1993), 23.

38 *GGG*, 26 June 1912, 8.

39 Ibid., 22 May 1912, 14; 9 Feb. 1910, 16.

40 Nearly all the persons with whom Sutton had economic relations (as indicated in his diary) are noted as UFA members in the minute book of his local, the Winona union. PAA, Winona local Minute Book, Acc. 66.119, Item 10.

41 *GGG*, 23 July 1919, 35.

42 Ibid., 27 Aug. 1919, 12; 6 Nov. 1912, 8.

43 Ernest B. Ingles, 'The Custom Threshermen in Western Canada, 1890–1925,' in David C. Jones and Ian MacPherson, eds, *Building Beyond the Homestead* (Calgary: University of Calgary Press, 1985; 1988 reprint), 135–60; *GGG*, 3 Apr. 1912, 20; 19 June 1912, 8; 20 Sept. 1916, 18–19.

44 *GGG*, 6 Dec. 1916, 27; 13 Oct. 1920, 48; MRAC, 1921, 77.

45 *GGG*, 3 Apr. 1918, 54; 5 Feb. 1919, 10; 20 Sept. 1916, 7.

46 AGI, SF, M1157, File 183, clipping from the *Farmers' Sun*, 5 Sept. 1923.

47 Ian MacPherson and John Herd Thompson, 'The Business of Agriculture: Prairie Farmers and the Adoption of "Business Methods," 1880–1950,' in Peter Baskerville, ed., *Canadian Papers in Business History* 1 (Victoria: Public History Group, 1988), 247–8.

48 *GGG*, 14 June 1911, 16–17.

49 Ibid., 7 Sept. 1910, 17; 21 Dec. 1921, 9; 26 Oct. 1910, 16; Barbara Villy Cormack, *Perennials and Politics: The Life Story of Hon. Irene Parlby, LL.D.* (Sherwood Park, AB: Professional Printing, 1968), 35.

50 MRAC, 1910, 28; *GGG*, 16 Nov. 1910, 25.

51 *GGG*, 6 Nov. 1912, 28; Census, 1921, vol. V, cvi.

52 Voisey, *Vulcan*, 93.

53 See R.W. Sandwell, 'Rural Reconstruction: Towards a New Synthesis in Canadian History,' *Histoire sociale / Social History* 27, 53 (May 1994), 1–32.

54 *GGG*, 31 Oct. 1917, 33; 27 Feb. 1918, 51; 5 June 1918, 49; 9 Oct. 1918, 38; MRAC, 1918, 279.

55 I am indebted here to Marjorie Griffen Cohen's *Women's Work, Markets, and Economic Development in Nineteenth-Century Ontario* (Toronto: University of Toronto Press, 1988).

56 AGI, Rice Sheppard, M1135, 'Twenty Years in the Great North-West,' unpublished manuscript, 1922, 37; COR, Keen to Clarke, 16 Oct. 1905.

Chapter Four: Creating and Defining the Community

1 *GGG*, 10 Apr. 1918, 49.

2 John Mack Faragher, 'Open Country Community: Sugar Creek, Illinois, 1820–1850,' in Stephen Hahn and John Prude, eds, *The Countryside in the Age*

of Capitalist Transformation: Essays in the Social History of Rural America (Chapel Hill: University of North Carolina Press, 1985; 1987 reprint), 236; Ronald Rees, *New and Naked Land: Making the Prairies Home* (Saskatoon: Western Producer Prairie Books, 1988).

3 *GGG*, 16 Dec. 1914, 15; 2 Mar. 1910, 16.

4 Ibid., 17 Dec. 1919, 34; AGI, UFAF, M1749, Box 3, File 51.

5 *GGG*, 20 July 1910, 17.

6 UFAF, Box 1, File 10, UFA constitution, 1912, 5; 1921, 2; *GGG*, 7 July 1915, 23; 24 July 1918, 41.

7 *GGG*, 3 Mar. 1915, 28; 16 July 1919, 10.

8 UFA constitution, 1909, 13; 1914, 15; 1921, 21; AGI, *FRR*, 5 Dec. 1918, 1348; *GGG*, 20 Nov. 1918, 12–13; 22 Jan. 1919, 13.

9 *GGG*, 23 Sept. 1921, 7.

10 Ibid., 12 Apr. 1916, 43; 26 June 1918, 83.

11 Ibid., 5 June 1918, 48–9; 30 Oct. 1918, 12.

12 AGI, UFWA, 4–5; AGI, MRAC, 1919, 94; *GGG*, 21 Aug. 1918, 35.

13 MRAC, 1916, 97; *GGG*, 9 June 1915, 12.

14 *WI*, 31 Mar. 1920, 14.

15 Ibid., 1 Oct. 1919, 4; UFAF, Box 1, File 13, SC, 1919, 15.

16 *GGG*, 28 Apr. 1920, 40; 12 Mar. 1919, 92.

17 MRAC, 1912, 57; *GGG*, 13 Sept. 1911, 13; 9 Aug. 1911, 20; 11 Oct. 1911, 22. The term 'moral economy' was coined by E.P. Thompson. It refers to popular ideas about the proper economic roles of social groups. John Strickland, 'Traditional Culture and Moral Economy: Social and Economic Change in the South Carolina Low Country, 1865–1910,' in Hahn and Prude, eds, *The Countryside in the Age of Capitalist Transformation*, 144.

18 *GGG*, 14 Sept. 1910, 16–17; 5 Oct. 1910, 16; MRAC, 1911, 16–17.

19 *GGG*, 9 June 1915, 12; 8 Mar. 1916, 28; 3 May 1916, 11; 15 Feb. 1911, 26; MRAC, 1912, 21.

20 *GGG*, 9 Nov. 1910, 25.

21 Ibid., 3 Aug. 1910, 17; 9 Nov. 1910, 24–5.

22 Ibid., 14 May 1913, 11; Feb. 1909, 37–8, 47.

23 Barbara Villy Cormack, *Perennials and Politics: The Life Story of Hon. Irene Parlby, LL.D.* (Sherwood Park, AB: Professional Printing, 1968), 74–5; *GGG*, 29 June 1921, 3; 17 Aug. 1921, 7; AGI, SF, 1157, File 186, *Farmers' Weekly*, 25 Oct. 1922, 638.

24 Bill Maciejko makes a structural argument in 'Ukrainians and Prairie School Reform, 1896–1921: Ethnic and Domestic Ideologies in Modern State Formation,' *Canadian Ethnic Studies* 22, 2 (1990), 19–40. A good psychological and intellectual analysis of racism in British Columbia is W. Peter Ward,

White Canada Forever: Popular Attitudes and Public Policy Toward Orientals in British Columbia (Montreal & Kingston: McGill-Queen's University Press, 1978). Two well-rounded studies of nativism that consider a variety of causes are Patricia E. Roy, *A White Man's Province: British Columbia Politicians and Chinese and Japanese Immigrants, 1858–1914* (Vancouver: UBC Press, 1984); Howard Palmer, *Patterns of Prejudice: A History of Nativism in Alberta* (Toronto: McClelland & Stewart, 1982).

25 *SN*, 15 Apr. 1908, 6.
26 J.R. Miller, *Skyscrapers Hide the Heavens: A History of Indian-White Relations in Canada* (Toronto: University of Toronto Press, 1989), 212; David Demeritt, 'Visions of Agriculture in British Columbia,' *BC Studies* 108 (Winter 1995–96), 42.
27 *GGG*, 4 Dec. 1912, 11; 16 Oct. 1912, 26; 13 Nov. 1912, 15.
28 MRAC, 1911, 43; 1912, 58.
29 *SN*, 14 Dec. 1907, 4.
30 *GGG*, 21 Aug. 1918, 10.
31 AGI, Rice Sheppard, M1135, 'Twenty Years in the Great North-West,' unpublished manuscript, 1922, 32; *WI*, 11 Feb. 1920, 8; *GGG*, 9 Nov. 1921, 17.
32 *GGG*, 21 June 1911, 16; 28 June 1911, 49; 5 July 1911, 20; Judith S. Hill, 'Alberta's Black Settlers: A Study of Canadian Immigration Policy and Practice' (MA thesis: University of Alberta, 1981), iv, 77–8, 94, 96.
33 *GGG*, 28 June 1911, 34.
34 Ward, *White Canada Forever,* 169; *GGG*, 28 June 1911, 49; Hill, 'Alberta's Black Settlers,' v.
35 *GGG*, 3 May 1911, 24–5; Hill, 'Alberta's Black Settlers,' v, 20–1, 95; Howard Palmer with Tamara Palmer, *Alberta: A New History* (Edmonton: Hurtig, 1990), 83–4.
36 *GGG*, 3 May 1911, 25.
37 Ibid., 9 Aug. 1911, 20.
38 Ibid., 18 Apr. 1917, 12.
39 Ibid., 20 Sept. 1920, 19; AGI, MREB, 1917, 233.
40 *FRR*, 20 Feb. 1918, 198; MRAC, 1918, 193; *GGG*, 2 Mar. 1921, 35; *CAR*, 1912, 548; 1913, 553.
41 PAA, Premiers' Papers, Acc. 69.289, File 472, newspaper clipping, 'Determination Shown,' 26 June 1920; *GGG*, 1 Jan. 1919, 11.
42 MRAC, 1919, 72, 67; *GGG*, 15 May 1912, 13; 30 Sept. 1914, 4; SC, First Day's Proceedings, Edmonton, 1918, 27.
43 *CAR*, 1917, 740, 382; 1916, 724; Census of Canada, 1921, vol. V, 79.
44 *SN*, 14 Dec. 1907, 1; 8 June 1907, 6. Along the same lines, an article in the *Guide* objects to J.T.M. Anderson's notion of Anglo-Saxon superiority and his

contention that 'foreigners' were morally and racially inferior. The author
decries the exploitation of the foreigner and the attempts made to 'dena-
tionalize him, to get him to forget his ancient traditions, his literature, and
his language' (26 Nov. 1919, 41).

45 Census, 1921, vol. V, 79. About 36 per cent of the association's officers in
1916, 1918, and 1920 were ex-Americans (three UFWA officers were
included in the count for 1918). Calculated from MRAC, 1916, 4–12; 1918,
7–17; *GGG*, 25 Feb. 1920, 43.

46 Howard Palmer, 'Strangers and Stereotypes: The Rise of Nativism, 1880–
1920,' in R. Douglas Francis and Howard Palmer, eds, *The Prairie West: Historical Readings* (Edmonton: Pica Pica Press, 1985), 311; Census, 1921, vol. V, 79;
GGG, 11 Aug. 1915, 12; 11 July 1917, 9; 12 Dec. 1917, 35. The secretaries'
reports in the *Guide* bear out these statements about the ethnic composition
of locals, as do the names of unions and their members listed in those
reports.

47 Andrij Borys Makuch, 'In the Populist Tradition: Organizing the Ukrainian
Farmer in Alberta, 1909–1935' (MA thesis: University of Alberta, 1983), 84,
96–7; MRAC, 1919, 51.

48 MRAC, 1919, 72; *CAR*, 1913, 654–5.

49 *GGG*, 19 May 1920, 21.

50 Ibid., 19 Oct. 1921, 14.

51 Ibid., 2 June 1920, 32; 12 May 1920, 27.

52 Ibid., 25 Feb. 1920, 43; MRAC, 1916, 4–12; 1918, 7–17.

53 *GGG*, 6 July 1910, 16; 20 July 1910, 16; 11 Dec. 1912, 14; MRAC, 1913, 12.

54 MRAC, 1915, 49, 42; 1916, 39; 1918, 209; MREB, 1916, 90; 1915, 22; *GGG*, 29
Nov. 1916, 10; 21 July 1915, 12.

55 *GGG*, 14 May 1919, 10; 6 Aug. 1919, 10; 14 Jan. 1920, 26; MRAC, 1920, 62–3;
1921, 63; MREB, 1920, 69–70.

56 *GGG*, Feb. 1909, 37–8; MRAC, 1912, 51, 53; 1913, 19–20; 1918, 43, 105–13,
123, 127.

57 *GGG*, 26 July 1911, 20; MRAC, 1912, 59.

58 MRAC, 1913, 40–1; 1916, 99.

59 *GGG*, 5 Apr. 1911, 17; 29 Nov. 1911, 14; Feb. 1909, 38; Mar. 1909, 56; MRAC,
1911, 12; 1912, 5.

60 MRAC, 1914, 58; 1915, 46–7, 49–50; *GGG*, 20 Dec. 1916, 22; MREB, 1918, 95.

61 MRAC, 1911, 39; 1912, 32–3, 53; MREB, 1918, 95; *GGG*, 3 Feb. 1915, 13;
17 Apr. 1918, 11.

62 *GGG*, 28 Jan. 1920, 47; MRAC, 1916, 19.

63 *GGG*, 19 May 1920, 39.

64 Jean Burnet, in particular, emphasizes this tension in *Next-Year Country: A*

Study of Rural Social Organization in Alberta (Toronto: University of Toronto Press, 1951).

65 *GGG*, 17 Sept. 1913, 14; 18 June 1913, 14.

66 Ibid., 17 Dec. 1919, 34; 16 Apr. 1919, 10.

67 Ibid., 6 July 1910, 17.

68 Ibid., 19 Apr. 1911, 7; 15 May 1912, 14.

69 Ibid., 24 Dec. 1913, 9; 24 Mar. 1915, 12.

70 Ibid., 9 Dec. 1914, 19; 23 May 1917, 13; 23 Dec. 1914, 10; 16 Feb. 1916, 13; 6 Sept. 1916, 7.

71 Ibid., 25 June 1913, 15; 22 Oct. 1913, 9; MRAC, 1912, 28–9; 1916, 33; MREB, 1921, 15.

72 AGI, Alberta Farmers' Association, M1745, Minutes of Conventions and Directors' Meetings, 72, 74. The convention did not pass other board of trade resolutions judged to be inimical to farmers' interests (71, 75).

73 *GGG*, 5 Oct. 1910, 21; 2 June 1920, 23; 9 Mar. 1921, 10–11.

74 Ibid., 1 Mar. 1911, 4; 14 Dec. 1921, 22–3; 3 Sept. 1913, 16; 3 Dec. 1913, 10; MRAC, 1918, 143, 149, 317, 319; MREB, 1921, 28, 55–6.

75 *GGG*, 8 Sept. 1915, 12; 31 May 1916, 9, 22; 12 June 1918, 11; MRAC, 1916, 23.

76 *GGG*, May 1909, 4, 6; MRAC, 1910, 5–6.

77 *GGG*, Mar. 1909, 5; Feb. 1909, 3; MRAC, 1911, 11.

78 MRAC, 1913, 12; *GGG*, 31 July 1912, 4.

79 *GGG*, 6 Apr. 1910, 16; 31 Aug. 1910, 7–9; MRAC, 1911, 6, 11–12, 22–4.

80 MRAC, 1911, 37–8; 1912, 42–3, 59.

81 *GGG*, 28 Feb. 1912, 16.

82 Ibid., 5 June 1912, 12.

83 Ibid., 26 June 1912, 16; 18 Sept. 1912, 11.

84 Ibid., 18 Sept. 1912, 11; 28 Aug. 1912, 8; 24 July 1912, 11; *CAR*, 1913, 629; Warren Caragata, *Alberta Labour: A Heritage Untold* (Toronto: James Lorimer, 1979), 36; MRAC, 1913, 41.

85 MRAC, 1915, 50; *GGG*, 15 Nov. 1911, 16; 24 Apr. 1912, 16; 20 Aug. 1919, 9; 26 Nov. 1919, 40; 6 Apr. 1921, 20–1; *ANP*, 19 June 1919, 8; UFAF, Box 1, File 14, Minutes of Conventions and Executive of UFA Political Association, 24, 29.

86 AGI, GC, M260, Box 17, File 161, 'Alberta Plan of Co-operation between Groups Spreading'; *GGG*, 12 Oct. 1921, 4, 35; 23 Nov. 1921, 7; Cecilia Danysk, *Hired Hands: Labour and the Development of Prairie Agriculture, 1880–1930* (Toronto: McClelland & Stewart, 1995), 135–6; William Kirby Rolph, *Henry Wise Wood of Alberta* (Toronto: University of Toronto Press, 1950), 107–8, 32; Paul F. Sharp, *The Agrarian Revolt in Western Canada: A Survey Showing American Parallels*, with introductions by William Pratt and Lorne Brown

(Regina: Canadian Plains Research Center, 1997; originally published by the University of Minnesota Press, Minneapolis, 1948), 110.

87 *GGG*, 14 Jan. 1920, 26; Paul Grayson and L.M. Grayson, 'The Social Base of Interwar Political Protest in Urban Alberta,' *Canadian Journal of Political Science* 7, 2 (June 1974), 289–313.

88 *GGG*, 9 July 1919, 8; GC, Box 7, File 50, Constitution and By-Laws of the Macleod U.F.A.P. League, 4.

89 *GGG*, 2 June 1920, 23.

Chapter Five: The Building of the Movement, 1914–1918

1 AGI, MRAC, 1918, 283, 285.

2 *GGG*, 19 Dec. 1917, 10; 10 July 1918, 9. Of the 171 unions formed from the beginning of 1914 to May 1915, 141 were organized locally; only sixteen were organized by directors and fourteen by paid organizers. AGI, MREB, 1915, 34.

3 *GGG*, 26 December 1917, 10; 8 May 1918, 10; 17 July 1918, 10; 23 Oct. 1918, 11.

4 MRAC, 1915, 7, 24–8; 1916, 25; 1917, 49; 1918, 55; 1919, 28; 1920, 32, 110; *GGG*, 18 Dec. 1918, 11.

5 MRAC, 1913, 34; 1914, 39; 1915, 42; 1916, 74–5; 1917, 37; *GGG*, 26 Aug. 1914, 9; Eva Carter, *Thirty Years of Progress: History of United Farm Women of Alberta* (1944), 18–19; AGI, UFWA, 2.

6 Carter, *Thirty Years of Progress*, 22; UFWA, 10; Leslie May Robinson, 'Agrarian Reformers: Women and the Farm Movement in Alberta, 1909–1925' (MA thesis: University of Calgary, 1979), 51; MRAC, 1916, 82; AGI, UFAF, M1749, Box 1, File 10, UFA constitution, 1917, 6–7.

7 UFAF, Box 1, File 13, SC, 1919, 46.

8 The older literature includes Catherine Cleverdon, *The Woman Suffrage Movement in Canada: The Start of Liberation, 1900–1920*, with an introduction by Ramsay Cook (Toronto: University of Toronto Press, 1950; 1975 reprint); Barbara J. Nicholson, 'Feminism in the Canadian Prairie Provinces to 1916' (MA thesis: University of Calgary, 1974); Robinson, 'Agrarian Reformers.' The newer scholarship includes Catherine Cavanaugh, 'The Limitations of the Pioneering Partnership: The Alberta Campaign for Homestead Dower, 1909–25,' *Canadian Historical Review* 74, 2 (June 1993), 198–225; Veronica Strong-Boag, 'Pulling in Double Harness or Hauling a Double Load: Women, Work, and Feminism on the Canadian Prairie,' *Journal of Canadian Studies* 21, 3 (Fall 1986), 32–52; Alvin Finkel, 'Populism and Gender: The UFA and Social Credit Experiences,' *Journal of Canadian Studies* 27, 4 (Winter

1992–93), 76–97. Nanci Langford's *Politics, Pitchforks, and Pickle Jars: 75 Years of Organized Farm Women in Alberta* (Calgary: Detselig, 1997) falls into the latter category inasmuch as it describes gender inequality in the organization.

9 Alvin Finkel comes close to making the argument being refuted here; he contends that 'social feminists often used maternalist rhetoric to achieve an equal rights agenda.' 'Populism and Gender,' 94.

10 In the 1970s Susan Gunn, UFWA secretary from 1925 to 1929 and a prominent UFWA leader in the period of this study, wrote: 'Let me emphasize that we never thought of ourselves as a feminist movement per se. We were an organized group of women working hand in glove with our men for better economic conditions.' PAA, Susan M. Gunn Letters, Acc. 83.507, Gunn to Robinson, 31 Oct. 1977.

11 *GGG*, 29 May 1918, 11; 14 Aug. 1918, 10. Regarding women UFA officers or delegates see ibid., 11 Mar. 1914, 14; 3 Feb. 1915, 13; 11 Aug. 1915, 12; 15 Mar. 1916, 12; 20 Sept. 1916, 10; 16 Jan. 1918, 10.

12 *GGG*, 16 Dec. 1914, 15; 17 Nov. 1915, 12; MRAC, 1912, 56; 1918, 31, 181, 183; *SN*, 15 Aug. 1908, 6; AGI, Rice Sheppard, M1135, 'Twenty Years in the Great North-West,' unpublished manuscript, 1922, 37.

13 Ramsay Cook, introduction to Cleverdon, *The Woman Suffrage Movement*, xvi; Janice Newton, 'The Alchemy of Politicization: Socialist Women and the Early Canadian Left,' in Franca Iacovetta and Mariana Valverde, eds, *Gender Conflicts: New Essays in Women's History* (Toronto: University of Toronto Press, 1992), 118–48; Joan Sangster, 'The Role of Women in the Early CCF, 1933–1940,' in Linda Kealey and Joan Sangster, eds, *Beyond the Vote: Canadian Women and Politics* (Toronto: University of Toronto Press, 1989), 118–38.

14 *GGG*, 31 May 1911, 21; 8 Jan. 1913, 9; 18 Mar. 1914, 11; 22 May 1912, 27; 10 Sept. 1913, 9; 8 Jan. 1913, 9; 12 Nov. 1913, 10; Robinson, 'Agrarian Reformers,' 88–90.

15 MRAC, 1915, 39–40; *GGG*, 19 May 1915, 11; 28 Apr. 1915, 12; Margaret E. McCallum, 'Prairie Women and the Struggle for a Dower Law, 1905–1920,' *Prairie Forum* 18, 1 (Spring 1999), 20–2, 26–7; Cavanaugh, 'The Limitations of the Pioneering Partnership,' 202–4, 212–17.

16 MRAC, 1918, 315, 215; 1917, 141; MREB, 1918, 41; 1917, 175, 177.

17 MRAC, 1918, 315, 217, 317.

18 UFA constitution, 1917, 16; MRAC, 1918, 39; Finkel, 'Populism and Gender,' 79. Early in 1918 the UFA board determined that directors would be paid $6.00 per day when they were on UFA business, but a month later the secretary was instructed to pay Irene Parlby only $2.00 per day for her UFWA work in 1917. It was later decided, however, to allow Winnifred Ross a director's expenses while she was on UFWA organization work. MREB, 1918, 32, 37,

101. In 1919 all UFWA directors were given the same per diem allowance as their UFA counterparts. MREB, 1919, 207.

19 AGI, *FRR*, 20 May 1918, 596; *GGG*, 4 Dec. 1918, 25; 11 Dec. 1918, 34.

20 Resolutions on matters internal to the organization were not included in this calculation and only resolutions the conventions voted on were counted.

21 MRAC, 1916, 126–9 (quotation on p. 126); AGI, SF, M1157, File 183, clipping from the *CH*, 29 July 1921, 'Interesting Pen Picture'; *GGG*, 18 July 1917, 10. A biographer of Parlby concluded that 'first and foremost the home was Irene Parlby's concern.' Barbara Villy Cormack, *Perennials and Politics: The Life Story of Hon. Irene Parlby LL.D.* (Sherwood Park, AB: Professional Printing, 1968), 59.

22 MRAC, 1916, 137. See also ibid., 1918, 289.

23 MRAC, 1918, 313; *GGG*, 3 Apr. 1918, 51; 24 Apr. 1918, 49; 24 Dec. 1919, 18; SC, 1919, 30.

24 *GGG*, 5 Sept. 1917, 29; 21 Nov. 1917, 10; 12 Dec. 1917, 35; MRAC, 1918, 275, 291.

25 MRAC, 1916, 136–7; 1913, 30; 1914, 8–9; Paul F. Sharp, *The Agrarian Revolt in Western Canada: A Survey Showing American Parallels*, with introductions by William Pratt and Lorne Brown (Regina: Canadian Plains Research Center, 1997; originally published by the University of Minnesota, Minneapolis, 1948), 55; Donald Page, 'The Development of a Western Canadian Peace Movement,' in S.M. Trofimenkoff, ed., *The Twenties in Western Canada* (Ottawa: National Museum of Man, National Museums of Canada, 1972), 77; *GGG*, 26 Jan. 1910, 24; 4 Sept. 1912, 8; 29 Jan. 1913, 9; 15 Apr. 1914, 27; 5 Aug. 1914, 3.

26 MRAC, 1915, 33; 1913, 20; *CAR*, 1913, 299, 574; 1914, 615.

27 *GGG*, 31 May 1911, 21; MRAC, 1917, 173; 1918, 297, 299.

28 Catherine Cavanaugh comments that the early dower debate 'was conducted entirely within the parameters established by maternal feminism.' 'The Women's Movement in Alberta as Seen Through the Campaign for Dower Rights, 1909–1928' (MA thesis: University of Alberta, 1986), 32.

29 Howard Palmer with Tamara Palmer, *Alberta: A New History* (Edmonton: Hurtig, 1990), 174–6; Diane Kathryn Stretch, 'From Prohibition to Government Control: The Liquor Question in Alberta, 1909–1929' (MA thesis: University of Alberta, 1979), 4–8.

30 MRAC, 1918, 277, 49, 143, 149, 317, 319; 1917, 27, 35, 37, 91, 93, 127, 143; 1919, 90; *GGG*, 26 June 1918, 87.

31 MRAC, 1918, 277; Angus McLaren, *Our Own Master Race: Eugenics in Canada, 1885–1945* (Toronto: McClelland & Stewart, 1990).

32 MRAC, 1920, 84; 1917, 143, unnumbered section (indicates that the UFA

endorsed all UFWA resolutions); 1918, 319, 217; *CAR*, 1919, 392, 397; 1920, 774.

33 PAA, Winnifred Ross Papers, Acc. 71.420/19, address by Irene Parlby, 'Mental Deficiency' (1924), 3; McLaren, *Our Own Master Race*; Susan M. Gunn Letters, Gunn to Robinson, 31 Oct. 1977.

34 *GGG*, 23 July 1919, 33; 26 Feb. 1919, 57.

35 Ibid., 4 Nov. 1914, 13; 11 Sept. 1918, 11.

36 MRAC, 1917, 109; *CAR*, 1916, 652; 1917, 779.

37 W.L. Morton, *The Progressive Party in Canada* (Toronto: University of Toronto Press, 1950), 57–8, 301.

38 Richard Allen, *The Social Passion: Religion and Social Reform in Canada, 1914–28* (Toronto: University of Toronto Press, 1971), 4; *GGG*, 28 June 1916, 10; 28 Feb. 1917, 41–3; 22 July 1914, 8; 3 May 1916, 10; 23 May 1917, 29; 20 June 1917, 34; MRAC, 1916, 126–9; *FRR*, 20 July 1916, 571.

39 *GGG*, 18 Apr. 1917, 12; 25 Apr. 1917, 11. Wood's social philosophy became less spiritual and more material after the war.

40 *GGG*, 18 Sept. 1918, 38–9; 8 Nov. 1916, 10; MRAC, 1917, 55; 1918, 63.

41 Sharp, *The Agrarian Revolt*, 81.

42 The following discussion of state control of the grain trade is based primarily on Charles F. Wilson, *A Century of Canadian Grain: Government Policy to 1951* (Saskatoon: Western Producer Prairie Books, 1978), chaps 4–5; Robert E. Ankli, 'The North American Wheat Futures Market During World War I,' in Donald H. Akenson, ed., *Papers in Rural History*, Vol. VI (Gananoque, Ont.: Langdale Press, 1988), 172–91; Louis Aubrey Wood, *A History of Farmers' Movements in Canada: The Origins and Development of Agrarian Protest, 1872–1924*, with an introduction by Foster J.K. Griezic (Toronto: University of Toronto Press, 1975; originally published by Ryerson Press, Toronto, 1924), 321.

43 *GGG*, 29 Aug. 1917, 19; 14 Nov. 1917, 16; 27 Feb. 1918, 19; 26 Dec. 1917, 10; MRAC, 1918, 165–9; 179, 193.

44 MRAC, 1915, 49; *GGG*, 4 Feb. 1914, 7; 5 May 1915, 8, 17; 2 May 1917, 14–15; 25 Sept. 1918, 11.

45 In the section on democratic reform, the 1916 Farmers' Platform expressed farmers' alarm over the government's growing use of Orders-in-Council, and it advocated greater participation for individual members of Parliament in law making. Morton, *The Progressive Party*, 305.

46 MRAC, 1914, 65–6; 46–8. The latter is apparently what was done with certain radical credit resolutions. Ibid., 1915, 52; 1916, 113.

47 MRAC, 1918, 105–41.

48 William McIntosh, 'The United Farmers of Alberta, 1909–1920' (MA thesis:

University of Calgary, 1971), iii, 5, 44, 110–11; MRAC, 1917, 109; 1918, 105–27.

49 MRAC, 1918, 201, 203; 1915, 13.

50 *GGG*, 26 Jan. 1916, 11; MRAC, 1916, 70, 78; 1918, 77, 79, 159. The report is on pp. 71–9. A delegate from the union demanding that the report be improved was satisfied with the 1918 report (93).

51 *GGG*, 9 Feb. 1916, 13; UFA constitution, 1917, 9, 7; MREB, 1918, 92.

52 MRAC, 1914, 38; 1916, 74. One of the very few times officers did not carry out the wishes of a convention occurred in 1917 when the board failed to submit the UFA platform to politicians to obtain their views on it. The resolution is in MRAC, 1917, 111; the directors' justification for their inaction – after being taken to task by rank-and-file members – is in ibid., 1918, 47.

53 *GGG*, 11 Nov. 1914, 14; MRAC, 1915, 31–2. At the delegates' request, the officers considered resolutions sent in too late for the 1916 convention. They did so in a generally fair manner, forwarding many to the relevant authorities or UFA committee. MRAC, 1916, 116; MREB, 1916, 87–92.

54 Morton, *The Progressive Party*, 305.

55 *GGG*, 18 Aug. 1915, 11; 15 Sept. 1915, 12; 2 Sept. 1914, 4; 3 Nov. 1915, 12; John Herd Thompson, *The Harvests of War: The Prairie West, 1914–1918* (Toronto: McClelland & Stewart, 1978), 113; MRAC, 1914, 13, 59–60; 1915, 12–13; 1916, 17, 19.

56 *GGG*, 23 Aug. 1916, 10; 27 Sept. 1916, 10; 4 Oct. 1916, 10; MRAC, 1917, 107; 1918, 71.

57 MRAC, 1914, 7.

58 Ibid., 1916, 105; 1917, 107, 109; 1915, 10; 1918, 81, 129, 131, 179, 181, 199; MREB, 1918, 3–4.

59 MRAC, 1915, 33–4; *GGG*, 16 Feb. 1916, 26; *FRR*, 20 Feb. 1918, 198.

60 MRAC, 1916, 78–9; *GGG*, 17 May 1916, 27; Morton, *The Progressive Party*, 43.

61 *GGG*, 18 Feb. 1914, 12; 18 Sept. 1918, 11; 29 Aug. 1917, 21; 18 Sept. 1918, 11; Morton, *The Progressive Party*, 300, 303.

62 UFWA, 15; MRAC, 1919, 91.

63 L.G. Thomas, *The Liberal Party in Alberta: A History of Politics in the Province of Alberta, 1905–1921* (Toronto: University of Toronto Press, 1959), 166; William Kirby Rolph, *Henry Wise Wood of Alberta* (Toronto: University of Toronto Press, 1950), 52; *GGG*, 3 May 1916, 11; MRAC, 1917, 63; 1919, 23–6.

64 *FRR*, 5 Jan. 1918, 10; *GGG*, 25 Dec. 1918, 10.

65 MRAC, 1916, 153; *GGG*, 5 Feb. 1919, 10; Hopkins Moorhouse, *Deep Furrows* (Toronto and Winnipeg: George J. McLeod, 1918).

66 MRAC, 1916, 149; *GGG*, 20 June 1917, 12–13; 19 Sept. 1917, 10.

67 *FRR*, 5 Apr. 1915, 223; *GGG*, 6 Nov. 1918, 40.

68 MRAC, 1918, 283, 285.

69 *GGG*, 17 Jan. 1917, 38; MRAC, 1916, 153.

70 *GGG*, 12 Apr. 1916, 48; 23 Feb. 1916, 13; 1 Mar. 1916, 12; 15 Mar. 1916, 12.

71 Ibid., 1 Mar. 1916, 12; 20 Nov. 1918, 13.

72 Ibid., 10 June 1914, 12; 31 July 1918, 35; 12 July 1916, 12; 4 Dec. 1918, 94.

73 Ibid., 10 Feb. 1915, 25; 14 Apr. 1915, 8; Sharp, *The Agrarian Revolt*, 84–5.

74 *GGG*, 26 May 1915, 13; 7 July 1915, 13; MRAC, 1915, 53; 1916, 107–8.

75 *GGG*, 7 July 1915, 13.

76 Morton, *The Progressive Party*, 44–5, 17.

77 *CAR*, 1919, 377–8; Sharp, *The Agrarian Revolt*, 58.

78 *ANP*, 7 June 1918, 10; Morton, *The Progressive Party*, 48.

79 It was reported at the 1916 convention, which met in January, that 2,500 UFA men had joined the forces. MRAC, 1916, 115. Undoubtedly, more UFA members volunteered after that time.

80 MRAC, 1917, 41; *GGG*, 29 Mar. 1916, 20; MREB, 1916, 139–40, 151–4; 1917, 185, 187, 196.

81 Sharp, *The Agrarian Revolt*, 91; MRAC, 1918, 165. The act disfranchised pacifists and persons of 'alien birth' who had not been naturalized in Canada since 1902.

82 *CAR*, 1918, 411; MREB, 1918, 64–6; *ANP*, 10 May 1918, 9; *GGG*, 17 July 1918, 10.

83 *GGG*, 26 June 1918, 25; AGI, John Hooper Ford Fonds, Box E, Non-Partisan League, Correspondence, NPL, 1918(2), S. Stevenson to H. Higginbothom, 17 June 1918; Stevenson to the chairman and UFA executive, 'An Open Letter'; SC, 1918, First Day's Proceedings, Calgary, 14; Second Day's Proceedings, Edmonton, 37; Rolph, *Henry Wise Wood*, 69–70.

84 Cited in Rolph, *Henry Wise Wood*, 69.

85 *GGG*, 30 Oct. 1918, 29; *FRR*, 5 Dec. 1918, 1318.

86 *ANP*, 8 Nov. 1918, 8; 4 Dec. 1918, 10; *GGG*, 27 Nov. 1918, 26.

Chapter Six: Co-operation in the Movement

1 *GGG*, 27 Apr. 1910, 17.

2 Lawrence Goodwyn, *Democratic Promise: The Populist Moment in America* (New York: Oxford University Press, 1976); Robert W. Cherny, 'Lawrence Goodwyn and Nebraska Populism: A Review Essay,' *Great Plains Quarterly* 1, 3 (Summer 1981), 181–94. Stanley B. Parsons et al. in 'The Role of Co-operatives in the Development of the Movement Culture of Populism,' *Journal of American History* 69 (1983), 866–85, found that co-operatives were not always numerous in Populist states and that where they existed, 'co-ops, a radical monetary policy,

and politics often occurred simultaneously, not in the sequence of co-op to ideology to political revolt that the Goodwyn hypothesis demands' (868).

3 Stephen Hahn, *The Roots of Southern Populism: Yeoman Farmers and the Transformation of the Georgia Upcountry, 1850–1890* (New York: Oxford University Press, 1983); Robert C. McMath, Jr, 'Sandy Land and Hogs in the Timber: (Agri)cultural Origins of the Farmers' Alliance in Texas,' in Stephen Hahn and Jonathan Prude, eds, *The Countryside in the Age of Capitalist Transformation: Essays in the Social History of Rural America* (Chapel Hill: University of North Carolina Press, 1985; 1987 reprint), 205–29; Bruce Palmer, *'Man Over Money': The Southern Populist Critique of American Capitalism* (Chapel Hill: University of North Carolina Press, 1980); David Laycock, *Populism and Democratic Thought in the Canadian Prairies, 1910–1945* (Toronto: University of Toronto Press, 1990), 87–8, 123, 283; Ian MacPherson, *Each for All: A History of the Co-operative Movement in English Canada, 1900–1945* (Toronto: Macmillan, 1979), 77–9, and 'Selected Borrowings: The American Impact upon the Prairie Co-operative Movement, 1920–39,' *Canadian Review of American Studies* 10, 2 (Fall 1979), 137–51.

4 MacPherson, *Each for All*, 46–7, 106.

5 *SN*, 3 Aug. 1907, 5.

6 AGI, MREB, 1915, 34.

7 *GGG*, 2 Dec. 1914, 12.

8 Agriculture and Agri-Food Canada, Canadian Agricultural Library, *CC*, Oct. 1912, 13; Dec. 1912, 1; Oct. 1913, 18; Nov. 1913, 18; July 1918, 8–9. The society's principles included 'one man, one vote' and the payment of profits in proportion to purchases. *GGG*, 16 Oct. 1912, 16.

9 AGI, MRAC, 1911, 16–17; 1910, 32; *CC*, Aug. 1911, 8; Nov. 1911, 8; *GGG*, 19 May 1915, 11; 8 Nov. 1916, 10; 1 June, 1910, 16; 2 Mar. 1910, 26. By 1913 farmers were also writing to the Eckville co-op manager for advice. *CC*, Mar. 1913, 16.

10 *GGG*, 24 Apr. 1912, 16; 6 July 1910, 12; 4 July 1911, 10; 16 Feb. 1910, 10; 3 Dec. 1913, 9.

11 MRAC, 1910, 21; 1912, 55; *GGG*, 28 Dec. 1910, 11.

12 MRAC, 1911, 41; 1913, 31.

13 Ibid., 1913, 25, 17–19; 1911, 27; 1912, 30–2; Harald S. Patton, *Grain Growers' Co-operation in Western Canada* (Cambridge: Harvard University Press, 1928), 117–21.

14 Patton, *Grain Growers' Co-operation*, 121–2; William Kirby Rolph, *Henry Wise Wood of Alberta* (Toronto: University of Toronto Press, 1950), 32–3; MacPherson, *Each for All*, 15; MRAC, 1913, 42; 1914, 23–5; *GGG*, 3 Sept. 1913, 18; 15 Oct. 1913, 4.

15 *GGG*, 17 Sept. 1913, 14; 3 Sept. 1913, 16; 4 June 1913, 11; QUA, CP, Coll.
2117, Box 181, File 6, UFA, Woodbridge, official circular no. 8, 2 Nov. 1914;
Box 194, pamphlets, United Farmers of Alberta; MRAC, 1917, 39, 41.

16 MREB, 1916, 142; NAC, CUC, MG 28 I15, vol. 19, File U-1917, Woodbridge
to Keen, 28 Apr. 1917; *CC*, Mar. 1919, 13. Most, though not all, of these sixty-
five societies involved UFA/UFWA locals.

17 *GGG*, 12 Sept. 1917, 7; 5 Mar. 1919, 15; 12 May 1920, 27; AGI, UFAF, M1749,
Box 1, File 13, SC, 1917, 13, 8.

18 *GGG*, 12 Sept. 1917, 7; 26 Sept. 1917, 10; 12 Apr. 1916, 8, 41.

19 These principles are outlined in MacPherson, *Each for All*, 2–3.

20 *GGG*, 25 Mar. 1914, 7; 10 Mar. 1915, 12; 1 Sept. 1915, 19; 12 Jan. 1916, 16.

21 UFA president James Speakman made this suggestion, as did the proposed
by-law form the central office sent to prospective UFA co-ops, although it
also permitted co-op boards to admit non-UFA members. MREB, 1915, 50;
UFAF, Box 1, File 12, 'Incorporation Procedure.'

22 He was strongly against any form of 'class-conscious co-operation.' *CC*,
Dec. 1912, 11.

23 *GGG*, 5 Aug. 1914, 10; 28 Nov. 1917, 36; SC, 1918, Second Day's Proceedings,
Calgary, 3–4.

24 MRAC, 1915, 36; 1916, 15, 17; *GGG*, 11 Feb. 1914, 11, 23; 11 Mar. 1914, 14;
26 May 1915, 9; MREB, 1915, 8–9, 13–14, 19–20.

25 SC, 1917, 12; 1918, Second Day's Proceedings, Calgary, 6–9, 14–15, 19–20,
Second Day's Proceedings, Edmonton, 25–6, 28–9, 31, 34–6; UFAF, Box 1,
File 13, Report of Meeting of Representatives of Local Co-operative Associa-
tions and Local Secretaries of the UFA, 1917, 4, 13, 21–4, 27, 33–8.

26 CUC, vol. 22, General Files, A-1919, Minutes of Meeting, 6 Feb. 1919; vol. 23,
General Files, W-1919, Woodbridge to Keen, 19 Apr. 1919; MacPherson, *Each
for All*, 54.

27 MREB, 1919, 177.

28 MacPherson, *Each for All*, 107.

29 Ibid., 54–5.

30 *GGG*, 2 Feb. 1921, 15; 9 Nov. 1921, 17; MRAC, 1920, 62; MREB, 1920, 58.

31 MREB, 1916, 163–4; 1917, 171–2, 202; MRAC, 1917, 43–5, 111; 1918,
43–5.

32 MRAC, 1910, 23, 25; *GGG*, 13 Apr. 1910, 10.

33 *GGG*, 22 June 1910, 17; 13 Apr. 1910, 23, 10, 13–14, 16; 16 Mar. 1910, 16;
19 July 1911, 20.

34 MRAC, 1912, 61, 34; 1911, 3, 28, 37–8; *GGG*, 20 Aug. 1913, 11.

35 *GGG*, 13 Apr. 1910, 23; 15 June 1910, 16; 16 Mar. 1910, 16; 24 May 1911, 15;
3 Aug. 1910, 17; 21 June 1911, 16–17.

36 MRAC, 1914, 22–3; *GGG*, 24 Nov. 1915, 14; 22 Nov. 1916, 16; 6 Dec. 1916, 5; 28 Nov. 1917, 36.

37 MRAC, 1915, 15–16; *GGG*, 19 May 1915, 7; Patton, *Grain Growers' Co-operation*, 127.

38 *GGG*, 26 Jan. 1916, 18; MRAC, 1917, 81, 83.

39 CUC, vol. 21, File W-1918, Woodbridge to Keen, 26 May 1918; Vol. 23, File W-1919, Woodbridge to Keen, 19 Apr. 1919; MacPherson, *Each for All*, 54; *GGG*, 22 Nov. 1916, 12.

40 MRAC, 1912, 41–2, 51, 55–6.

41 Ibid., 1913, 19–20; *GGG*, 6 Mar. 1912, 17, 24–6; 6 Sept. 1916, 20–1; 9 May 1917, 25; 12 Dec. 1917, 10; *CAR*, 1913, 606–7.

42 MRAC, 1918, 43, 105–13.

43 Ibid., 123, 127; 1920, 11–13.

44 *GGG*, 6 June 1917, 12; 17 Oct. 1917, 13.

45 Ibid., 28 Nov. 1917, 9; 24 Nov. 1915, 12; *CAR*, 1919, 747, 394.

46 T.D. Regehr, 'Bankers and Farmers in Western Canada, 1900–1939,' in John E. Foster, ed., *The Developing West: Essays on Canadian History in Honor of Lewis H. Thomas* (Edmonton: University of Alberta Press, 1983), 306.

47 *GGG*, 2 Oct. 1912, 10; 28 Aug. 1912, 12; 4 Sept. 1912, 10; MRAC, 1912, 52; 1913, 35–6; *CAR*, 1913, 609. The convention resolution asked the government to 'enact legislation enabling farmers to form co-operative credit associations or to take such other steps as may be necessary to enable them to secure cheap and extended loans over a period of years with a small annual installment of principal and interest.'

48 MRAC, 1915, 47, 35; *GGG*, 25 Aug. 1915, 10.

49 *GGG*, 13 Oct. 1915, 12; 8 Sept. 1915, 12; 25 Aug. 1915, 10; 1 Sept. 1915, 11; 15 Sept. 1915, 12; 13 Oct. 1915, 12; MRAC, 1916, 21; *CAR*, 1916, 652.

50 MREB, 1915, 47, 56–8; MRAC, 1916, 78; *GGG*, 8 Mar. 1916, 7, 33–6.

51 MRAC, 1917, 147–69, 43, 105, 107; *GGG*, 2 May 1917, 24, 36; 16 Jan. 1918, 18; 10 Mar. 1920, 49, 54–5; *CAR*, 1917, 797; 1919, 350–1, 748; 1920, 791; 1921, 842.

52 MacPherson, *Each for All*, 51; MRAC, 1917, 109.

53 *GGG*, 29 Jan. 1919, 33, 48; 2 Apr. 1919, 10; 16 Apr. 1919, 10; 21 May 1919, 12; 31 Dec. 1919, 3; *CAR*, 1919, 391.

54 AGI, Norman F. Priestley Fonds, M1003, File 31, clipping from the *MA*, 21 Jan. 1920.

55 *GGG*, 30 June 1920, 37; 21 July 1920, 12; Rolph, *Henry Wise Wood*, 126; MacPherson, *Each for All*, 71.

56 MREB, 1920, 68.

57 *GGG*, 3 Nov. 1920, 29; 21 July 1920, 3; 15 Dec. 1920, 3–4; 26 Jan. 1921, 35.

58 Ibid., 22 Dec. 1920, 16; 17 Nov. 1920, 18; 29 Dec. 1920, 16; 15 Dec. 1920, 14.
59 Ibid., 12 Jan. 1921, 21; 1 Dec. 1920, 14; 5 Jan. 1921, 4; 19 Jan. 1921, 16; 15 June 1921, 4; MRAC, 1921, 61.
60 Rolph, *Henry Wise Wood*, 127–9; *CAR*, 1921, 798–9.
61 AGI, *Vulcan Advocate*, 15 Dec. 1920, 4.
62 MREB, 1921, 82; *GGG*, 28 Dec. 1921, 3.
63 AGI, Earl G. Cook Fonds, 1918–1947, M255, File 41, 'Report of Committee on Co-operative Marketing ... of the Pincher Creek District Association, 4 Feb. 1922; Rolph, *Henry Wise Wood*, 159; MRAC, 1922, 131.
64 *GGG*, 1 May 1912, 14; 14 Feb. 1912, 14; 6 Sept. 1911, 24; 23 Oct. 1918, 11; 22 May 1912, 14; 3 May 1916, 11.
65 Ibid., 31 July 1912, 15; SC, 1919, 28.
66 *GGG*, 21 May 1913, 8; 14 Sept. 1921, 39.
67 Ibid., 20 Aug. 1919, 35–6.
68 Ibid., 22 June 1921, 19; 23 Feb. 1921, 33; MRAC, 1917, 133; 1918, 317.
69 PAA, Susan M. Gunn Letters, Acc. 83.507, Gunn to Robinson, n.d., 1; MRAC, 1918, 285.

Chapter Seven: Education in the Movement

 1 *GGG*, 19 Apr. 1911, 9.
 2 Louis Aubrey Wood, *A History of Farmers' Movements in Canada: The Origins and Development of Agrarian Protest, 1872–1924*, with an introduction by Foster J.K. Griezic (Toronto: University of Toronto Press, 1975; originally published by Ryerson Press, Toronto, 1924), 46; Carrol Jaques, 'The U.F.A.: A Social and Educational Movement' (MA thesis: University of Calgary, 1991), 15–17, 24–46, 58–63.
 3 AGI, MRAC, 1912, 9.
 4 AGI, UFAF, M1749, Box 1, File 10, UFA constitution, 1909, 14; AGI, SF, M1157, File 102, Randolph Patton, *Saskatoon Star*, 14 Nov. 1921, 5, 'H.W. Wood on Federal Election Prospects'; *GGG*, 26 Oct. 1910, 16.
 5 UFA constitution, 1911, 17, 2.
 6 *GGG*, 1 Sept. 1920, 28; 12 Apr. 1916, 15; 29 May 1918, 44.
 7 MRAC, 1917, 75.
 8 UFAF, Box 1, File 13, SC, 1919, 32; *GGG*, 28 Apr. 1915, 12; 2 Jan. 1918, 12.
 9 *GGG*, 8 June 1910, 16.
10 MRAC, 1917, 53; *GGG*, 7 July 1915, 23; 10 Oct. 1917, 28.
11 *GGG*, 1 Mar. 1911, 18.
12 Ibid., 29 Mar. 1911, 12; AGI, MREB, 1920, 38; SC, 1917, 12; 1918, First Day's Proceedings, Calgary, 12.

13 Paul F. Sharp, *The Agrarian Revolt in Western Canada: A Survey Showing American Parallels*, with introductions by William Pratt and Lorne Brown (Regina: Canadian Plains Research Center, 1997; originally published by the University of Minnesota Press, Minneapolis, 1948), 27; W.L. Morton, *The Progressive Party in Canada* (Toronto: University of Toronto Press, 1950), 61, 216; Paul D. Earl, 'Rhetoric, Reality, and Righteousness: The Ideological Debate between the Farm Organizations and the Grain Trade, 1917–1935' (PhD thesis: University of Manitoba, 1992), esp. 240–6, 320–30; MRAC, 1921, 69, 78. A pamphlet written by Dr R. Magill for farmers in the early 1920s provided historical data demonstrating that their ideas about price trends were false. AGI, AWP, M2369, File 810, 'Holding Wheat and Future Trading.'

14 MRAC, 1913, 39.

15 *GGG*, 15 Mar. 1911, 24; 31 Mar. 1920, 22. The CMA published its views in the 31 July 1918 edition of the *Guide*.

16 Sara M. Evans and Harry C. Boyte, *Free Spaces: The Sources of Democratic Change in America* (New York: Harper & Row, 1986), ix–x, 169.

17 Jeffrey M. Taylor, *Fashioning Farmers: Ideology, Agricultural Knowledge, and the Manitoba Farm Movement, 1890–1925* (Regina: Canadian Plains Research Center, 1994).

18 MRAC, 1919, 76; *ANP*, 23 Nov. 1917, 10.

19 *ANP*, 15 Mar. 1918, 10.

20 *GGG*, 5 Dec. 1917, 40; 1 May 1918, 10; MRAC, 1921, 54; Sheilagh S. Jameson, *Chautauqua in Canada* (Calgary: Glenbow-Alberta Institute, 1979), 3–5. Jameson shows that UFA vice-president S.S. Dunham played an important part in getting the 1917 Chautauqua started in Alberta.

21 AWP, Box 65, File 818, newspaper clipping, 20 July 1918, 'Good Programmes at Chautauqua'; *GGG*, 28 Aug. 1918, 11; 4 May 1921, 22; 1 May, 1918, 10.

22 Ralph J. Clark, 'A History of the Department of Extension at the University of Alberta, 1912–1956' (PhD thesis: University of Toronto, 1985), 8–9, 15–43, 59, 63–8, 88.

23 UAA, Report of the Department of Extension, 1914–15, 3; Report of the Department of Extension to 30 Apr. 1915 (1914–15), 1; Interim Report of the Department of Extension, 1916–17, 2; Clark, 'A History of the Department of Extension,' 97–8, 77–8, 105; *GGG*, 10 Mar. 1915, 15.

24 *GGG*, 28 Sept. 1921, 15; 21 Sept. 1921, 23; UAA, Annual Report of the Department of Extension for the year ending 30 June 1921, 4; Clark, 'A History of the Department of Extension,' 56, 80–1; *CAR*, 1921, 808.

25 *CAR*, 1917, 780; Clark, 'A History of the Department of Extension,' 54, 58; UAA, Final Report of the Department of Extension, 1915–16, 3–4; Interim Report, 1916–17, 2.

26 There were packages specifically on 'economics,' 'political economy,' 'marketing,' 'sociology,' 'household science,' 'co-operation,' and 'home economics,' but only the latter two were at all popular. Department of Extension Reports, 1914–16.

27 AGI, UFWA, 16; *GGG*, 30 Mar. 1921, 20.

28 Wood, *A History of Farmers' Movements*, 45; UFA constitution, 1909, 3; AGI, COR, AFA constitution, 1; *GGG*, 23 Nov. 1910, 24.

29 MRAC, 1911, 17; *GGG*, 14 Sept. 1910, 17.

30 MRAC, 1911, 4–5; 1912, 8–9; 1913, 7; 1914, 10.

31 Ibid., 1918, 139.

32 Paul Voisey, *Vulcan: The Making of a Prairie Community* (Toronto: University of Toronto Press, 1988), 77–97.

33 Ibid., 104–6; *GGG*, 14 Aug. 1912, 7, 18.

34 *CAR*, 1921, 815; *GGG*, 4 May 1921, 8.

35 William L. Bowers, *The Country Life Movement in America, 1900–1920* (Port Washington, NY: Kennikat Press, 1974); John MacDougall, *Rural Life in Canada: Its Trend and Tasks* (Toronto: Westminster, 1913); David Demeritt, 'Visions of Agriculture in British Columbia,' *BC Studies* 108 (Winter 1995–6), 29–59.

36 Ibid.

37 *GGG*, 25 Nov. 1914, 20; 3 Nov. 1915, 12.

38 MRAC, 1919, 89; 1918, 263; 1920, 102.

39 Ibid., 1910, 30; 1912, 55; 1913, 36; 1918, 267. The *Canadian Annual Review* shows that Manitoba had more consolidated districts than Alberta or Saskatchewan in the period under study.

40 *CAR*, 1917, 811; *GGG*, 14 Apr. 1920, 7, 43; 12 Oct. 1921, 31; MRAC, 1920, 115.

41 MRAC, 1920, 57; 1922, 155; *GGG*, 16 June 1920, 24; 15 Dec. 1920, 11; 26 Jan. 1921, 32; *CAR*, 1916, 723; 1921, 771.

42 MRAC, 1921, 104; 1919, 95; *GGG*, 26 Jan. 1921, 3, 31, 39; 29 June 1921, 15.

43 MREB, 1920, 1–2, 30, 49; 1921, 8, 101; *GGG*, 26 Jan. 1921, 3; 16 June 1920, 24; MRAC, 1920, 56.

44 MRAC, 1919, 89; *GGG*, 19 Nov. 1919, 17.

45 Taylor, *Fashioning Farmers*, 63; *GGG*, 13 Oct. 1920, 35.

46 *WI*, 14 Apr. 1920, 13; MRAC, 1920, 116–17.

47 *GGG*, 12 May 1920, 44.

48 Ibid., 9 Mar. 1921, 10; 12 Oct. 1921, 12, 25; MRAC, 1919, 84–5; 1920, 96; 1921, 96; 1922, 29, 124; AGI, *FRR*, 5 July 1916, 544; UAA, Department of Extension Directors' Files, RG 16, Acc. No. 74–23, Box 1, File 14, 'The History of the Farm Young People's Week at the University of Alberta,' 3–4.

49 *GGG*, 9 Mar. 1921, 39; 12 May 1920, 44.

50 Ibid., 9 Apr. 1919, 66; 20 Aug. 1919, 35; 7 July 1920, 41; 14 Sept. 1921, 8; 'History of the Farm Young People's Week,' 4–6; MRAC, 1921, 97, 100; 1922, 124–5.

51 *GGG*, 10 Dec. 1919, 40; 23 Feb. 1921, 33; MRAC, 1920, 100.

52 *GGG*, 22 Dec. 1920, 23–4.

53 MRAC, 1920, 100.

54 *GGG*, 28 Dec. 1921, 16–17.

55 'The U.F.W.A.: The Organization for Alberta Farm Women,' n.a., n.d., 4; *GGG*, 30 June 1920, 29.

56 *GGG*, 7 May 1919, 7.

57 SC, 1919, 17–18, 39; *GGG*, 17 Aug. 1921, 17.

58 *GGG*, 31 Aug. 1921, 26.

Chapter Eight: The Politicizing of the Movement, 1919–1921

1 *GGG*, 16 July 1919, 41.

2 This is an adaptation of a theory summarized in Ian Ross Robertson's *The Tenant League of Prince Edward Island, 1864–1867: Leasehold Tenure in the New World* (Toronto: University of Toronto Press, 1996), 75.

3 AGI, MRAC, 1920, 25, 110; 1921, 33, 119; 1922, 74. Membership data conflict in these and other sources. The figures provided are conservative estimates.

4 *GGG*, 23 Mar. 1921, 22; 18 Feb. 1920, 29.

5 Ibid., 1 Dec. 1920, 18; 2 Feb. 1921, 18; MRAC, 1922, 53.

6 *GGG*, 25 Feb. 1920, 43; 29 Jan. 1919, 30; 28 Jan. 1920, 13–14.

7 Ibid., 10 Dec. 1919, 46; 3 Mar. 1920, 26; MRAC, 1921, 47.

8 *ANP*, 5 June 1919, 9; *GGG*, 29 Jan. 1919, 33; 2 July 1919, 79; 17 Aug. 1921, 22; MRAC, 1921, 48. That the UFA did not rubber-stamp the Farmers' Platform was evident in its refusal to endorse the Canadian Council of Agriculture's proposal to add a plank favouring personal naturalization. *GGG*, 28 Jan. 1920, 16–17.

9 Ten per cent was required for a federal constituency convention, 20 per cent for a provincial constituency convention.

10 AGI, SF, M1157, File 102, clipping from the *Saskatoon Star*, 14 Nov. 1921, 'H.W. Wood on Federal Election Prospects, 1921'; *GGG*, 6 Apr. 1921, 9; 13 Apr. 1921, 3.

11 *GGG*, 8 Oct. 1919, 12; 17 Aug. 1921, 22. To give members the freedom to vote as they wished, farmers wanted the legislature to adopt a law providing that the defeat of a bill would not lead to the government's resignation.

MRAC, 1921, 59. The threat of resignation was the main way cabinets forced party members to vote for government bills they did not approve of.

12 SF, File 186, clipping from the *Manitoba Free Press*, 23 July 1921, UFA provincial platform; *GGG*, 16 Apr. 1919, 10. A recall is a measure whereby, upon petition of a defined percentage of the constituents, an elected representative can be unseated.

13 *GGG*, 6 Apr. 1921, 9; *ANP*, 19 June 1919, 13; AGI, UFAF, M1749, Box 1, File 14, Minutes of Conventions and Executive of UFA Political Association, 14–15; MRAC, 1920, 46, 73; W.L. Morton, *The Progressive Party in Canada* (Toronto: University of Toronto Press, 1950), 305.

14 *WI*, 29 Oct. 1919, 11; *GGG*, 14 Sept. 1921, 23.

15 QUA, CP, Coll. 2117, Box 139, United Farmers of Alberta, bulletin no. 5A; UFAF, Box 1, File 13, SC, 1919, 5, 20, 44–6.

16 *GGG*, 23 Mar. 1921, 22; 26 Mar. 1919, 84; 7 May 1919, 49; 3 Sept. 1919, 12; 8 Oct. 1919, 52; 20 Oct. 1920, 31; 23 Apr. 1919, 53.

17 Ibid., 22 Oct. 1919, 12; 24 Dec. 1919, 29; MRAC, 1922, 113.

18 AGI, MREB, 1920, 29, 57; *GGG*, 31 Mar. 1920, 37; 24 Mar. 1920, 55; 7 Apr. 1920, 42; *WI*, 14 Apr. 1920, 9; SC, 1919, 46.

19 *GGG*, 30 July 1919, 31; 21 May 1919, 46; 17 Sept. 1919, 8; 1 Dec. 1920, 14; 2 Feb. 1921, 18; 3 Apr. 1921, 20; 30 June 1920, 8; 11 Aug. 1920, 20; Minutes of Conventions and Executive of UFA Political Association, 17; AGI, GC, M260, File 50, Minutes of political convention of UFA locals in Macleod riding, 28 July 1920, 5. In some associations, the women were designated 'subdirectors,' denoting a lower status. The junior UFA elected an equal number of 'boy' and 'girl' directors to its board. *GGG*, 14 Sept. 1921, 8.

20 MRAC, 1920, 120; *GGG*, 30 June 1920, 37.

21 MREB, 1919, 131; MRAC, 1919, 63–4; 1920, 53, 65, 123–5; 1921, 66–7; Minutes of Conventions and Executive of UFA Political Association, 14. The other 'unimportant' resolutions included a request for Scripture readings in schools and another asking that two retiring directors remain on the board for an additional year to provide continuity. MRAC, 1919, 94, 97.

22 *GGG*, 10 Dec. 1919, 37; 12 Feb. 1919, 49; 26 Mar. 1919, 84; MREB, 1919, 146.

23 *ANP*, 19 June 1919, 8, 13; *GGG*, 2 Apr. 1919, 47; 15 June 1921, 31; 12 Oct. 1921, 12; 6 July 1921, 4.

24 *GGG*, 2 Apr. 1919, 10; AGI, HS, M1165, Box 2, File 21, 'The Farmers' Platform,' 2; MREB, 1919, 165.

25 MREB, 1919, 145; *GGG*, 5 Mar. 1919, 44; 19 Mar. 1919, 49; 2 July 1919, 40.

26 Morton, *The Progressive Party*, 304; *GGG*, 28 Jan. 1920, 19; 19 Mar. 1919, 13; MRAC, 1919, 55–6, 97; 1920, 61, 64.

27 *WI*, 11 Feb. 1920, 13.

28 MRAC, 1921, 113–14, 1919, 78.

29 *GGG*, 15 Oct. 1919, 44.

30 Franklin Lloyd Foster, 'The 1921 Alberta Provincial Election: A Consideration of Factors Involved with Particular Attention to Overtones of Millennialism within the U.F.A. and Other Reform Movements of the Period' (MA thesis: Queen's University, 1977), iii, chap. 1; *GGG*, 16 Nov. 1921, 15; 12 Nov. 1919, 26.

31 Foster, 'The 1921 Alberta Provincial Election,' iii; MRAC, 1922, 11; Christian Leithner, 'The National Progressive Party of Canada, 1921–1930: Agricultural Economic Conditions and Electoral Support,' *Canadian Journal of Political Science* 26, 3 (Sept. 1993), 448.

32 *GGG*, 31 Mar. 1920, 7; 10 Dec. 1919, 8; 5 May 1920, 22.

33 L.G. Thomas, *The Liberal Party in Alberta: A History of Politics in the Province of Alberta, 1905–1921* (Toronto: University of Toronto Press, 1959), 201; MRAC, 1921, 109–11; 1922, 126–7; HS, File 21, 'The U.F.A. and the Provincial Government.'

34 *WI*, 10 Mar. 1920, 3; MREB, 1919, 176–7; MRAC, 1920, 74, 119; 1921, 94; *GGG*, 28 Jan. 1920, 7; Mary Frances Doucedame, 'The Stormy, Liquor-Plagued Birth of the Alberta Provincial Police,' in Ted Byfield, ed., *Alberta in the 20th Century*, vol. 4, *The Great War and Its Consequences, 1914–1920* (Edmonton: United Western Communications, 1994), 276–8; Thomas, *Liberal Party in Alberta*, 192–3.

35 MRAC, 1919, 76, 95; 1920, 126; *GGG*, 19 Mar. 1919, 15.

36 MRAC, 1921, 118; 1919, 67; 1920, 58; 1922, 138; *GGG*, 8 Sept. 1920, 26; SF, File 50, directors' bulletin, 5 May 1921, 6; HS, File 21, 'The U.F.A. and the Provincial Government.'

37 *GGG*, 17 Aug. 1921, 3; *WI*, 24 Mar. 1920, 7.

38 *GGG*, 10 Mar. 1920, 49; 25 May 1921, 7; *WI*, 17 Mar. 1920, 15; *CAR*, 1920, 795; 1921, 839.

39 MRAC, 1919, 61; 1920, 73; *CAR*, 1917, 730, 750–1, 796–7; 1920, 791, 721, 761; 1921, 756, 792, 842.

40 *GGG*, 26 Jan. 1921, 34; 2 July 1919, 40; 30 June 1920, 37; 16 Mar. 1921, 7; GC, Box 7, File 56, directors' bulletin no. 20, 18 Nov. 1921, 'Some Opinions on the Causes of Agricultural and Industrial Depression'; SF, File 184, clipping from the *MA*, 28 Apr. 1922, 'Wood Says Worse Crimes Committed since War Than during It'; MRAC, 1919, 52. W.R. Ball argued that the implementation of a provincial banking system would 'require independent political action.' *GGG*, 15 Jan. 1919, 26.

41 *GGG*, 15 Dec. 1920, 18; 25 May 1921, 7; *CAR*, 1920, 141, 143, 788; MRAC, 1921, 57; Thomas, *Liberal Party in Alberta*, 190.

42 AGI, United Farmers of Alberta Oral History Project, Hugh Allen, M3864, interview with former UFA minister from Peace River by Una Maclean, 1961, transcript, 4–5; MRAC, 1919, 61, 70; 1921, 51; Thomas, *Liberal Party in Alberta*, 190–2.

43 *WI*, 19 Nov. 1919, 8. The premier promised to implement proportional representation in 1919, but there was little support for the measure in the government, which dragged its feet by appointing committees to study the issue. AGI, AWP, M2369, File 821, clipping from the *Edmonton Journal*, 20 Oct. 1919, 1; *WI*, 10 Mar. 1920, 8; *GGG*, 25 May 1921, 7.

44 *WI*, 31 Mar. 1920, 10; 11 Feb. 1920, 10.

45 Thomas, *Liberal Party in Alberta*, chap. 4, 203–5.

46 *GGG*, 2 June 1920, 23; 1 Sept. 1920, 21.

47 Ibid., 26 May 1920, 5; 13 Oct. 1920, 5; 18 May 1921, 5.

48 Ibid., 27 Apr. 1921, 5; 1 June 1921, 5.

49 *CAR*, 1921, 467; *GGG*, 5 Oct. 1921, 5.

50 *GGG*, 18 Feb. 1920, 47; 30 Nov. 1921, 10; 11 Feb. 1920, 19; 7 July 1920, 7, 69–72.

51 Ibid., 11 Feb. 1920, 19; *WI*, 17 Mar. 1920, 5; MRAC, 1920, 69; *CAR*, 1921, 580, 771.

52 MRAC, 1920, 61; 1921, 63.

53 Morton, *The Progressive Party*, 305; MRAC, 1919, 62.

54 *GGG*, 27 Apr. 1921, 5; 6 Apr. 1921, 9–10; 4 May 1921, 5; 28 July 1920, 5; 3 Sept. 1919, 37; MRAC, 1921, 15; 1920, 69.

55 *GGG*, 25 June 1919, 18; 2 July 1919, 40, 89; 14 Sept. 1921, 22; 17 Aug. 1921, 7–8.

56 *WI*, 14 Apr. 1920, 10; 31 Mar. 1920, 5; HS, File 20, 'Minutes of Meeting Re Incorporation for Political Purposes.'

57 *GGG*, 28 Apr. 1920, 40; 8 Dec. 1920, 8, 24–5; 21 July 1920, 27; *WI*, 10 Mar. 1920, 11; 17 Mar. 1920, 11; 24 Mar. 1920, 9.

58 *GGG*, 23 June 1920, 37.

59 Ibid., 3 Nov. 1920, 20–1; 9 Mar. 1921, 5; 15 June 1921, 3–5.

60 *WI*, 19 Nov. 1919, 12; *GGG*, 3 Nov. 1920, 18. In an empirical study, Christian Leithner concluded that 'voters who resided in areas which produced great amounts of price-inelastic agricultural commodities (such as grains and cattle) tended, at elections between 1921 and 1930, to vote for Progressive candidates.' Leithner, 'The National Progressive Party of Canada,' 442, 446–7.

61 *WI*, 14 Apr. 1920, 2.

62 *GGG*, 19 May 1920, 39; 5 Feb. 1919, 10; 4 Aug. 1920, 18; AGI, Cameron, James A., M3904, interview re UFA history in Medicine Hat area, transcript, 5.

63 MRAC, 1919, 53; MREB, 1919, 171–3, 186.
64 MREB, 1919, 186–7.
65 *GGG*, 25 June 1919, 14–16.
66 In the context of a discussion between the UFA executive and the Provincial
    Political Association about Wood's 'closed door policy,' it was agreed that the
    clauses of the UFA constitution stipulating that anyone 'directly interested in
    farming' could join the organization would not be changed. These clauses
    permitted non-farmer membership in the UFA/UFWA and thus in the UFA
    political movement, since the door to that movement was through the UFA/
    UFWA. It was decided to leave the application of the clauses 'to the locals,
    who could then interpret them according to local conditions and the indi-
    viduals applying for membership.' With the same end in view, the 1920 Bat-
    tle River convention defeated a proposed amendment to the constitution
    that would have limited membership in the political association to 'bona fide
    farmers.' MREB, 1919, 194; *GGG*, 30 June 1920, 4.
67 *GGG*, 25 June 1919, 16–18, 26; 16 Apr. 1919, 7. The East Edmonton conven-
    tion required only that its constituency's candidate be a resident of the
    riding; a provision that he or she must be a farmer was deleted (ibid., 9 July
    1919, 8). Similarly, the Macleod Association declared that 'any qualified elec-
    tor' living in the constituency was eligible for candidacy. GC, Box 7, File 50,
    Constitution and By-Laws of the Macleod U.F.A.P. League, 4.
68 AWP, File 821, clipping from the *MA*, 24 Oct. 1919, 'Class Organization Is
    Only Autocracy, States Jas. Weir'; clipping from the *CH*, 30 Oct. 1919, 'U.F.A.
    Speakers Repudiate H.W. Wood's Political Plan.'
69 *GGG*, 28 Jan. 1920, 20, 51; MRAC, 1920, 53; AGI, Norman F. Priestley Fonds,
    M1003, Box 4, File 31, clippings from the *MA*, 22 Jan. 1920, 'Political Fight in
    the U.F.A.'; 24 Jan. 1920, 'Political Association to U.F.A. Is Now Dissolved.'
70 MRAC, 1921, 133; Morton, *The Progressive Party*, 96; *GGG*, 26 Jan. 1921, 7;
    17 Aug. 1921, 6; 29 June 1921, 3, 17 Aug. 1921, 7; SF, File 186, *The Farmers'
    Weekly*, 25 Oct. 1922, 638.
71 Morton, *The Progressive Party*, 71–2, 82–3, 85, 98–9, 103, 110–11.
72 *WI*, 19 Nov. 1919, 3; *GGG*, 16 July 1919, 23; 14 Jan. 1920, 3; 15 Dec. 1920, 3;
    21 July 1920, 3.

Chapter Nine: The Philosophy of the Post-War UFA/UFWA

1 *GGG*, 2 July 1919, 7.
2 W.L. Morton, Paul Sharp, and W.K. Rolph emphasize the importance of
    Wood's education and American experience for the development of his phi-
    losophy. W.L. Morton, 'The Social Philosophy of Henry Wise Wood, the

Canadian Agrarian Leader,' *Agricultural History* 22, 2 (Apr. 1948), 114–23, and *The Progressive Party in Canada* (Toronto: University of Toronto Press, 1950), 86–94; Paul F. Sharp, *The Agrarian Revolt in Western Canada: A Survey Showing American Parallels*, with introductions by William Pratt and Lorne Brown (Regina: Canadian Plains Research Center, 1997; originally published by the University of Minnesota Press, Minneapolis, 1948), 105–7; William Kirby Rolph, *Henry Wise Wood of Alberta* (Toronto: University of Toronto Press, 1950), 9–12, 14, 62–6. In *Democracy in Alberta: Social Credit and the Party System* (Toronto: University of Toronto Press, 1953; 1962 reprint), C.B. Macpherson sees the UFA philosophy as a product of Wood's and Alberta farmers' class and hinterland status.

3 Anthony Mardiros, *William Irvine: The Life of a Prairie Radical* (Toronto: James Lorimer, 1979); John Edward Hart, 'William Irvine and Radical Politics in Canada' (PhD thesis: University of Guelph, 1972); David Laycock, *Populism and Democratic Thought in the Canadian Prairies, 1910–1945* (Toronto: University of Toronto Press, 1990), 63–135.

4 AGI, Leonard D. Nesbitt Fonds, M891, File 17, Wood, Henry Wise, Articles, 1925–59, Grant MacEwan, 'Man from Missouri: Henry Wise Wood,' *Western Producer*, 27 June 1957, 17.

5 Interviews with Mr and Mrs Don Wood, John O. Wood, Lois Hollingsworth, and Bessie Pointen, Mar.–Apr. 1993.

6 AGI, *The U.F.A.*, 15 Mar. 1922, 5.

7 Ibid.; *Canadian Forum*, Dec. 1922, 73.

8 *The U.F.A.*, 15 Mar. 1922, 5.

9 Ibid., 1 Apr. 1922, 5; AGI, AWP, M2369, Box 6, File 125, *Westralian Farmers' Gazette*, 21 Oct. 1926, 15–16.

10 AWP, Box 65, File 818, *British Columbia Farmer*, 20 Apr. 1920, 12; *GGG*, 11 Dec. 1918, 40; AGI, SF, M1157, File 102, 'Social Regeneration. Address by President H.W. Wood of the U.F.A. to the Calgary Labor Church, Apr. 30th, 1922,' 6–8.

11 *The U.F.A.*, 15 Apr. 1922, 25, 27; *GGG*, 4 Dec. 1918, 75–6; 'Social Regeneration,' 12–13; *Canadian Forum*, Dec. 1922, 73.

12 *GGG*, 11 Dec. 1918, 39; SF, File 50, 'Report of Speech Made by Mr. H.W. Wood, President, U.F.A., at Empress Theatre, Medicine Hat, on Saturday, June 25th, 1921,' 6.

13 AGI, MRAC, 1919, 9.

14 *The U.F.A.*, 15 Apr. 1922, 27; MRAC, 1921, 5.

15 MRAC, 1927, 5–6; Laycock, *Populism and Democratic Thought*, 120, 279; Rolph, *Henry Wise Wood*, 9, 62.

16 Sharp, *The Agrarian Revolt*, 105.
17 'Social Regeneration,' 2–3; *The U.F.A.*, 15 Mar. 1922, 5; Richard Hofstadter, *Social Darwinism in American Thought* (New York: George Braziller; originally published in Philadelphia by the University of Pennsylvania Press, 1944), 94, 97–8, 103–4.
18 Carl Berger, *The Sense of Power: Studies in the Ideas of Canadian Imperialism, 1867–1914* (Toronto: University of Toronto Press, 1970), 118–19, 130; Hofstadter, *Social Darwinism*, 174–6.
19 'I can only interpret God by tracing him through Nature and Nature's laws,' Wood wrote in response to a religious survey. 'My ideas of religion have undergone quite a change during the last ten or fifteen years. I think I would interpret my religion, if it may be called a religion, and my religious creed as being a desire to understand natural social law.' Nesbitt Fonds, File 17, Wood to R.W. Frayne, 17 Aug. 1925, 2.
20 'Social Regeneration,' 7.
21 Rolph, *Henry Wise Wood*, 11; M.P. Follett, *The New State: Group Organization the Solution of Popular Government* (Gloucester, MA: Peter Smith, 1965; originally published by Longmans, Green, 1918); Morton, *The Progressive Party*, 91; AGI, United Farmers of Alberta Oral History Project, taped interview with Ray Wood, RCT-24-1, conducted by Una Maclean, Glenbow Foundation, 11 May, no year.
22 There he observed the efficiency of business organizations and organized a mutual telephone company to challenge the Bell telephone system. Sharp, *The Agrarian Revolt*, 105–6.
23 *GGG*, 1 June 1910, 17; 3 Jan. 1917, 13.
24 Ibid., 27 Aug. 1913, 14; 15 Mar. 1915, 14; MRAC, 1912, 9.
25 AGI, GC, M260, Box 17, File 161, 'Co-operation between Organized Democratic Groups' and 'Alberta Plan of Co-operation Spreading'; *GGG*, 6 Apr. 1921, 10.
26 Laycock, *Populism and Democratic Thought*, 98.
27 AWP, Box 66, File 821, clipping from the *CH*, 21 Oct. 1919.
28 Laycock, *Populism and Democratic Thought*, 102; *The U.F.A.*, 23 Feb. 1928, 14.
29 Cited in Macpherson, *Democracy in Alberta*, 46; Walter F. Cooling, *Public Policy* (Chicago: Promethean, 1916), 5; Follett, *The New State*, 24–33.
30 Harold Laski, *Authority in the Modern State* (New Haven, CT: Yale University Press, 1919), 88; Follett, *The New State*, esp. chap. 26; Cooling, *Public Policy*, esp. xiii, 20–1, 28–30, 49.
31 *GGG*, 20 June 1917, 12–13; 19 Sept. 1917, 10.
32 Cited in Morton, *The Progressive Party*, 89.

33 MRAC, 1910, 32–3.
34 George Oake, 'Beatings, Bribery, Theft, Thuggery and Fraud,' in Ted Byfield, ed., *Alberta in the 20th Century*, vol. 3, *The Boom and the Bust, 1910– 1914* (Edmonton: United Western Communications, 1994), 237–9.
35 This was a controversy that erupted in 1921 over the federal government's decision to accept promissory notes for taxes from the Riordon corporation. Farmers saw this as clear evidence that the government favoured the 'big interests'; ordinary taxpayers did not have the right to give notes for their taxes. *CAR*, 1921, 499–500.
36 Cited in Morton, *The Progressive Party*, 75.
37 Macpherson, *Democracy in Alberta*, 26.
38 LeRoy John Wilson, 'The Education of the Farmer: The Educational Objectives and Activities of the United Farmers of Alberta and the Saskatchewan Grain Growers' Association, 1920–1930' (PhD thesis: University of Alberta, 1975), 55–6. Wood gave addresses on group political action and government at the constituency conventions, annual conventions, and the 1919 UFA secretaries' convention. Examples of Wood explaining his ideas to locals can be found in *WI*, 10 Mar. 1920, 15; AGI, *Vulcan Advocate*, 17 Mar. 1920, 1. The *Advocate* printed Wood's speeches in some detail. Farmers also read Wood's articles as well as summaries of his talks on group politics in such periodicals as the *GGG*, the *WI*, the *CH*, and *The U.F.A.*
39 AWP, File 821, clipping from the *MA*, 'U.F.A. and Politics'; File 819, newspaper clippings, 'Secretaries of U.F.A. Back Wood's Scheme' and 'U.F.A. Members Take Exception to Wood's Views'; SF, File 819, clippings from the *Montreal Witness*, 17 Feb. 1920; 24 Feb. 1920; *GGG*, 31 Dec. 1919, 17; 28 Jan. 1920, 51; 12 Oct. 1921, 3; *WI*, 11 Feb. 1920, 13–14; 10 Mar. 1920, 10.
40 *GGG*, 28 Dec. 1921, 9. The 1920 UFA annual convention and the 1919 UFA secretaries' convention endorsed his principles, as did UFA/UFWA political conventions. See, for example, ibid., 4 Aug. 1920, 30; 19 Oct. 1921, 23.
41 *ANP*, 12 Apr. 1918, 10.
42 Mardiros, *William Irvine*, 97–8; Hart, 'William Irvine and Radical Politics,' 66.
43 William Irvine, *The Farmers in Politics*, with an introduction by Reginald Whitaker (Toronto: McClelland & Stewart, 1976; originally published in 1920), 135–48, 55–85, 148–73, 182–3, 188–91, 207–13.
44 Ibid., 237–8.
45 Ibid., 75–90, 183–5, 100–2, 144–7, 230–2, 235, xxi–xxiii.
46 Ibid., 36, 38, 191, 210–11, 231–2; M. Marcia Smith, 'The Ideological Relationship between the United Farmers of Alberta and the Co-operative Commonwealth Federation' (MA thesis: McGill University, 1967), 3.

Epilogue

1 Scripture taken from the New King James Version. Copyright © 1979, 1980, 1982, by Thomas Nelson, Inc. Used by permission. All rights reserved.
2 AGI, MRAC, 1923, 11–12.
3 Andrij Borys Makuch, 'In the Populist Tradition: Organizing the Ukrainian Farmer in Alberta, 1909–1935' (MA thesis: University of Alberta, 1983), 97–102.
4 Phillip J. Lewis, 'The Alberta Wheat Pool, 1923–1935' (MA thesis: University of Calgary, 1980), 178.
5 Alvin Finkel, 'Populism and Gender: The UFA and Social Credit Experiences,' *Journal of Canadian Studies* 27, 4 (Winter 1992–3), 82–3; Carl Betke, 'The United Farmers of Alberta, 1921–35: The Relationship between the Agricultural Organization and the Government of Alberta' (MA thesis: University of Alberta, 1971); C.B. Macpherson, *Democracy in Alberta: Social Credit and the Party System* (Toronto: University of Toronto Press, 1953; 1962 reprint); Franklin L. Foster, *John Brownlee: A Biography* (Lloydminster, AB: Foster Learning, 1996), 265.
6 MRAC, 1923, 20–1.
7 W.L. Morton, *The Progressive Party in Canada* (Toronto: University of Toronto Press, 1950), 267; Ramsay Cook, *The Regenerators: Social Criticism in Late Victorian English Canada* (Toronto: University of Toronto Press, 1985).
8 Howard Palmer with Tamara Palmer, *Alberta: A New History* (Edmonton: Hurtig, 1990), 220.
9 Foster, *John Brownlee*, 158–9.
10 Morton, *The Progressive Party*, 292.
11 Ecclesiastes 1:13–14, New King James Version.

Index